Those Not-So-Sweet Boys

3

YOKO NOGIRI

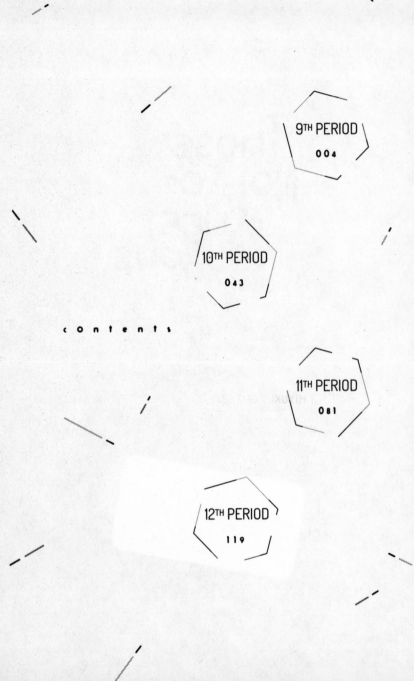

contents

characters

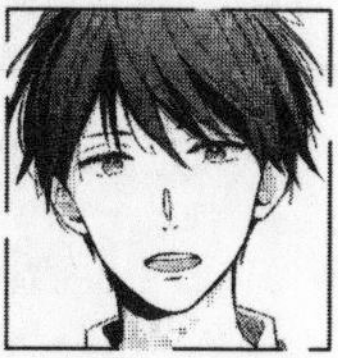

REI ICHIJO

Heir to the Ichijo Conglomerate.
Lives alone in a fancy apartment.

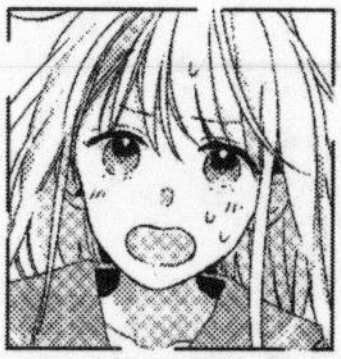

MIDORI NANAMI

Attends high school on a scholarship to help with her family's finances. Has Rei on her mind a lot.

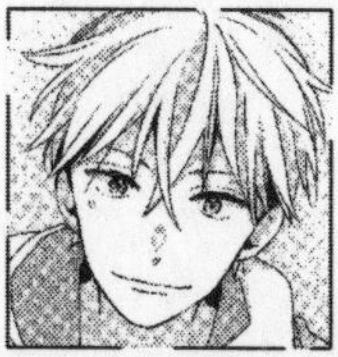

CHIHIRO GOSHIMA

Successor to the Goshima gang. Is used to the assumptions people make about him due to his family.

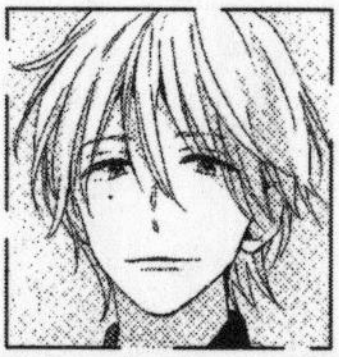

YUKINOJO IEIRI

Son of a doctor. A good friend to Rei and Chihiro, and an overall nice person, but...

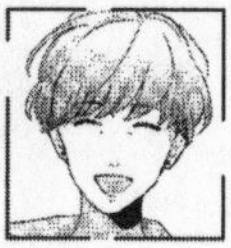

MIYUKI NAGATSUKI

Owner of the restaurant where Midori works. Has known Rei and his friends for 10 years.

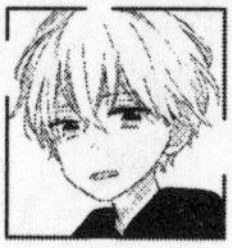

KON NANAMI

Midori's beloved little brother who's in junior high school. A great cook, and super reliable to boot.

story

Midori's school chairman catches her working a part-time job, which is against the school rules!! Instead of revoking her scholarship, the chairman suggests that he could let it go if she brings three truants back to school. At first, Rei, Yukinojo, and Chihiro refuse to give Midori the time of day, but her efforts pay off and they start going to school. During the school campout, Midori gradually closes the distance between herself and the boys, and finds herself drawn more and more to Rei, who always helps her when she's in trouble. Eventually, she realizes that she is in love with him!! But it would seem that Chihiro has feelings for Midori, too...

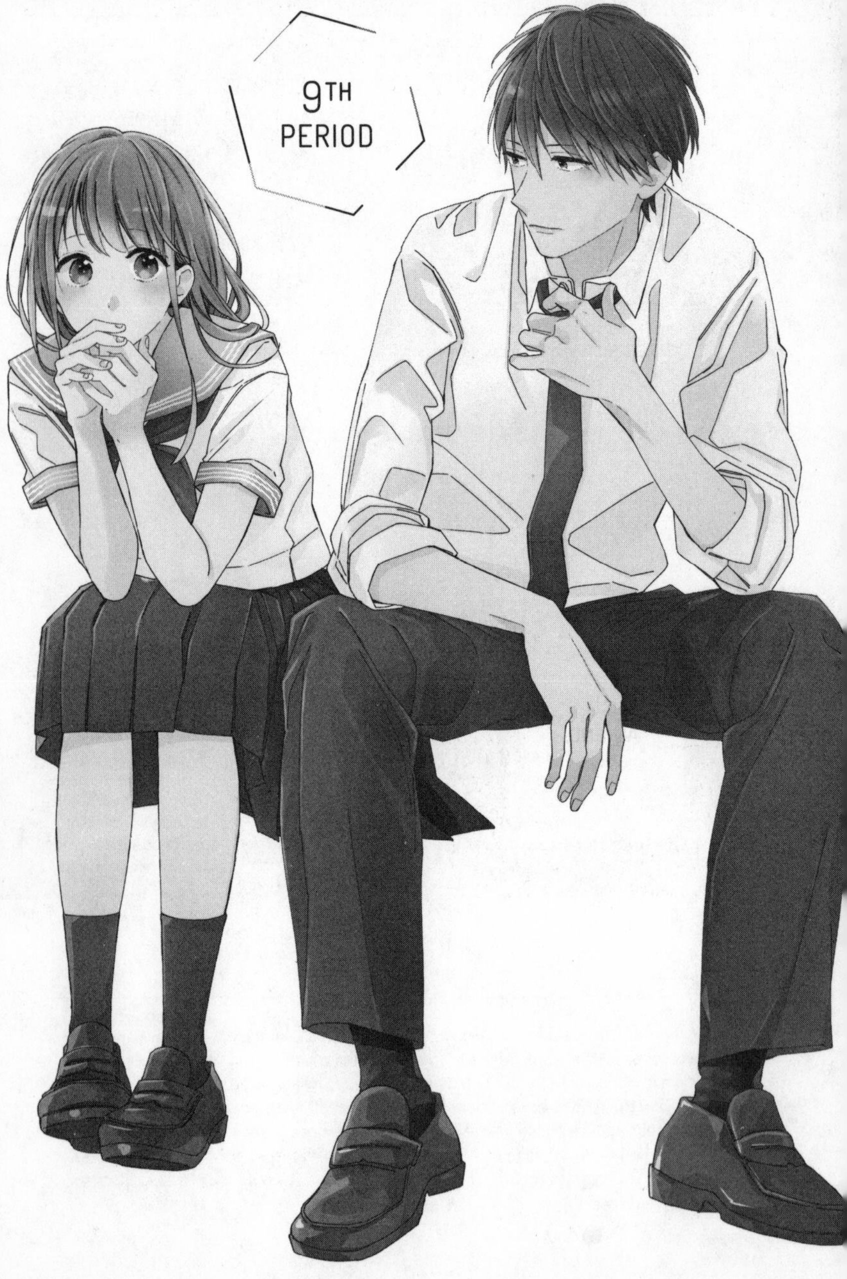
9TH
PERIOD

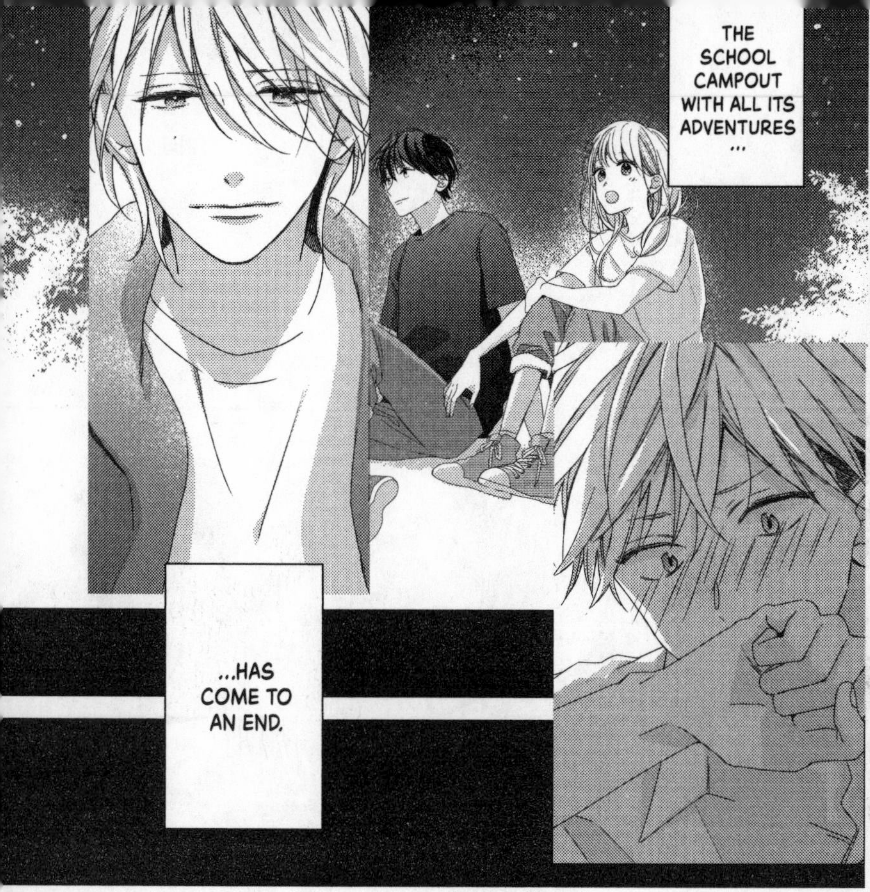
THE SCHOOL CAMPOUT WITH ALL ITS ADVENTURES ...
...HAS COME TO AN END.

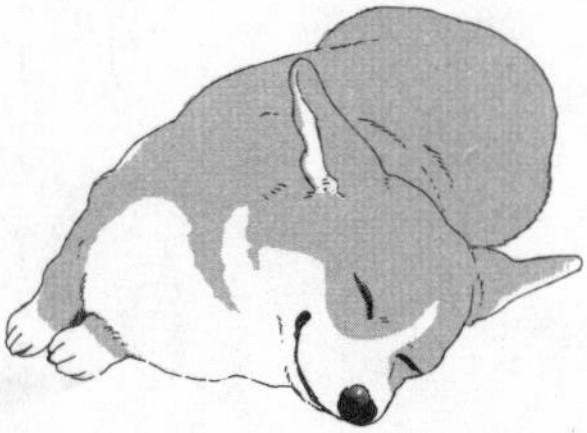

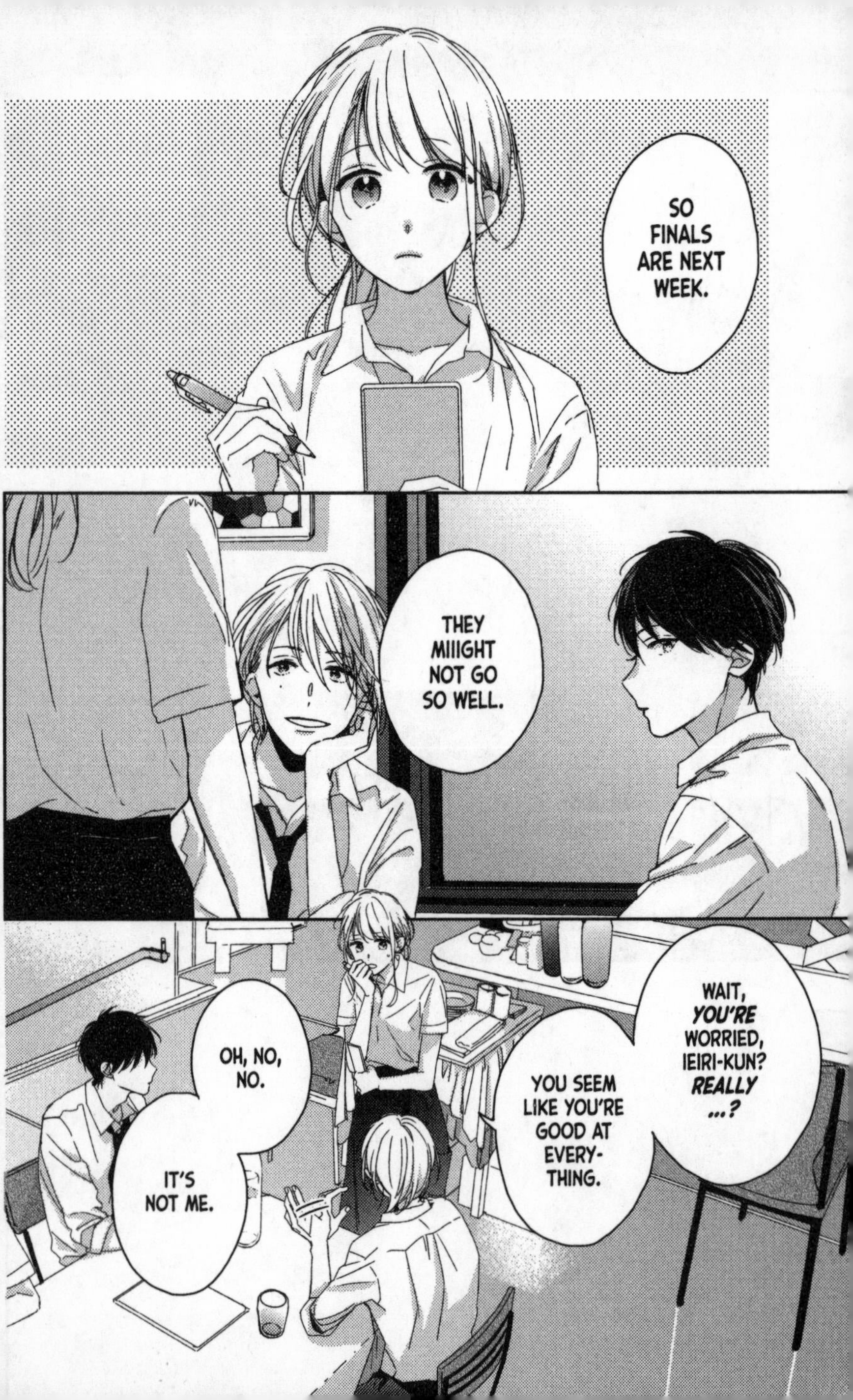
SO FINALS ARE NEXT WEEK.
THEY MIIIGHT NOT GO SO WELL.
WAIT, *YOU'RE* WORRIED, IEIRI-KUN? *REALLY* ...?
YOU SEEM LIKE YOU'RE GOOD AT EVERY-THING.
OH, NO, NO.
IT'S NOT ME.

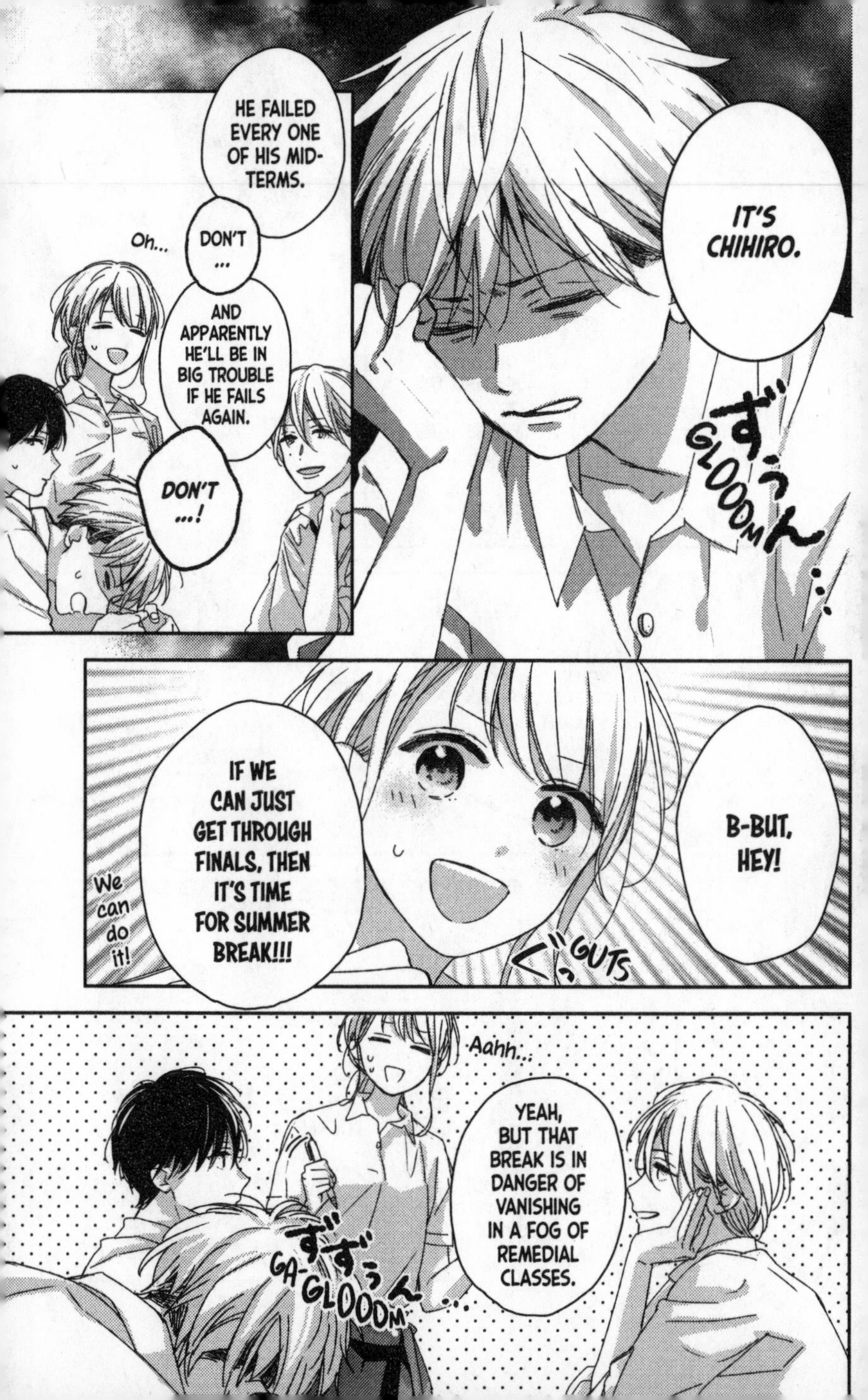
IT'S CHIHIRO.
ずうん
GLOOOM
HE FAILED EVERY ONE OF HIS MID-TERMS.
Oh...
DON'T ...
AND APPARENTLY HE'LL BE IN BIG TROUBLE IF HE FAILS AGAIN.
DON'T ...!
B-BUT, HEY!
IF WE CAN JUST GET THROUGH FINALS, THEN IT'S TIME FOR SUMMER BREAK!!!
ぐっ
GUTS
We can do it!
Aahh...
YEAH, BUT THAT BREAK IS IN DANGER OF VANISHING IN A FOG OF REMEDIAL CLASSES.
ずずうん
GA-GLOOOM

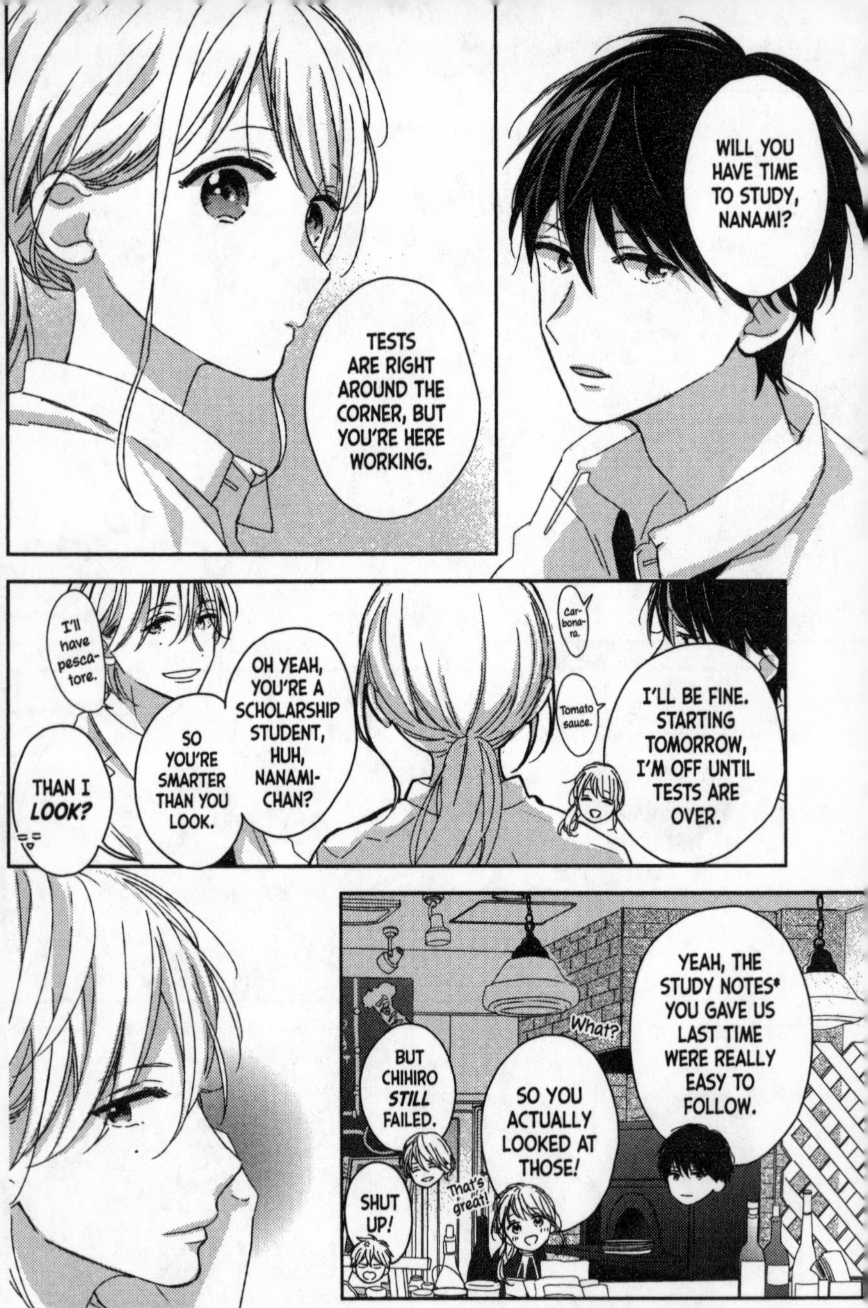
WILL YOU HAVE TIME TO STUDY, NANAMI?
TESTS ARE RIGHT AROUND THE CORNER, BUT YOU'RE HERE WORKING.
Carbonara.
Tomato sauce.
I'LL BE FINE. STARTING TOMORROW, I'M OFF UNTIL TESTS ARE OVER.
OH YEAH, YOU'RE A SCHOLARSHIP STUDENT, HUH, NANAMI-CHAN?
I'll have pescatore.
SO YOU'RE SMARTER THAN YOU LOOK.
THAN I *LOOK?*
YEAH, THE STUDY NOTES* YOU GAVE US LAST TIME WERE REALLY EASY TO FOLLOW.
What?
SO YOU ACTUALLY LOOKED AT THOSE!
That's great!
BUT CHIHIRO *STILL* FAILED.
SHUT UP!

(*See 1st Period)

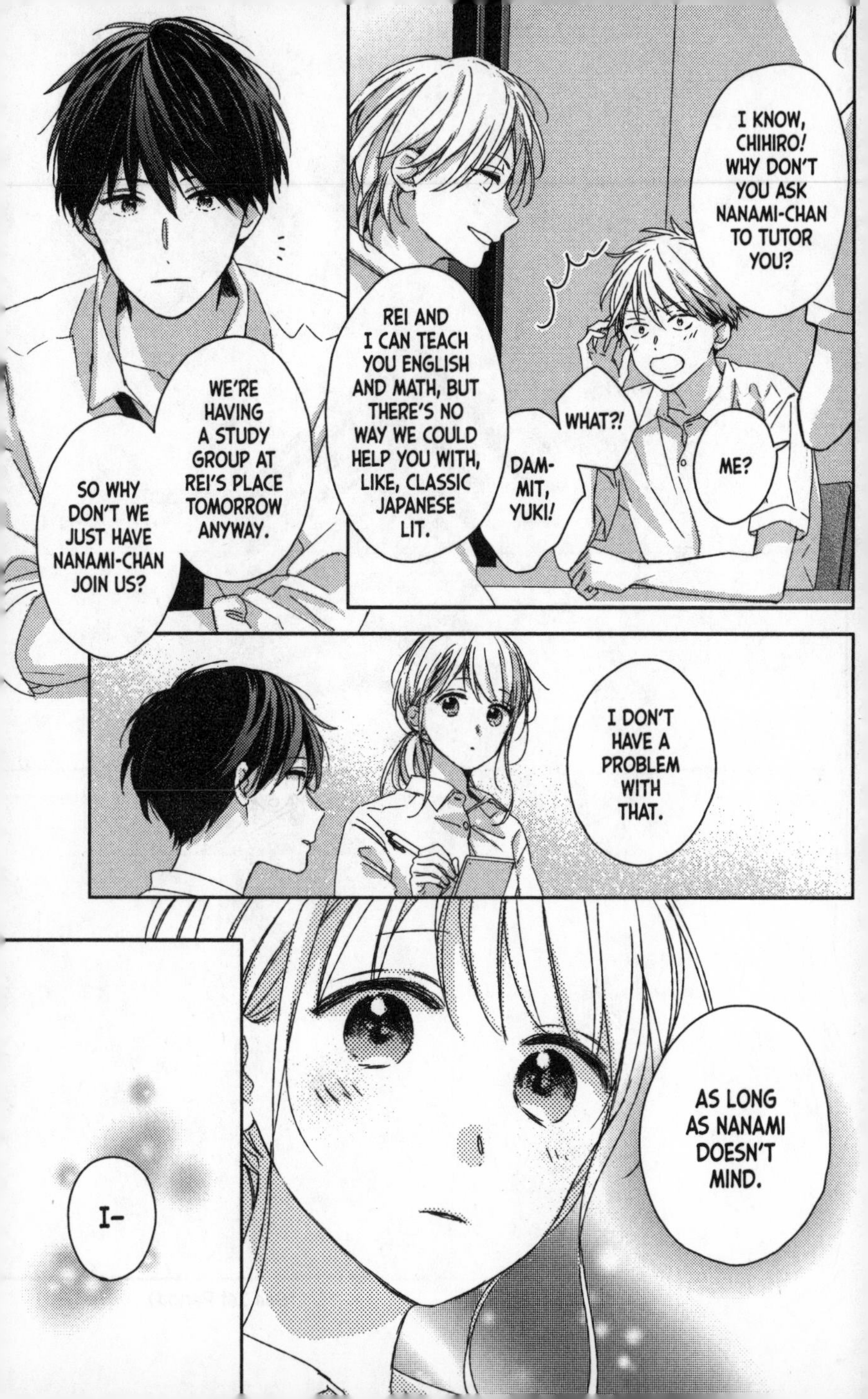
I KNOW, CHIHIRO! WHY DON'T YOU ASK NANAMI-CHAN TO TUTOR YOU?
ME?
WHAT?!
DAM-MIT, YUKI!
REI AND I CAN TEACH YOU ENGLISH AND MATH, BUT THERE'S NO WAY WE COULD HELP YOU WITH, LIKE, CLASSIC JAPANESE LIT.
WE'RE HAVING A STUDY GROUP AT REI'S PLACE TOMORROW ANYWAY.
SO WHY DON'T WE JUST HAVE NANAMI-CHAN JOIN US?
I DON'T HAVE A PROBLEM WITH THAT.
AS LONG AS NANAMI DOESN'T MIND.
I–

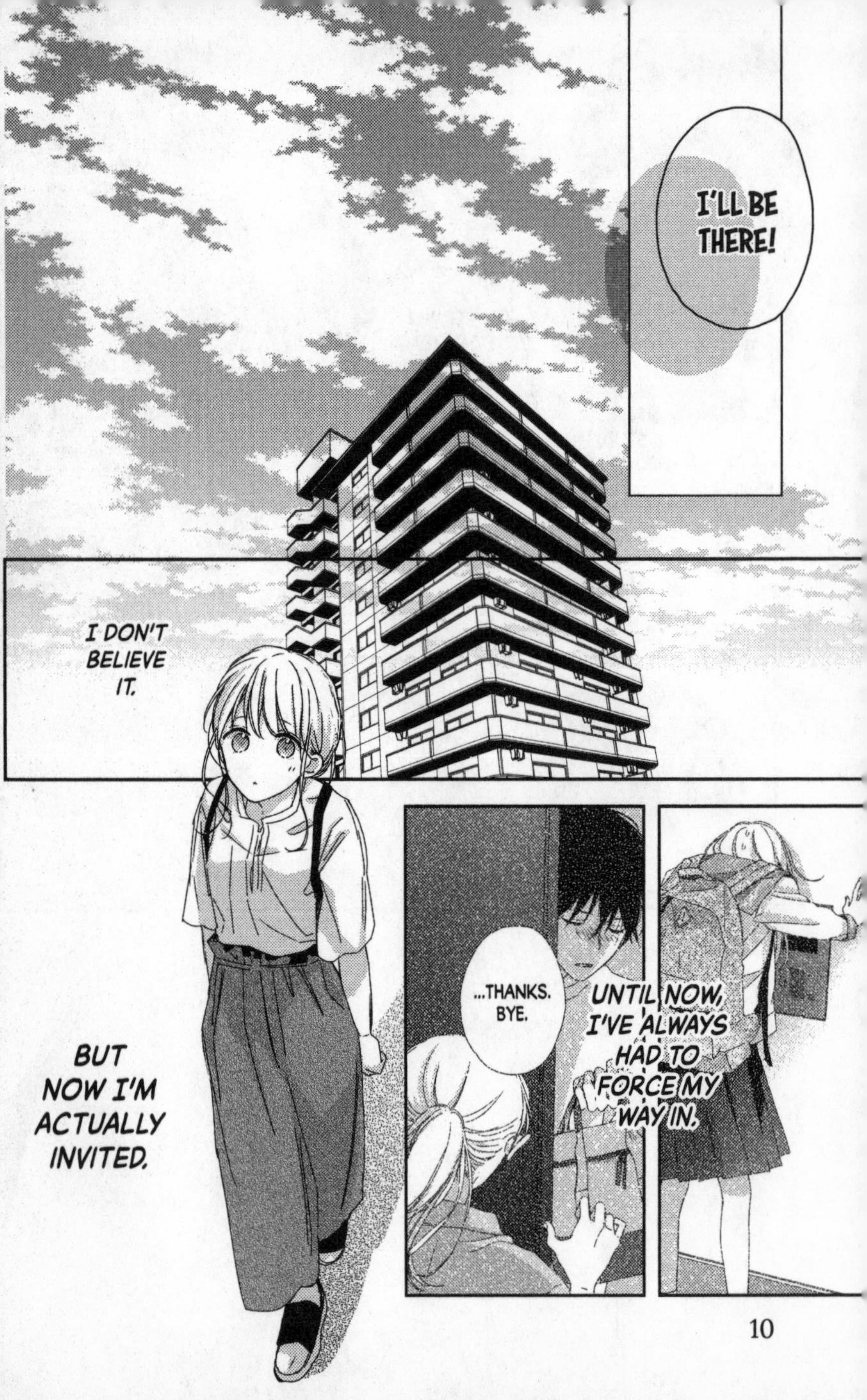
I'LL BE THERE!
I DON'T BELIEVE IT.
UNTIL NOW, I'VE ALWAYS HAD TO FORCE MY WAY IN.
...THANKS. BYE.
BUT NOW I'M ACTUALLY INVITED.

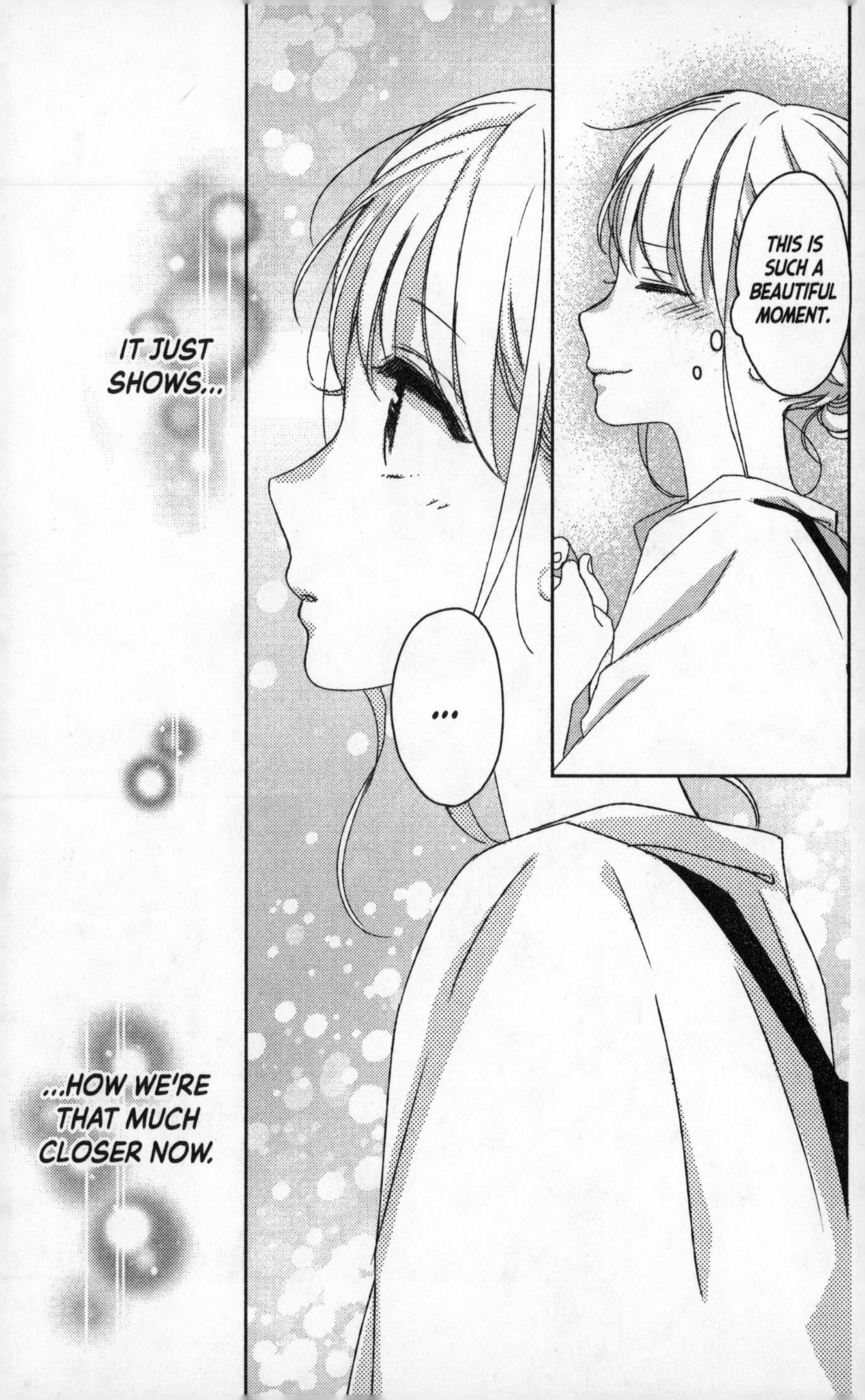
THIS IS SUCH A BEAUTIFUL MOMENT.
...
IT JUST SHOWS...
...HOW WE'RE THAT MUCH CLOSER NOW.

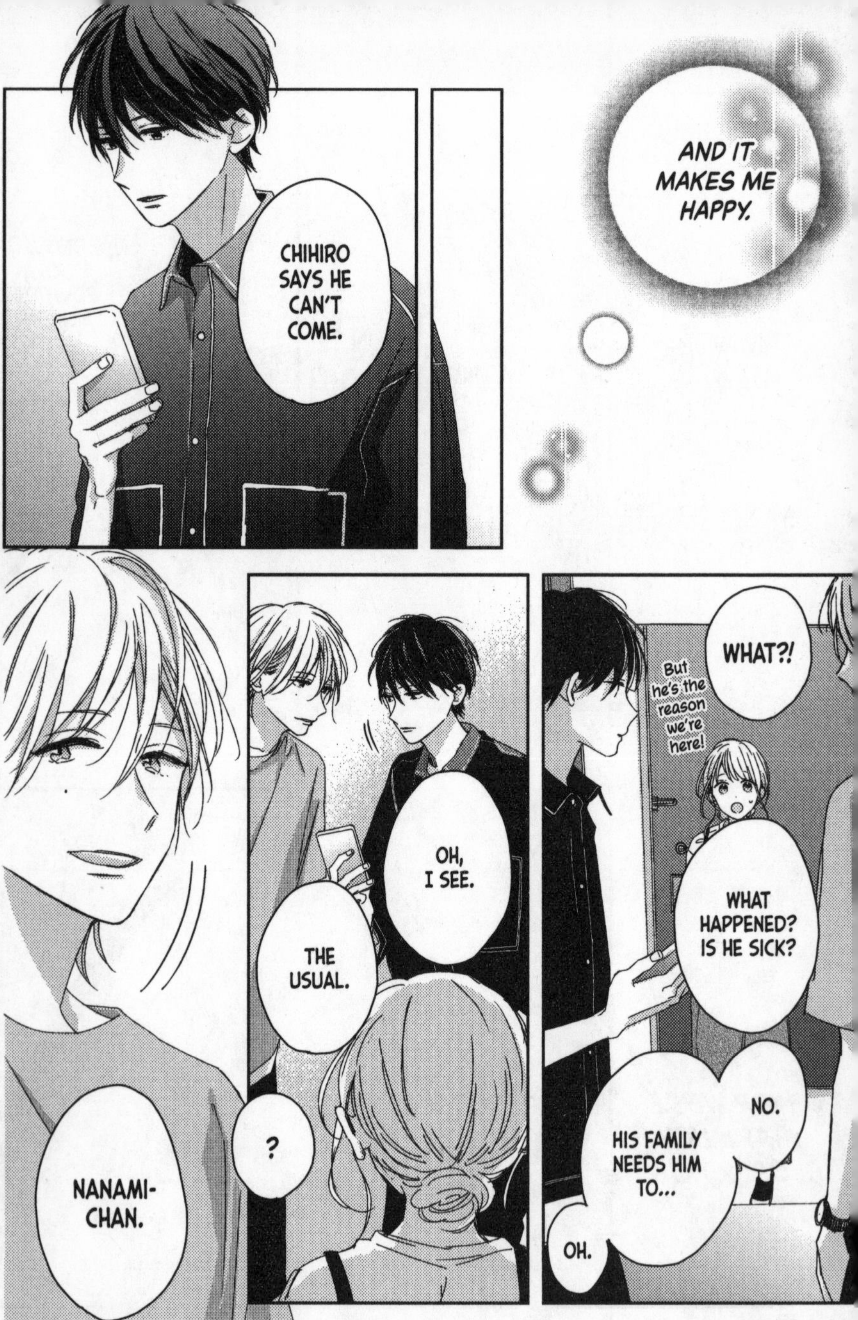
AND IT MAKES ME HAPPY.
CHIHIRO SAYS HE CAN'T COME.
WHAT?!
But he's the reason we're here!
WHAT HAPPENED? IS HE SICK?
NO.
HIS FAMILY NEEDS HIM TO...
OH.
OH, I SEE.
THE USUAL.
?
NANAMI-CHAN.

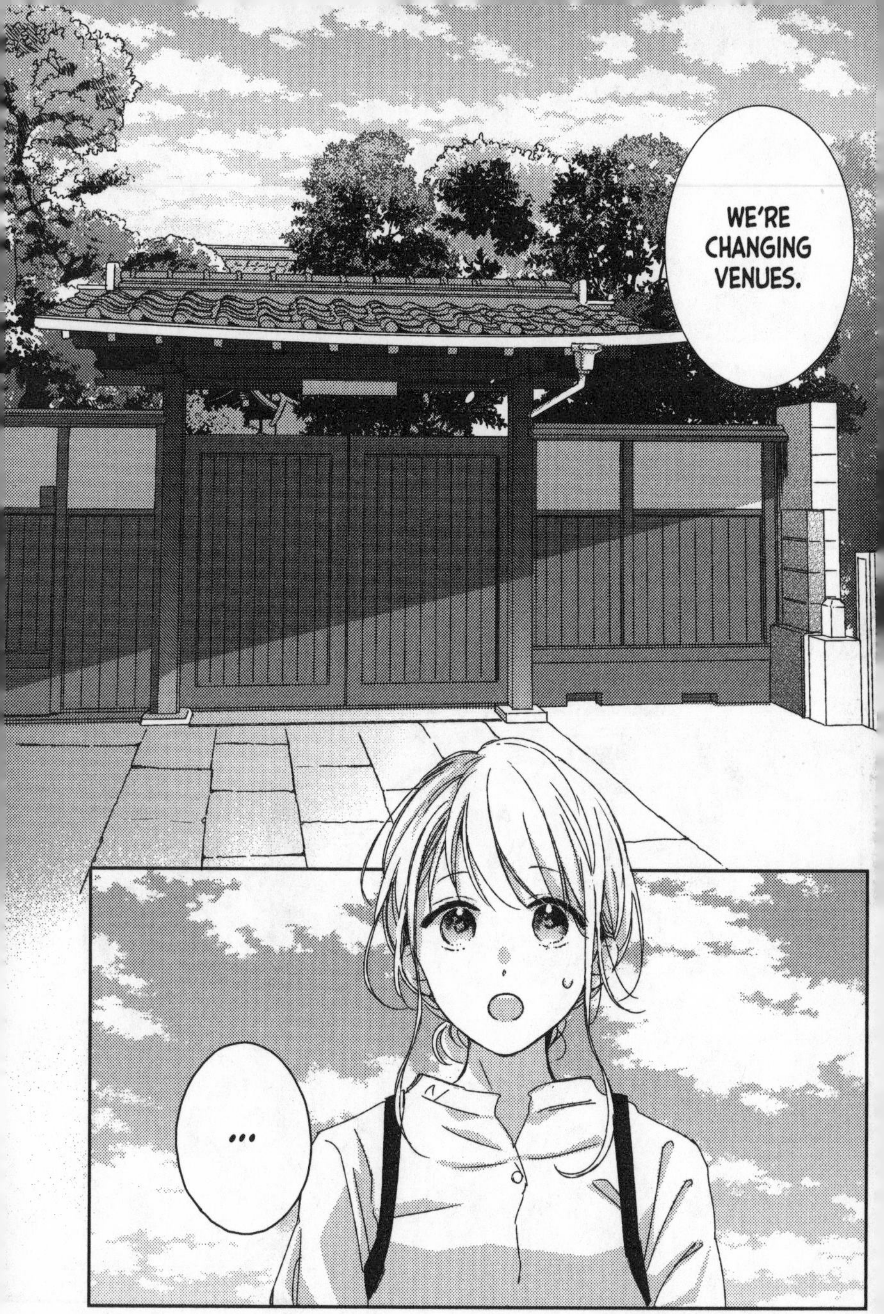
WE'RE CHANGING VENUES.
...

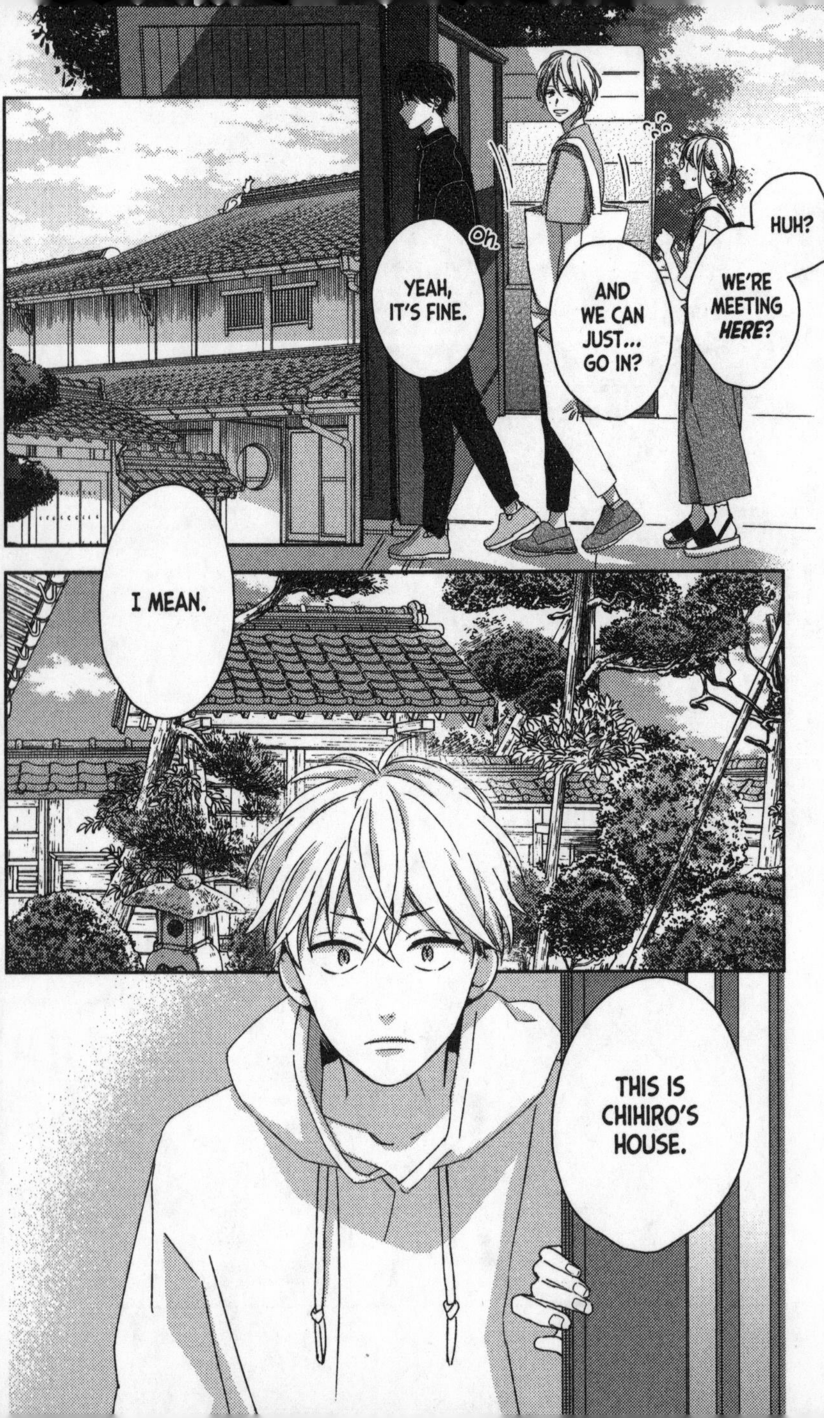
HUH?
WE'RE MEETING *HERE*?
AND WE CAN JUST... GO IN?
Oh.
YEAH, IT'S FINE.
I MEAN.
THIS IS CHIHIRO'S HOUSE.

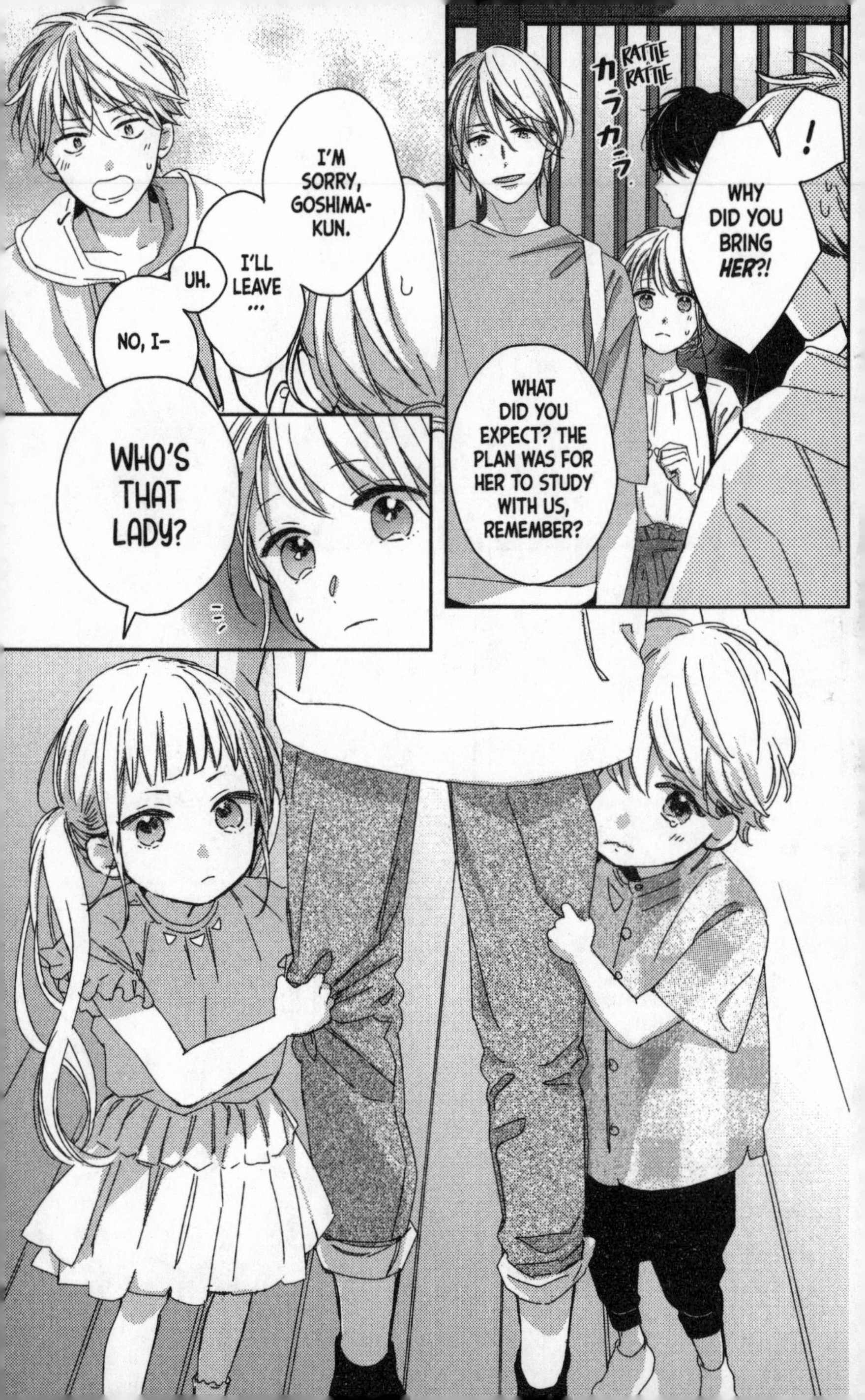
RATTLE RATTLE
カラカラ
!
WHY DID YOU BRING HER?!
WHAT DID YOU EXPECT? THE PLAN WAS FOR HER TO STUDY WITH US, REMEMBER?
I'M SORRY, GOSHIMA-KUN.
I'LL LEAVE...
UH.
NO, I-
WHO'S THAT LADY?

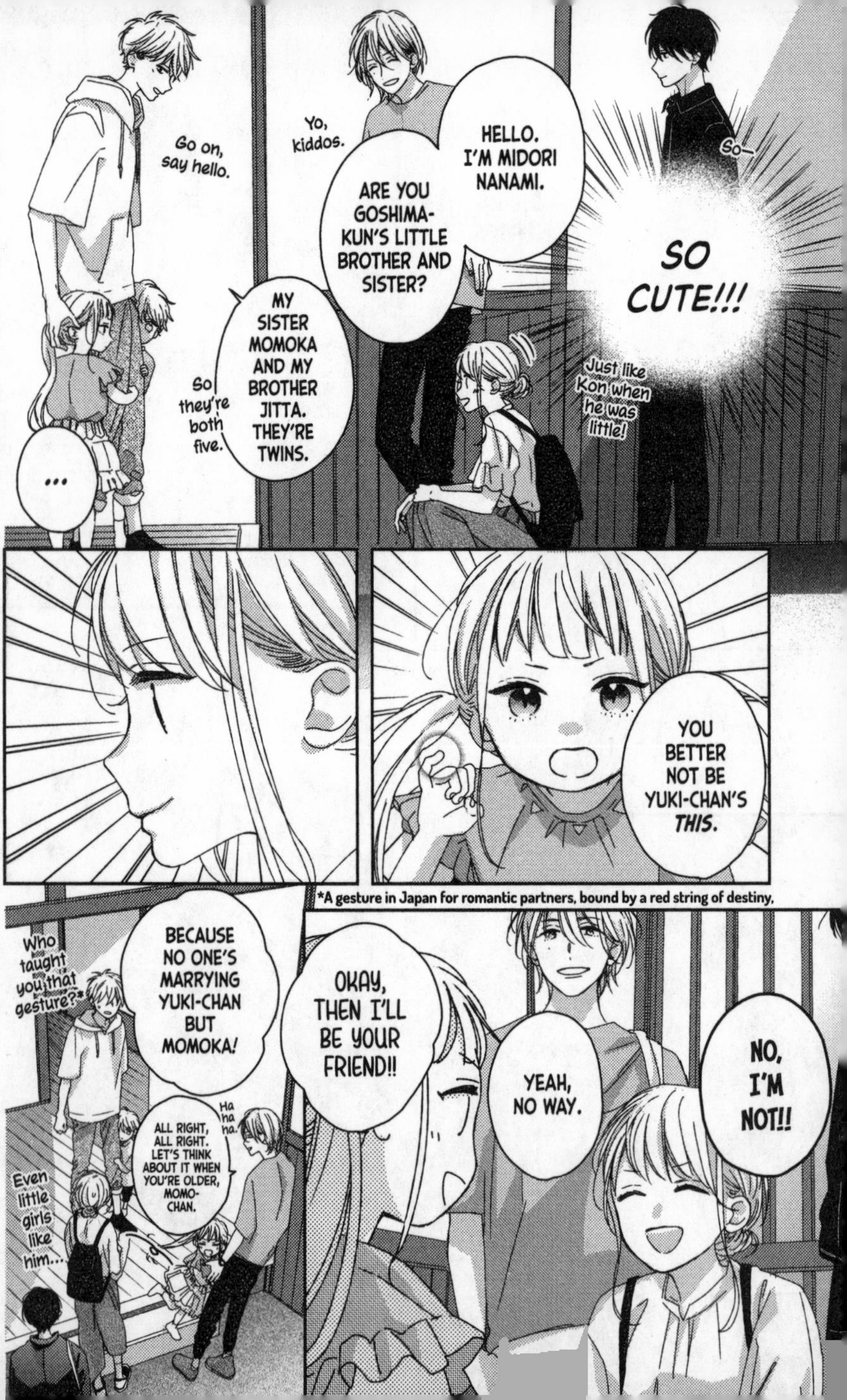
So—
SO CUTE!!!
HELLO. I'M MIDORI NANAMI.
ARE YOU GOSHIMA-KUN'S LITTLE BROTHER AND SISTER?
Just like Kon when he was little!
Yo, kiddos.
MY SISTER MOMOKA AND MY BROTHER JITTA. THEY'RE TWINS.
Go on, say hello.
So they're both five.
...
YOU BETTER NOT BE YUKI-CHAN'S THIS.
NO, I'M NOT!!
YEAH, NO WAY.
OKAY, THEN I'LL BE YOUR FRIEND!!
BECAUSE NO ONE'S MARRYING YUKI-CHAN BUT MOMOKA!
Who taught you that gesture?*
Ha ha ha.
ALL RIGHT, ALL RIGHT. LET'S THINK ABOUT IT WHEN YOU'RE OLDER, MOMO-CHAN.
Even little girls like him...

*A gesture in Japan for romantic partners, bound by a red string of destiny.

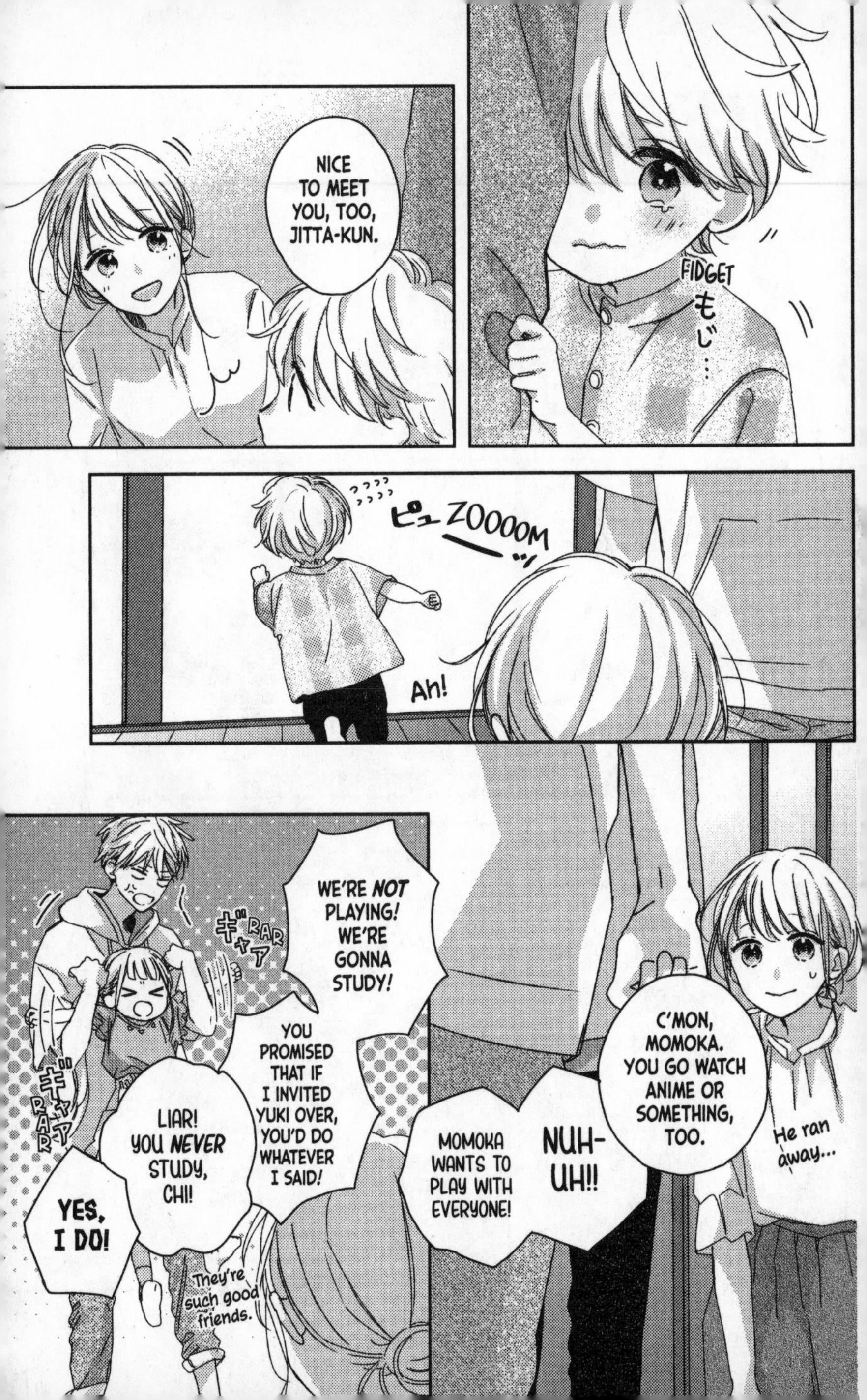
FIDGET
もじ…
NICE TO MEET YOU, TOO, JITTA-KUN.
ピュ ZOOOOM ッ
Ah!
He ran away...
C'MON, MOMOKA. YOU GO WATCH ANIME OR SOMETHING, TOO.
NUH-UH!!
MOMOKA WANTS TO PLAY WITH EVERYONE!
WE'RE *NOT* PLAYING! WE'RE GONNA STUDY!
ギャア RAR
YOU PROMISED THAT IF I INVITED YUKI OVER, YOU'D DO WHATEVER I SAID!
ギャア RAR
LIAR! YOU *NEVER* STUDY, CHI!
YES, I DO!
They're such good friends.

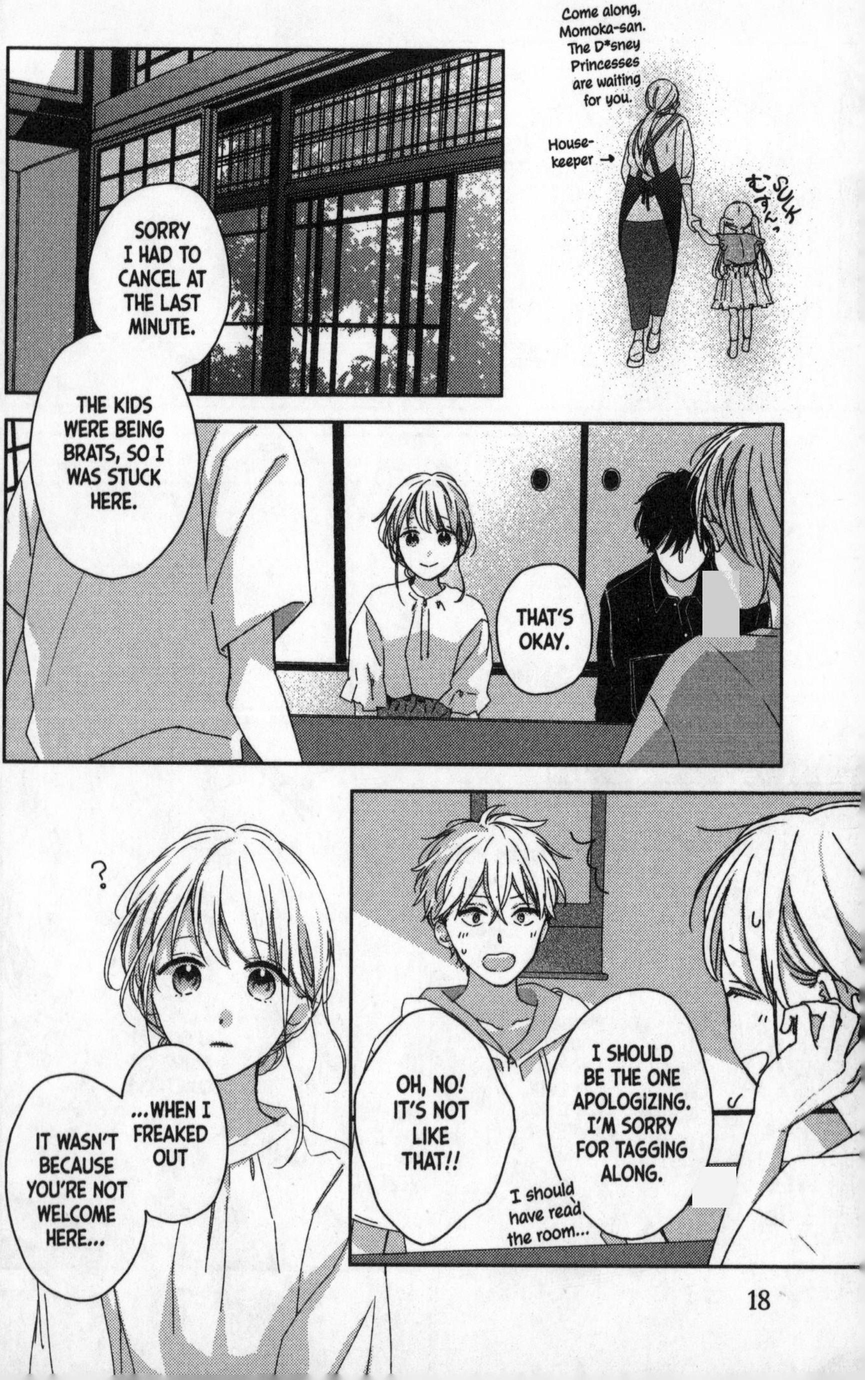
Come along, Momoka-san. The D*sney Princesses are waiting for you.
House-keeper →
SULK むすん
SORRY I HAD TO CANCEL AT THE LAST MINUTE.
THE KIDS WERE BEING BRATS, SO I WAS STUCK HERE.
THAT'S OKAY.
I SHOULD BE THE ONE APOLOGIZING. I'M SORRY FOR TAGGING ALONG.
I should have read the room...
OH, NO! IT'S NOT LIKE THAT!!
?
IT WASN'T BECAUSE YOU'RE NOT WELCOME HERE...
...WHEN I FREAKED OUT

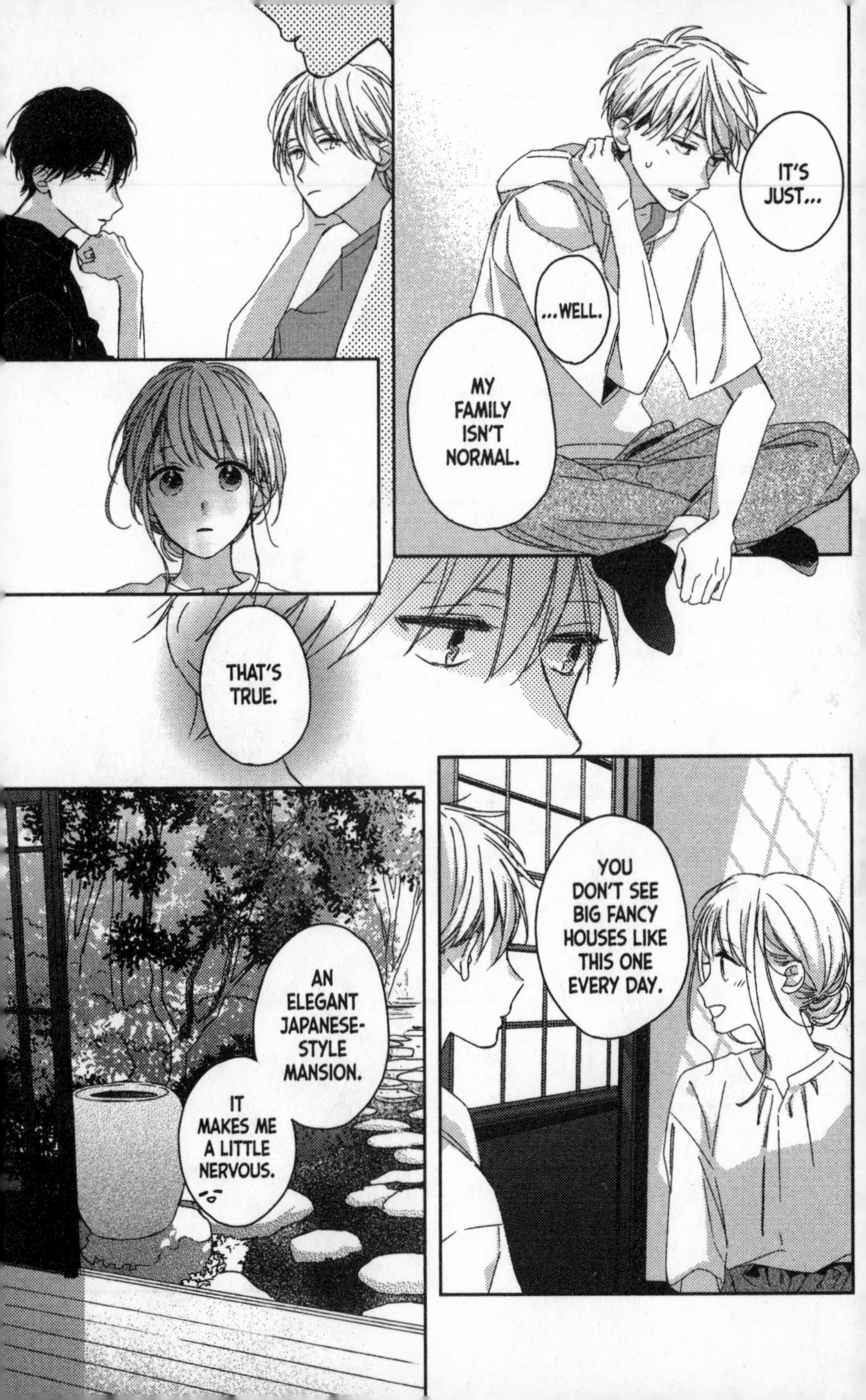
IT'S JUST...
...WELL.
MY FAMILY ISN'T NORMAL.
THAT'S TRUE.
YOU DON'T SEE BIG FANCY HOUSES LIKE THIS ONE EVERY DAY.
AN ELEGANT JAPANESE-STYLE MANSION.
IT MAKES ME A LITTLE NERVOUS.

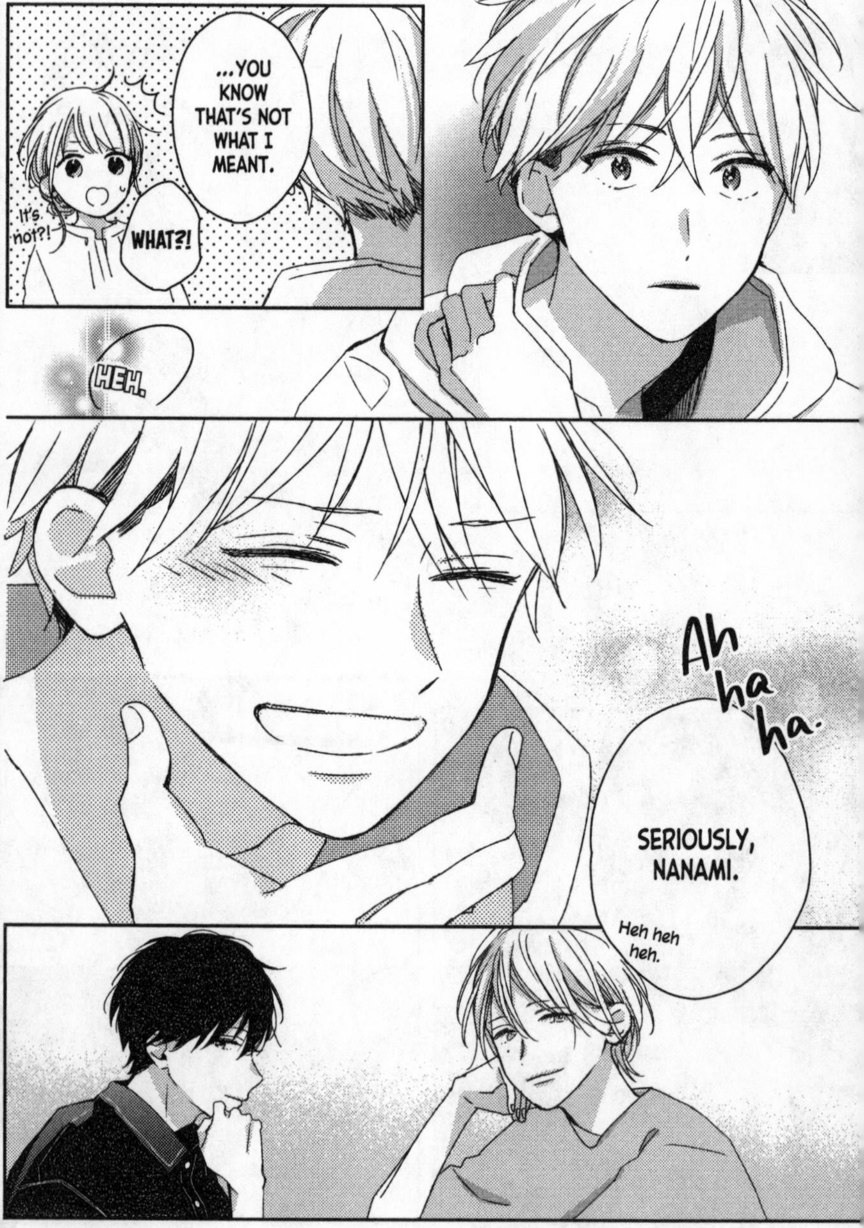
...YOU KNOW THAT'S NOT WHAT I MEANT.
WHAT?!
It's not?!
HEH.
Ah ha ha.
SERIOUSLY, NANAMI.
Heh heh heh.

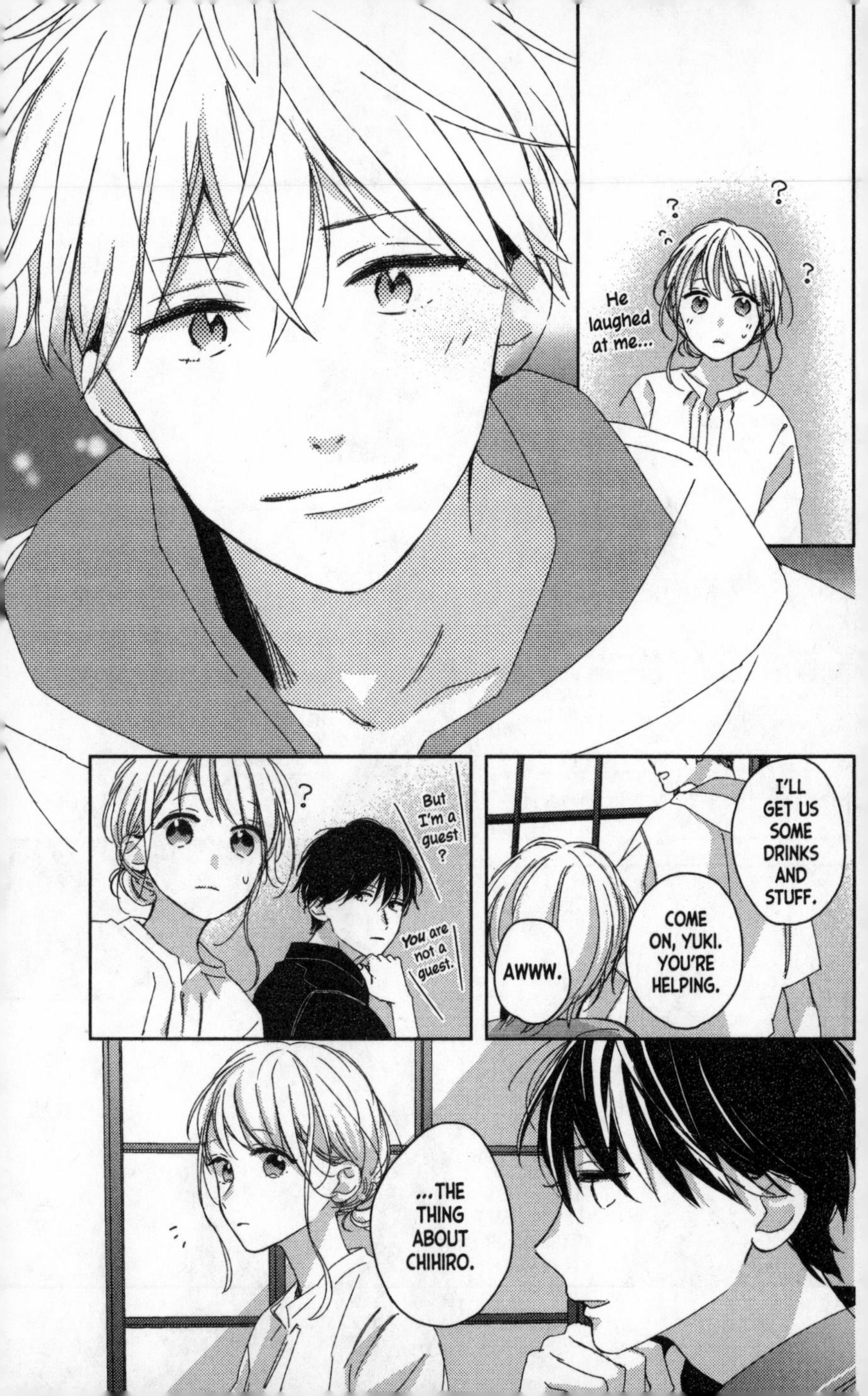
He laughed at me...
I'LL GET US SOME DRINKS AND STUFF.
COME ON, YUKI. YOU'RE HELPING.
AWWW.
But I'm a guest?
You are not a guest.
...THE THING ABOUT CHIHIRO.

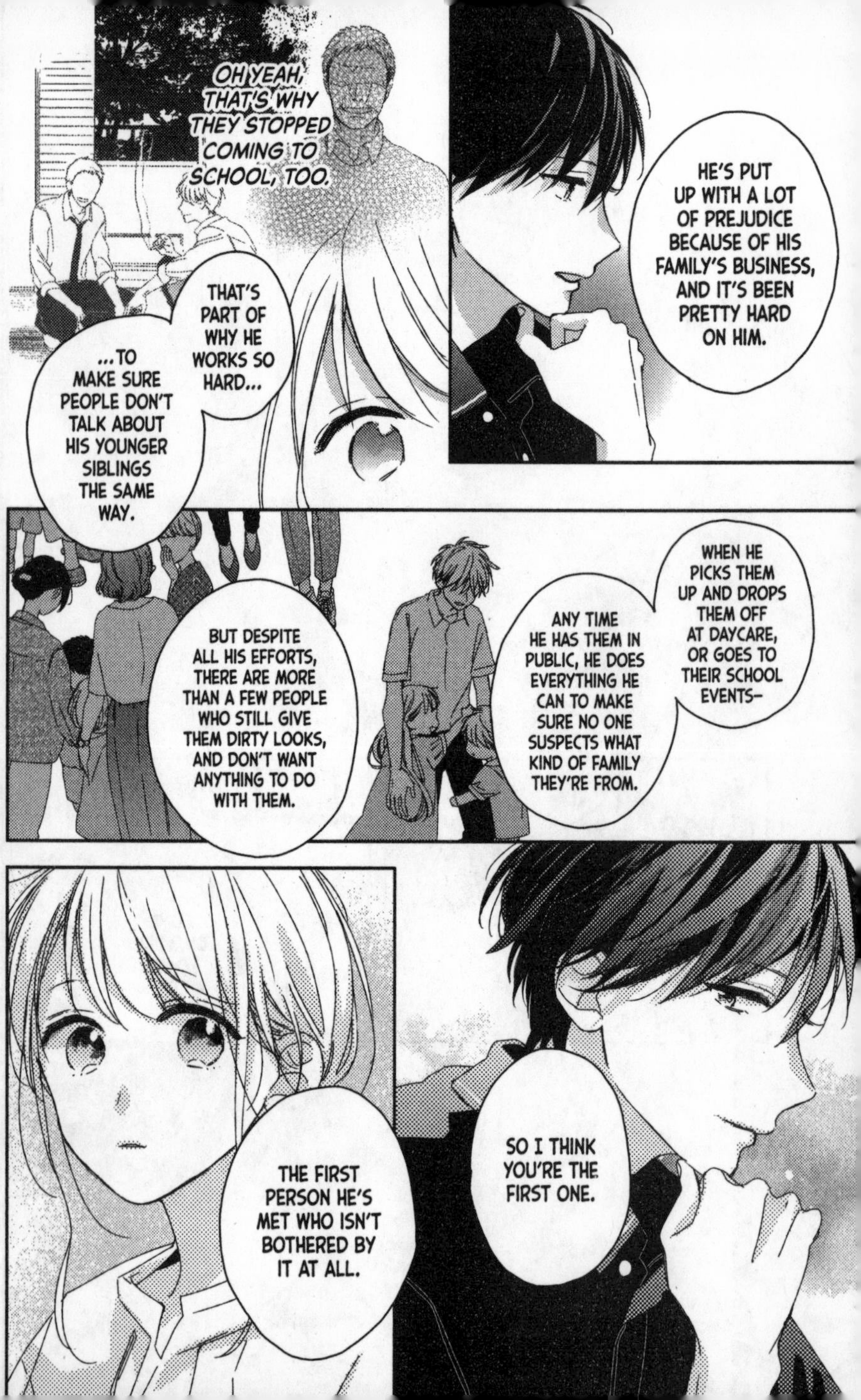
HE'S PUT UP WITH A LOT OF PREJUDICE BECAUSE OF HIS FAMILY'S BUSINESS, AND IT'S BEEN PRETTY HARD ON HIM.
OH YEAH, THAT'S WHY THEY STOPPED COMING TO SCHOOL, TOO.
THAT'S PART OF WHY HE WORKS SO HARD...
...TO MAKE SURE PEOPLE DON'T TALK ABOUT HIS YOUNGER SIBLINGS THE SAME WAY.
WHEN HE PICKS THEM UP AND DROPS THEM OFF AT DAYCARE, OR GOES TO THEIR SCHOOL EVENTS–
ANY TIME HE HAS THEM IN PUBLIC, HE DOES EVERYTHING HE CAN TO MAKE SURE NO ONE SUSPECTS WHAT KIND OF FAMILY THEY'RE FROM.
BUT DESPITE ALL HIS EFFORTS, THERE ARE MORE THAN A FEW PEOPLE WHO STILL GIVE THEM DIRTY LOOKS, AND DON'T WANT ANYTHING TO DO WITH THEM.
SO I THINK YOU'RE THE FIRST ONE.
THE FIRST PERSON HE'S MET WHO ISN'T BOTHERED BY IT AT ALL.

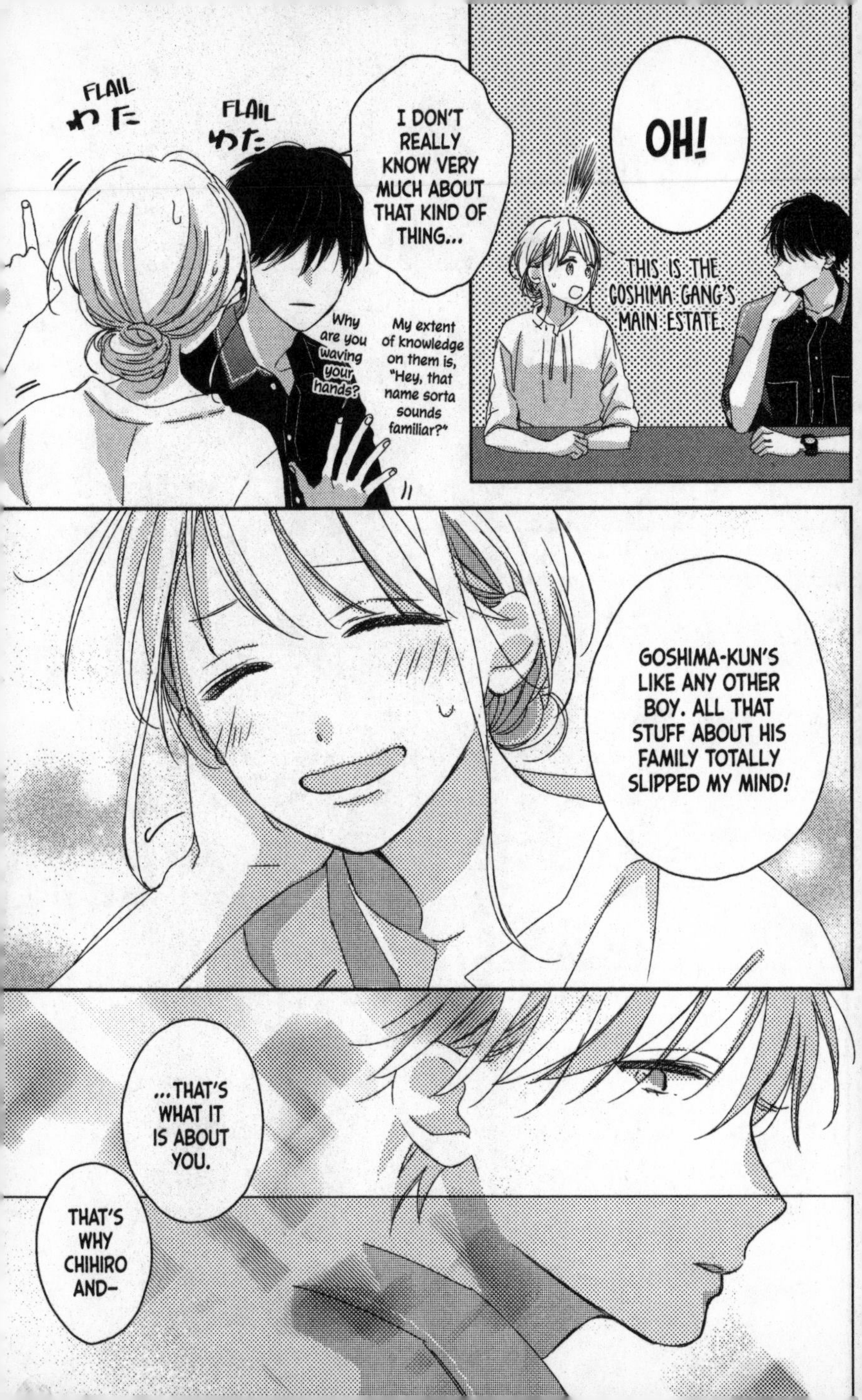
OH!
THIS IS THE GOSHIMA GANG'S MAIN ESTATE.
I DON'T REALLY KNOW VERY MUCH ABOUT THAT KIND OF THING...
FLAIL わた
FLAIL わた
My extent of knowledge on them is, "Hey, that name sorta sounds familiar?"
Why are you waving your hands?
GOSHIMA-KUN'S LIKE ANY OTHER BOY. ALL THAT STUFF ABOUT HIS FAMILY TOTALLY SLIPPED MY MIND!
...THAT'S WHAT IT IS ABOUT YOU.
THAT'S WHY CHIHIRO AND–

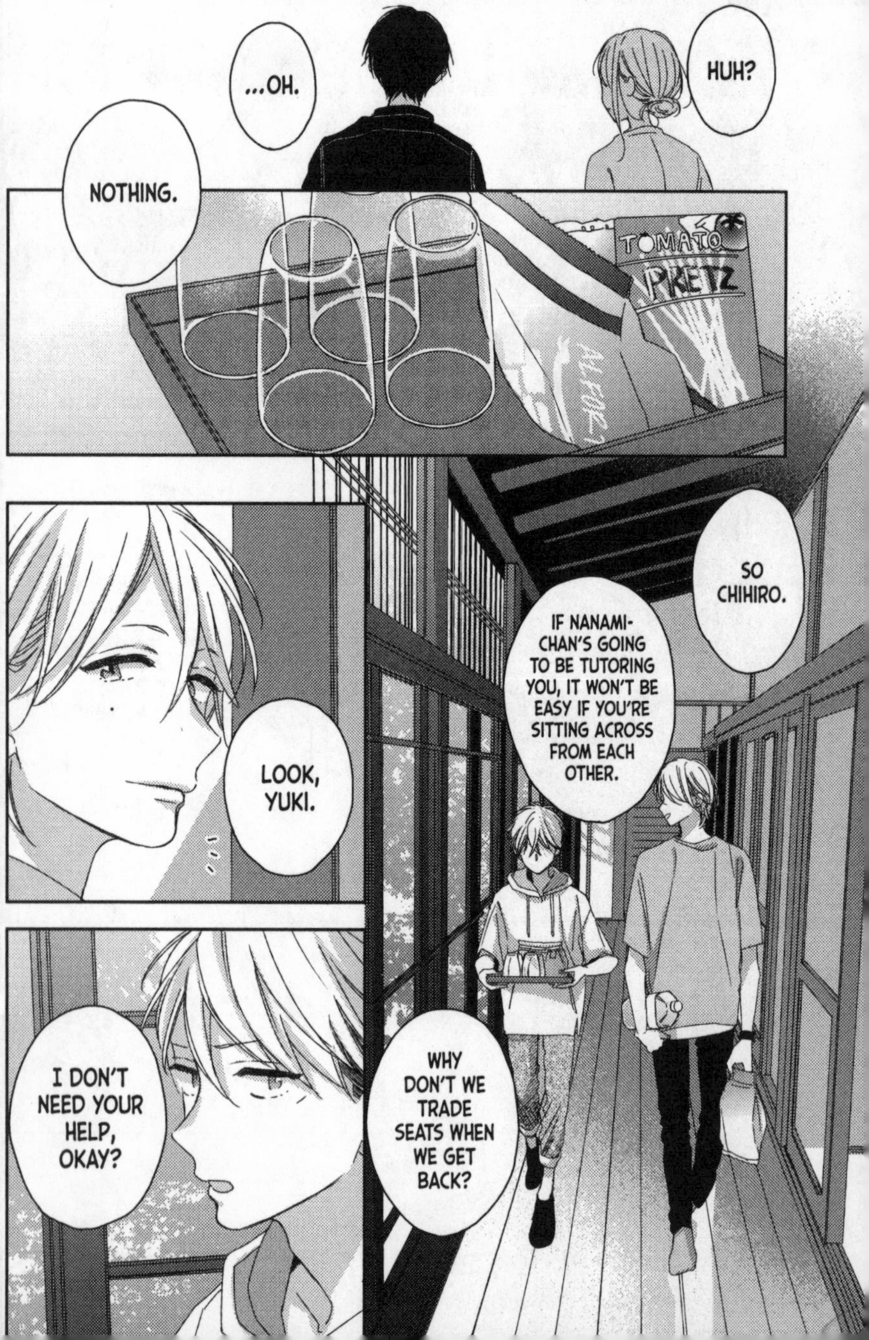
HUH?
...OH.
NOTHING.
TOMATO
PRETZ
SO CHIHIRO.
IF NANAMI-CHAN'S GOING TO BE TUTORING YOU, IT WON'T BE EASY IF YOU'RE SITTING ACROSS FROM EACH OTHER.
WHY DON'T WE TRADE SEATS WHEN WE GET BACK?
LOOK, YUKI.
I DON'T NEED YOUR HELP, OKAY?

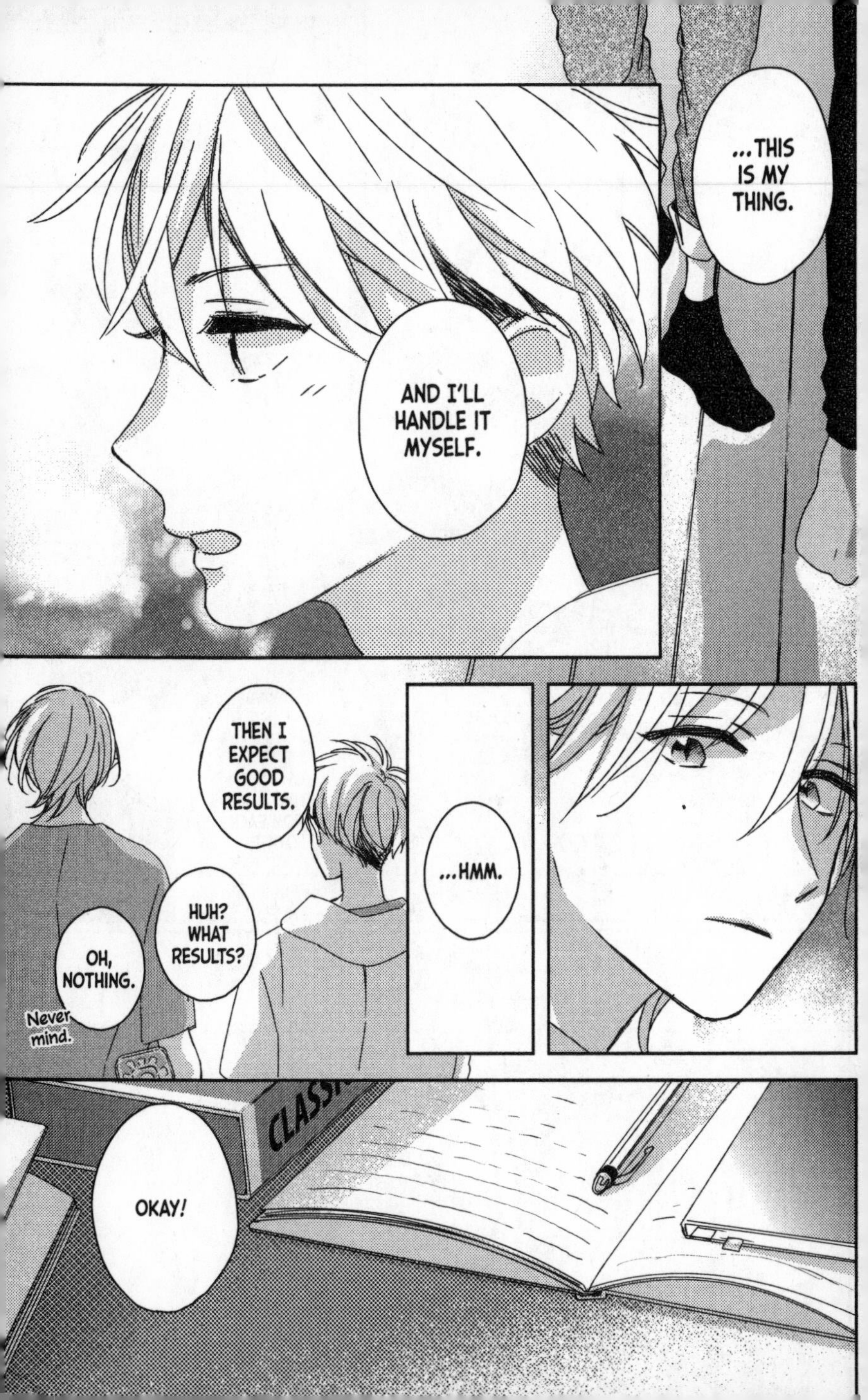
...THIS IS MY THING.
AND I'LL HANDLE IT MYSELF.
...HMM.
THEN I EXPECT GOOD RESULTS.
HUH? WHAT RESULTS?
OH, NOTHING.
Never mind.
CLASS
OKAY!

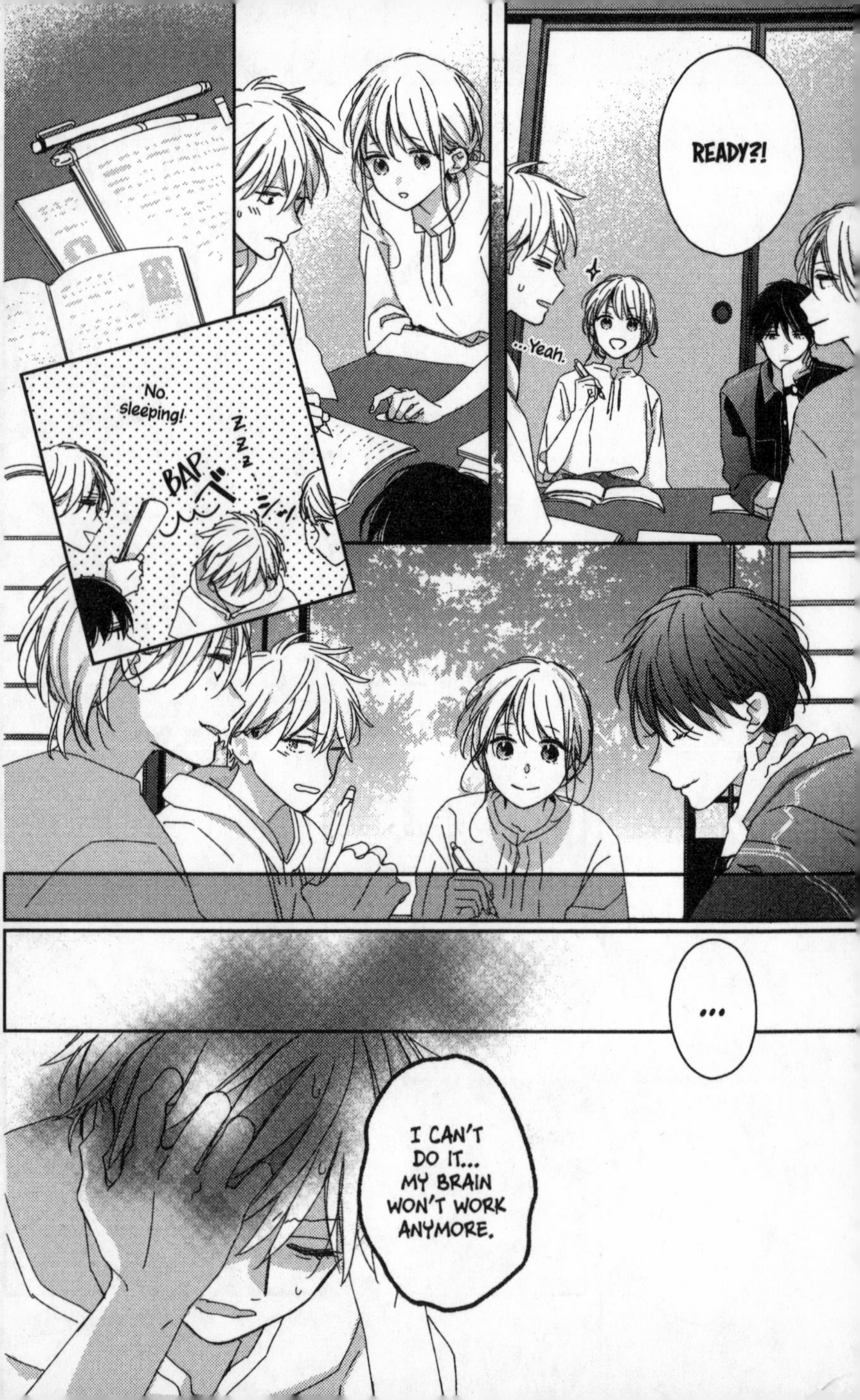
READY?!
...Yeah.
No sleeping!
Z Z Z
BAP
...
I CAN'T DO IT... MY BRAIN WON'T WORK ANYMORE.

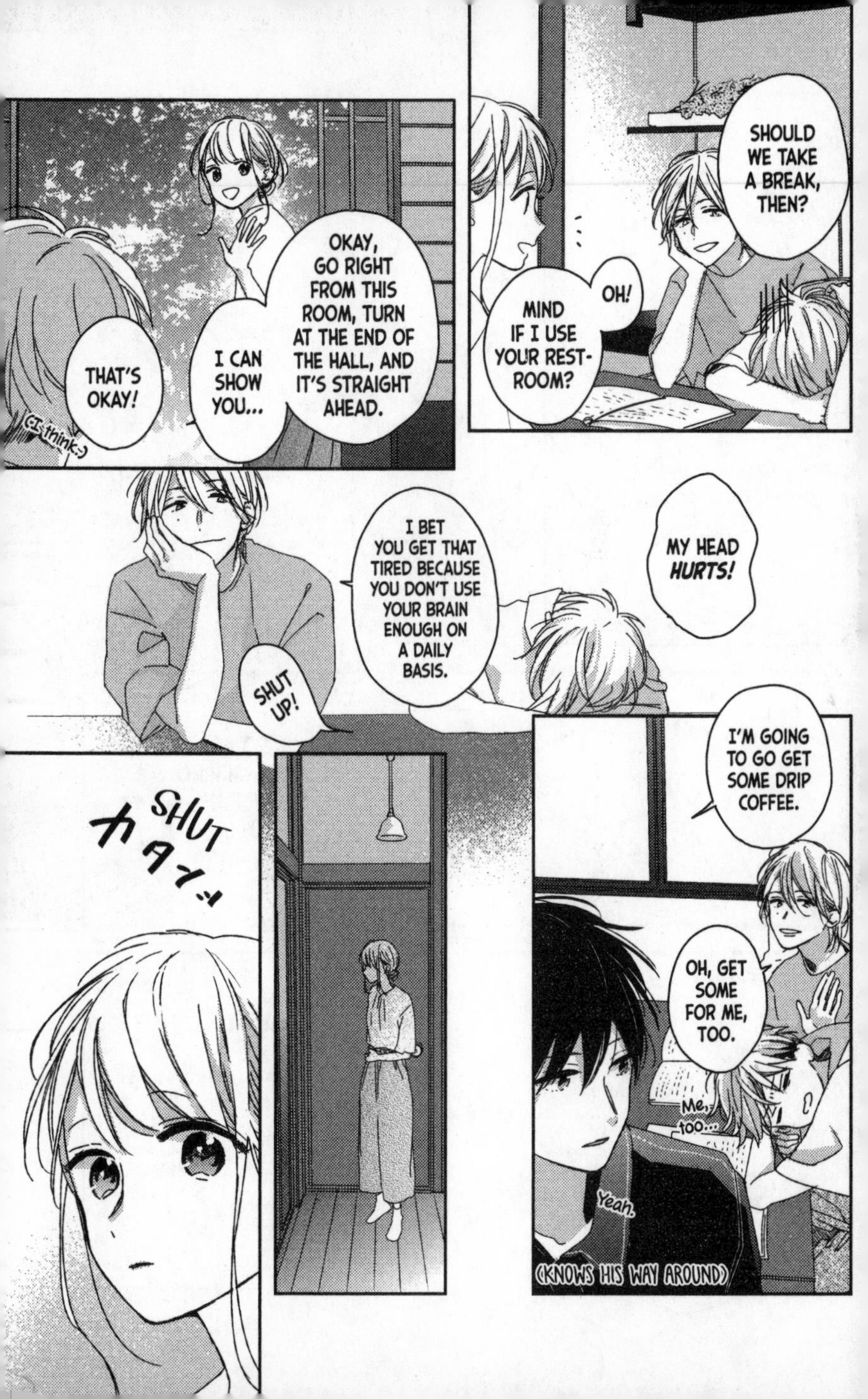
SHOULD WE TAKE A BREAK, THEN?
OH!
MIND IF I USE YOUR REST-ROOM?
OKAY, GO RIGHT FROM THIS ROOM, TURN AT THE END OF THE HALL, AND IT'S STRAIGHT AHEAD.
I CAN SHOW YOU...
THAT'S OKAY!
(I think.)
MY HEAD *HURTS!*
I BET YOU GET THAT TIRED BECAUSE YOU DON'T USE YOUR BRAIN ENOUGH ON A DAILY BASIS.
SHUT UP!
I'M GOING TO GO GET SOME DRIP COFFEE.
OH, GET SOME FOR ME, TOO.
Me, too...
Yeah.
(KNOWS HIS WAY AROUND)
SHUT
カタッ

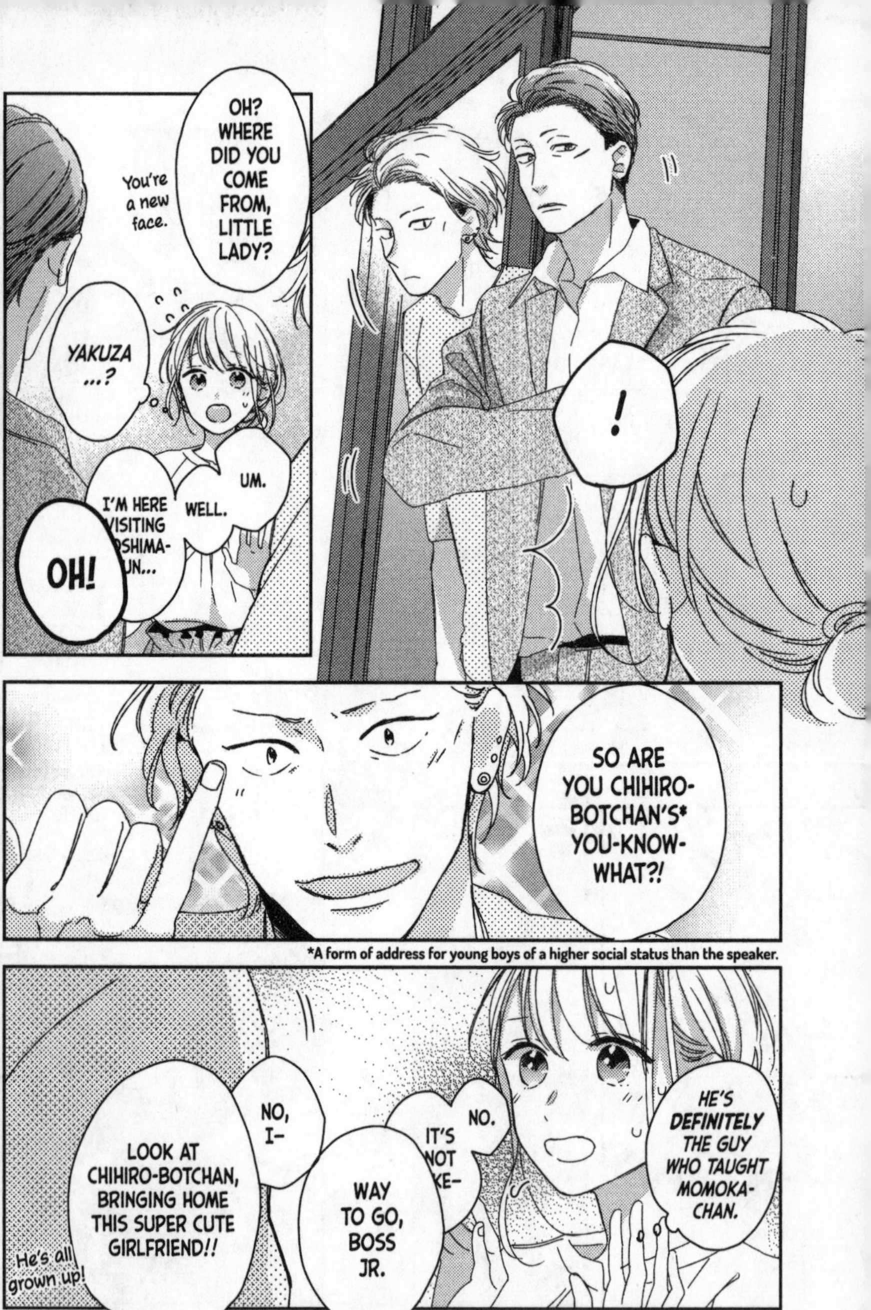
!
OH? WHERE DID YOU COME FROM, LITTLE LADY?
You're a new face.
YAKUZA ...?
UM.
WELL.
I'M HERE VISITING OSHIMA- UN...
OH!
SO ARE YOU CHIHIRO-BOTCHAN'S* YOU-KNOW-WHAT?!
HE'S DEFINITELY THE GUY WHO TAUGHT MOMOKA-CHAN.
NO.
IT'S NOT KE-
NO, I-
WAY TO GO, BOSS JR.
LOOK AT CHIHIRO-BOTCHAN, BRINGING HOME THIS SUPER CUTE GIRLFRIEND!!
He's all grown up!
*A form of address for young boys of a higher social status than the speaker.

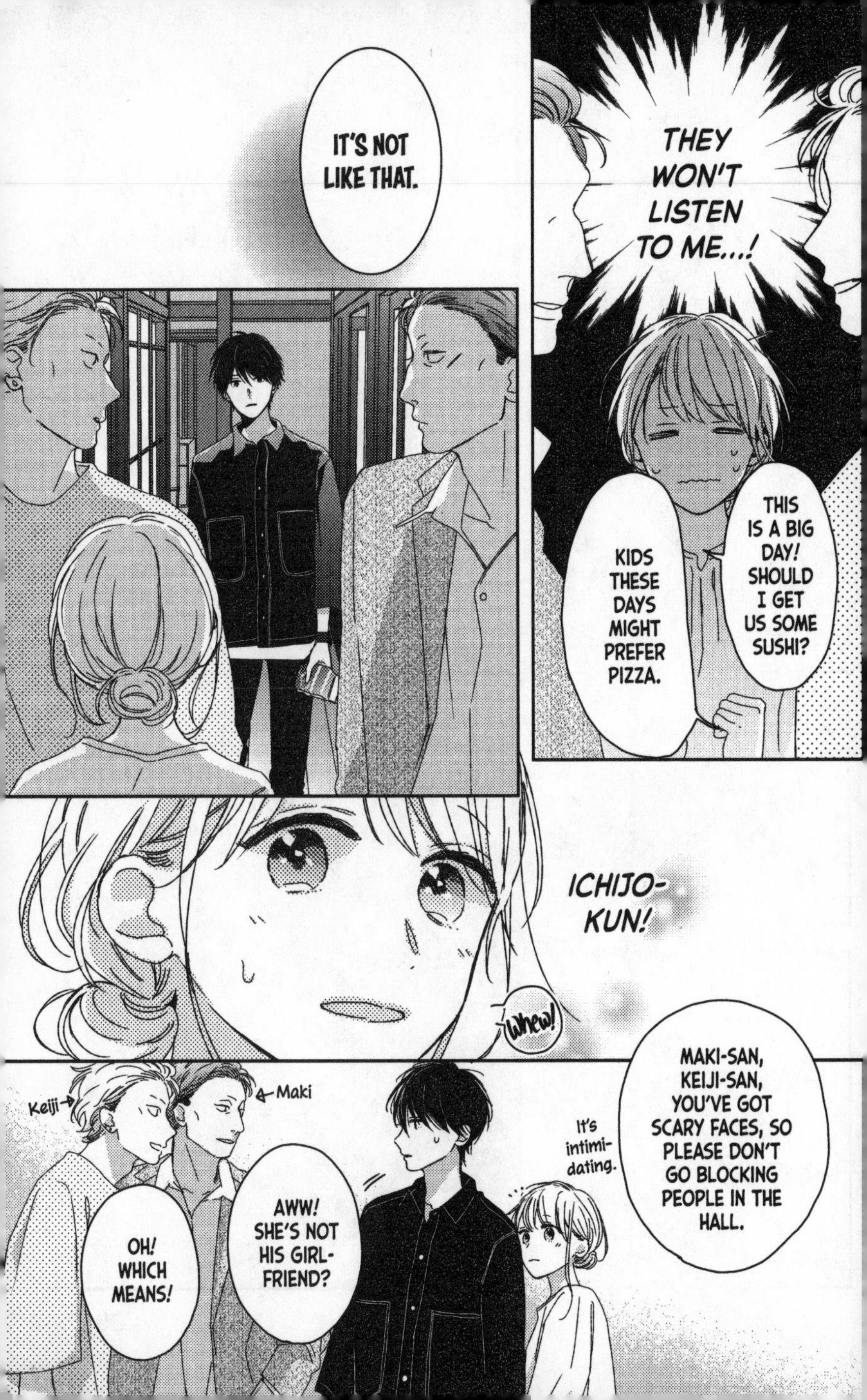
THEY WON'T LISTEN TO ME...!
THIS IS A BIG DAY! SHOULD I GET US SOME SUSHI?
KIDS THESE DAYS MIGHT PREFER PIZZA.
IT'S NOT LIKE THAT.
ICHIJO-KUN!
Whew!
MAKI-SAN, KEIJI-SAN, YOU'VE GOT SCARY FACES, SO PLEASE DON'T GO BLOCKING PEOPLE IN THE HALL.
It's intimi-dating.
Maki
Keiji
AWW! SHE'S NOT HIS GIRL-FRIEND?
OH! WHICH MEANS!

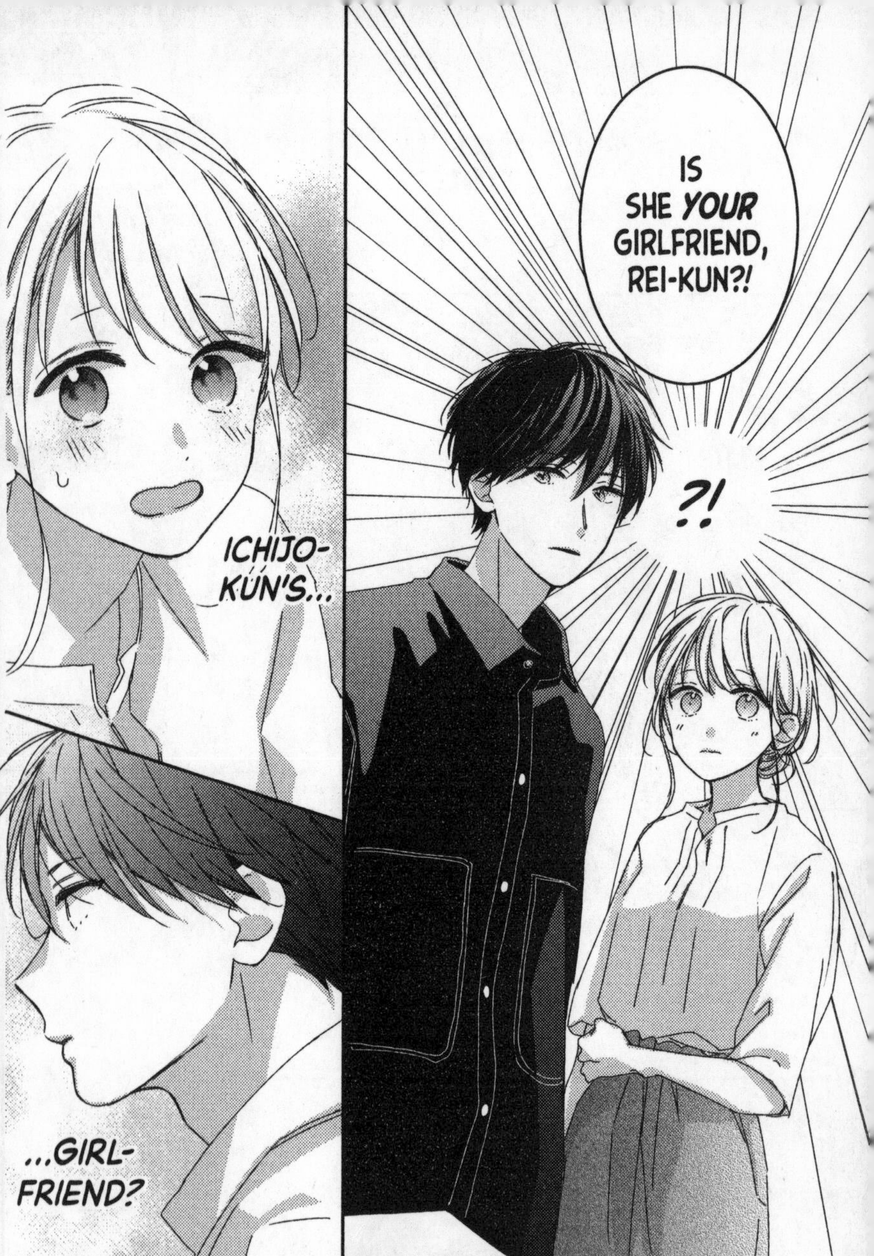
IS SHE *YOUR* GIRLFRIEND, REI-KUN?!
?!
ICHIJO-KUN'S...
...GIRL-FRIEND?

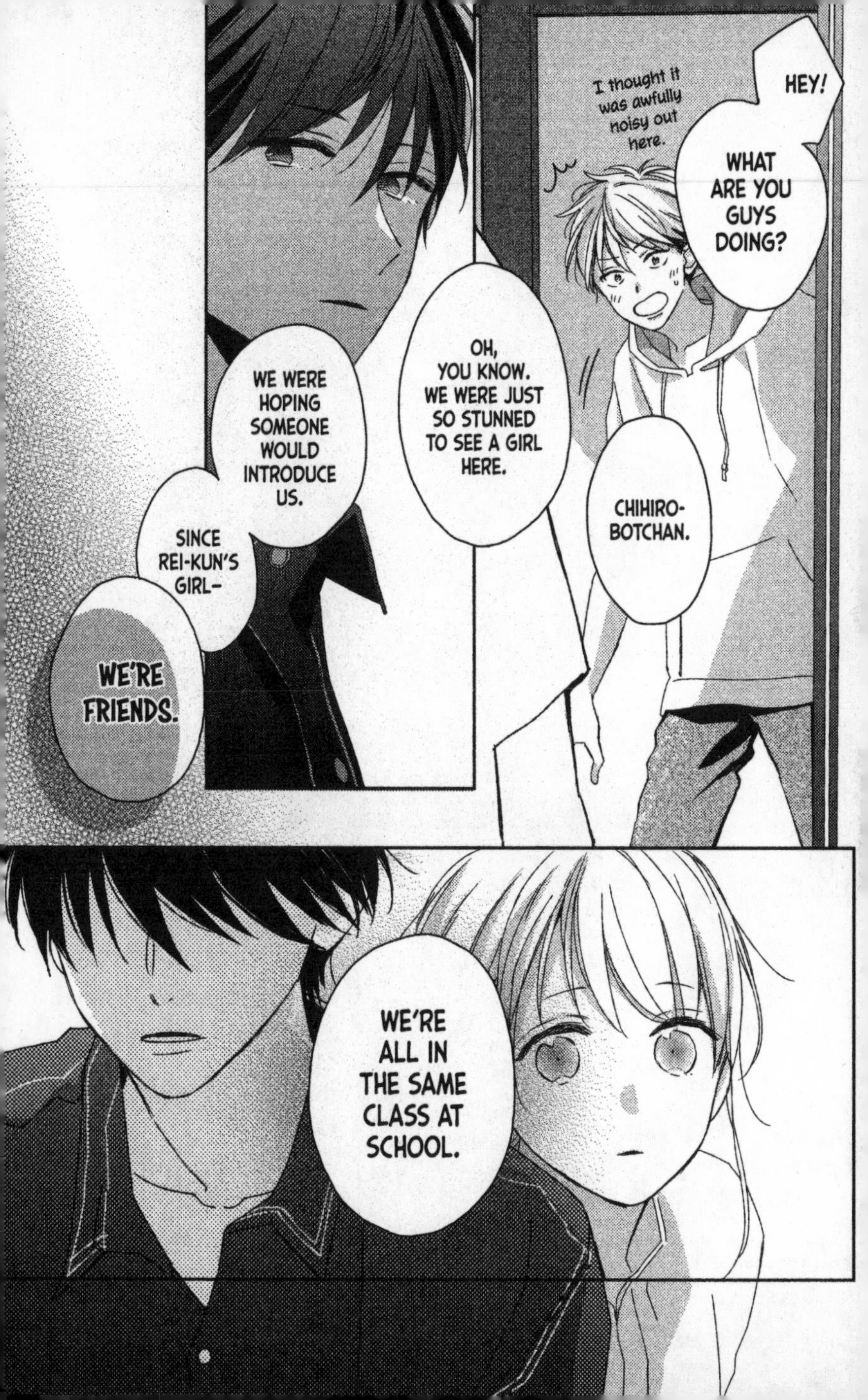
HEY!
I thought it was awfully noisy out here.
WHAT ARE YOU GUYS DOING?
OH, YOU KNOW. WE WERE JUST SO STUNNED TO SEE A GIRL HERE.
CHIHIRO-BOTCHAN.
WE WERE HOPING SOMEONE WOULD INTRODUCE US.
SINCE REI-KUN'S GIRL–
WE'RE FRIENDS.
WE'RE ALL IN THE SAME CLASS AT SCHOOL.

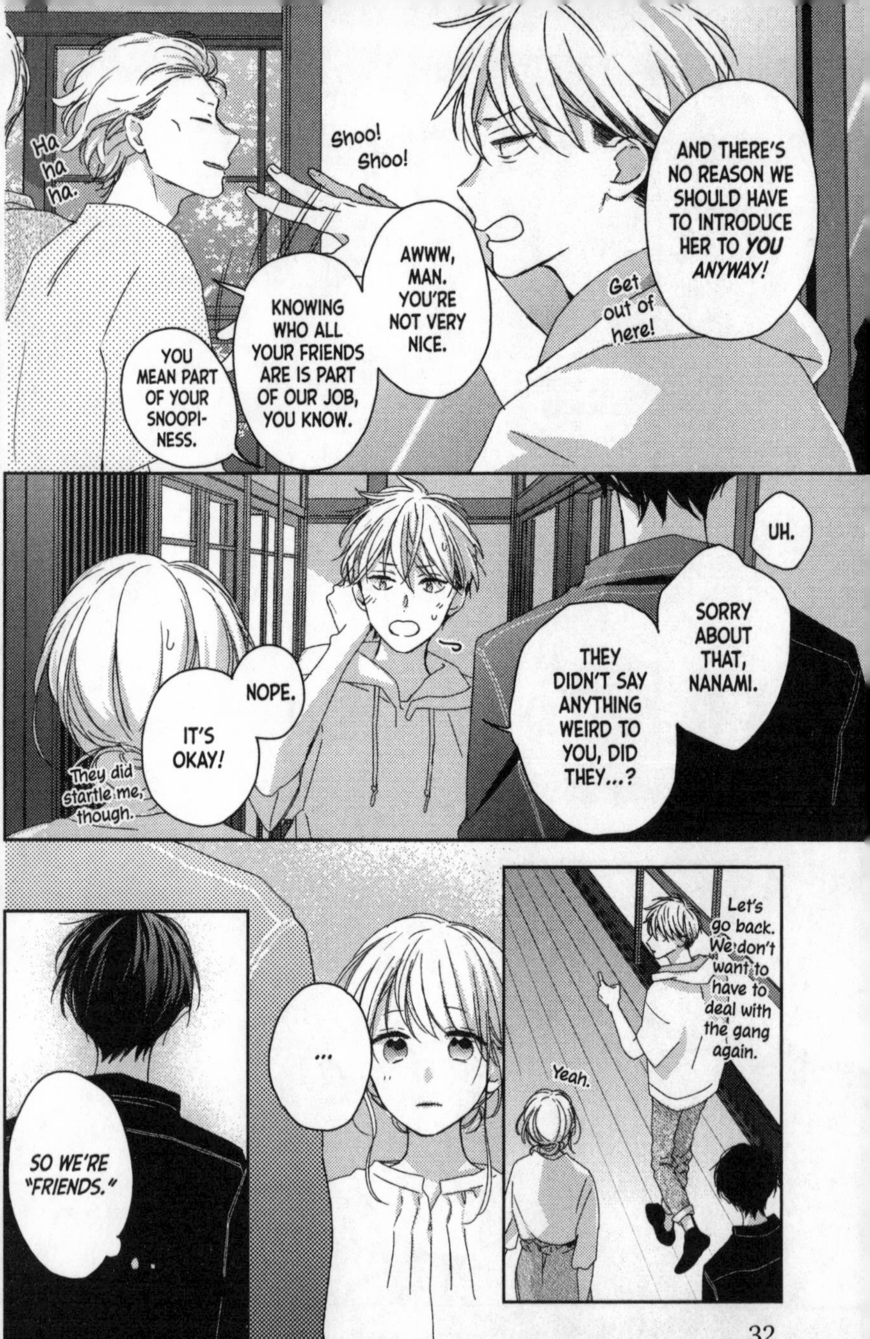
AND THERE'S NO REASON WE SHOULD HAVE TO INTRODUCE HER TO *YOU ANYWAY!*
Get out of here!
Shoo! Shoo!
AWWW, MAN. YOU'RE NOT VERY NICE.
Ha ha ha.
KNOWING WHO ALL YOUR FRIENDS ARE IS PART OF OUR JOB, YOU KNOW.
YOU MEAN PART OF YOUR SNOOPI-NESS.
UH.
SORRY ABOUT THAT, NANAMI.
THEY DIDN'T SAY ANYTHING WEIRD TO YOU, DID THEY...?
NOPE.
IT'S OKAY!
They did startle me, though.
Let's go back. We don't want to have to deal with the gang again.
Yeah.
...
SO WE'RE "FRIENDS."

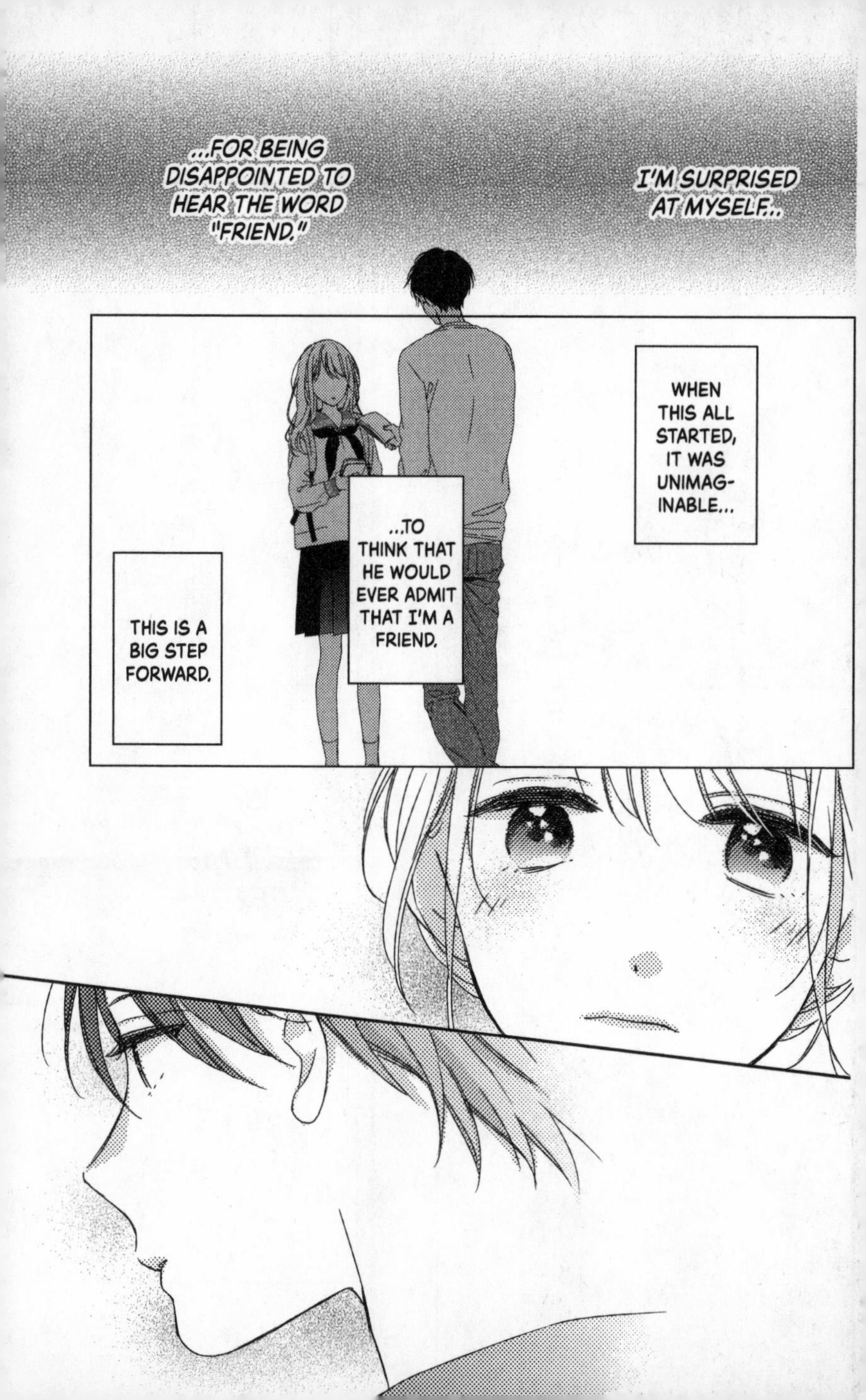
I'M SURPRISED AT MYSELF...
...FOR BEING DISAPPOINTED TO HEAR THE WORD "FRIEND."
WHEN THIS ALL STARTED, IT WAS UNIMAG-INABLE...
...TO THINK THAT HE WOULD EVER ADMIT THAT I'M A FRIEND.
THIS IS A BIG STEP FORWARD.

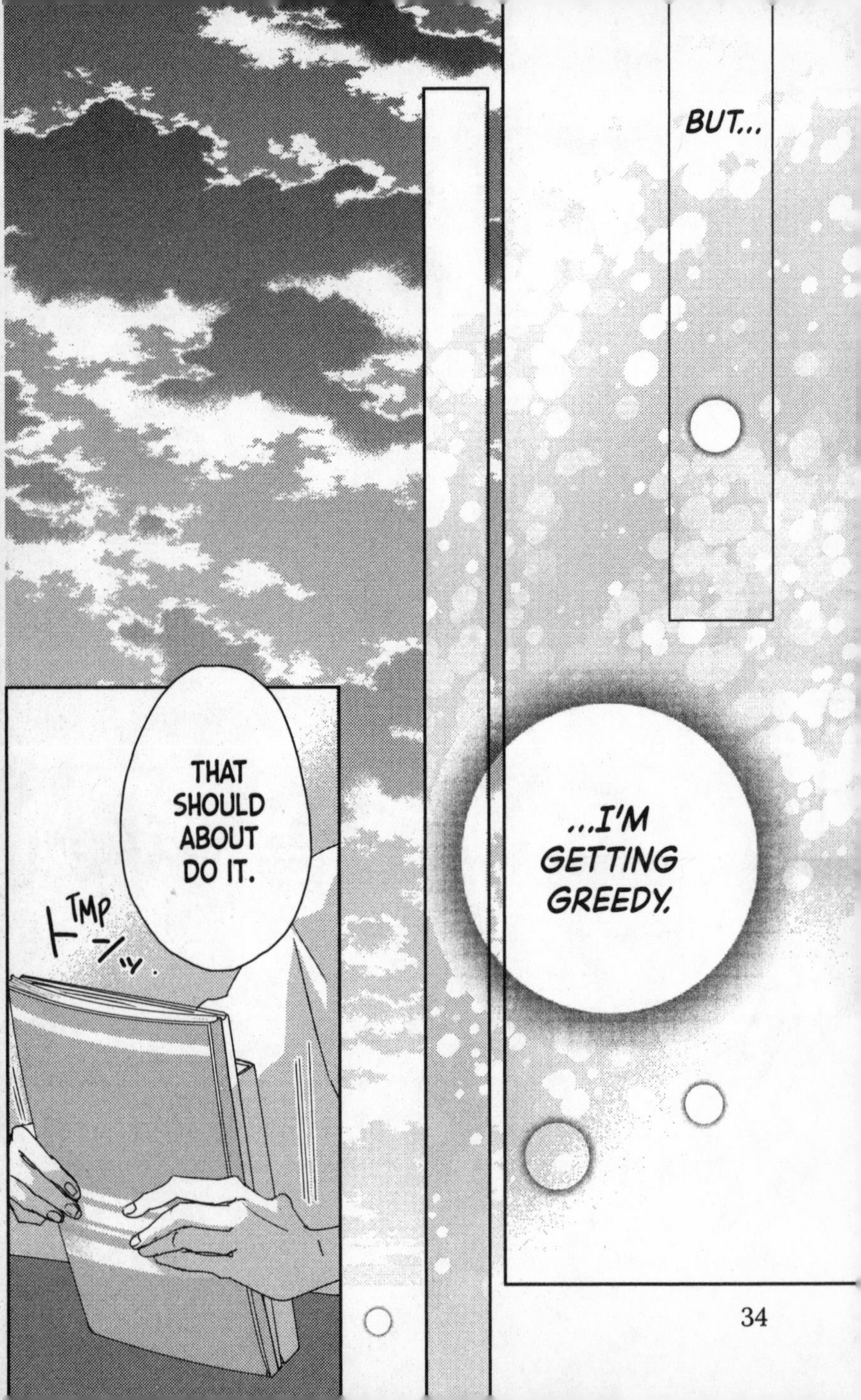
BUT...
...I'M GETTING GREEDY.
THAT SHOULD ABOUT DO IT.
TMP

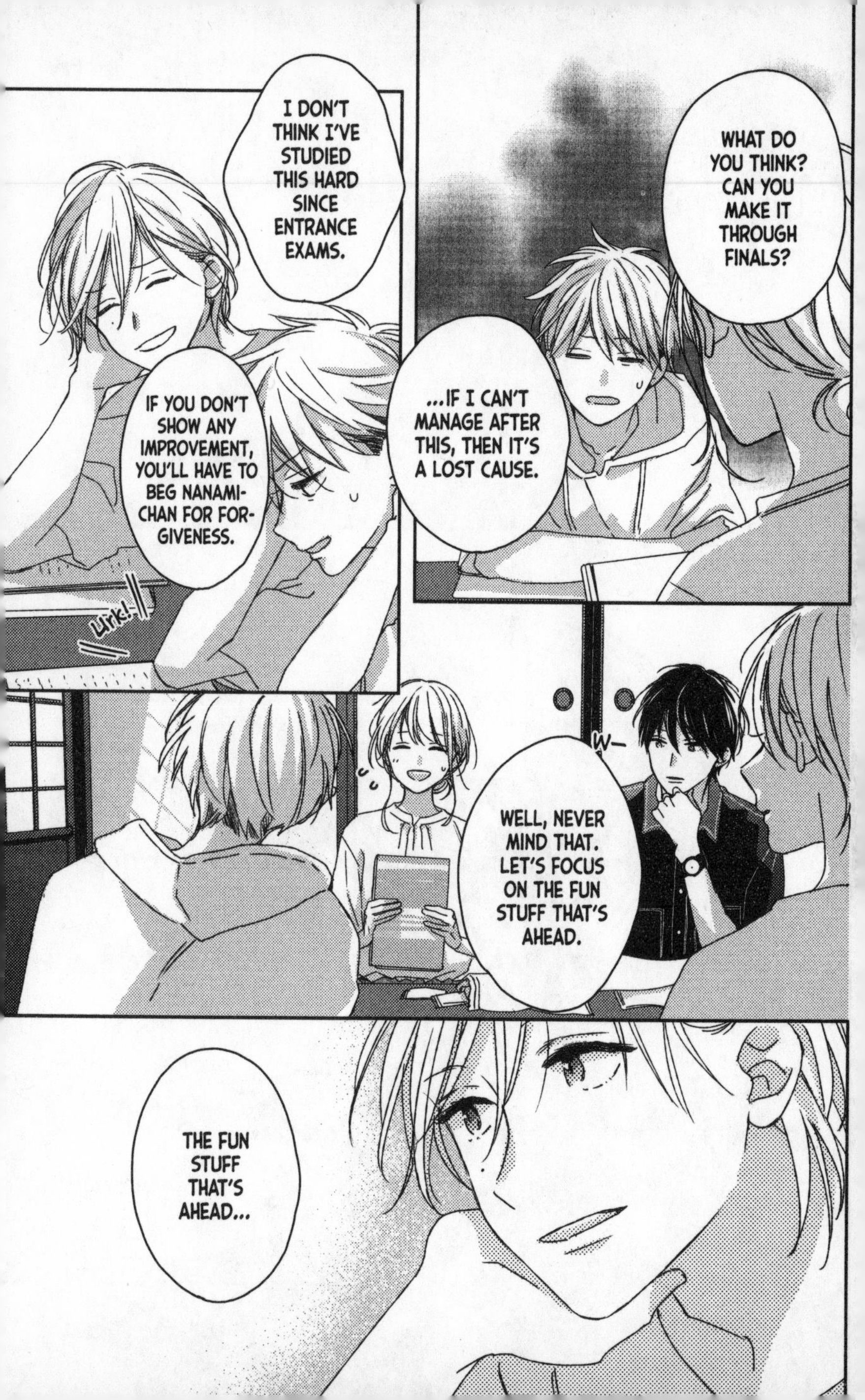
WHAT DO YOU THINK? CAN YOU MAKE IT THROUGH FINALS?
...IF I CAN'T MANAGE AFTER THIS, THEN IT'S A LOST CAUSE.
I DON'T THINK I'VE STUDIED THIS HARD SINCE ENTRANCE EXAMS.
IF YOU DON'T SHOW ANY IMPROVEMENT, YOU'LL HAVE TO BEG NANAMI-CHAN FOR FORGIVENESS.
Urk!
W—
WELL, NEVER MIND THAT. LET'S FOCUS ON THE FUN STUFF THAT'S AHEAD.
THE FUN STUFF THAT'S AHEAD...

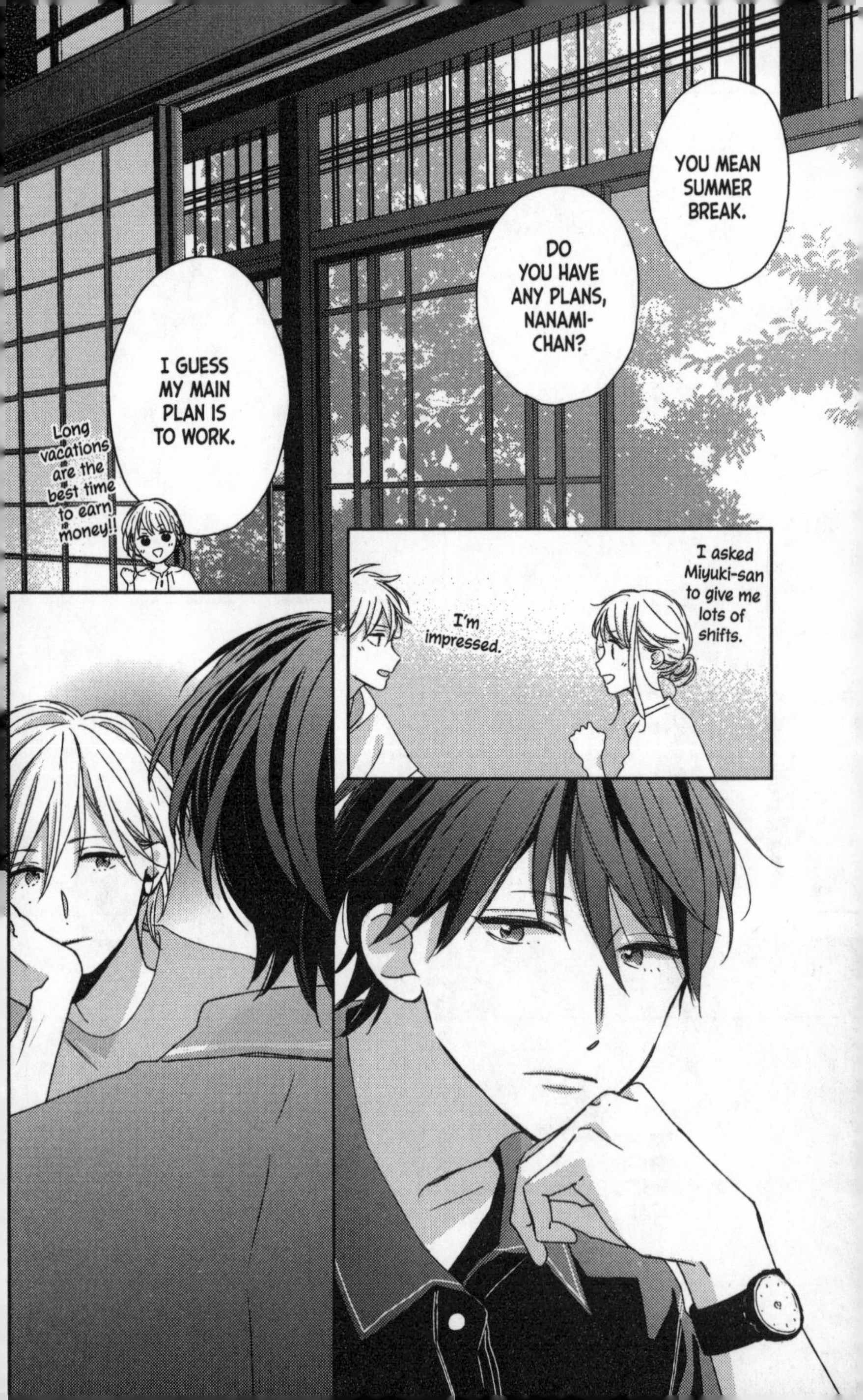
YOU MEAN SUMMER BREAK.
DO YOU HAVE ANY PLANS, NANAMI-CHAN?
I GUESS MY MAIN PLAN IS TO WORK.
Long vacations are the best time to earn money!!
I asked Miyuki-san to give me lots of shifts.
I'm impressed.

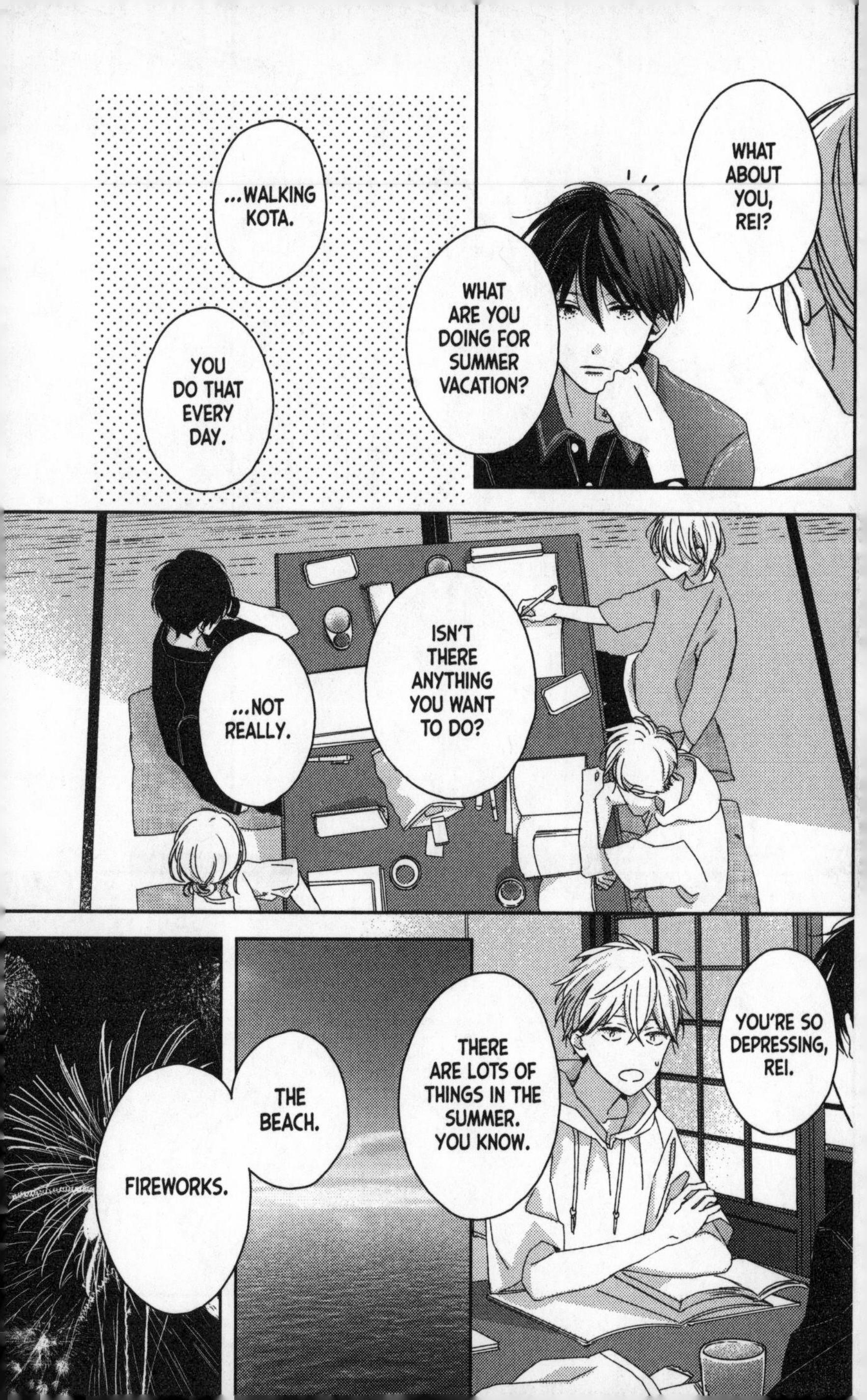
WHAT ABOUT YOU, REI?
WHAT ARE YOU DOING FOR SUMMER VACATION?
...WALKING KOTA.
YOU DO THAT EVERY DAY.
ISN'T THERE ANYTHING YOU WANT TO DO?
...NOT REALLY.
YOU'RE SO DEPRESSING, REI.
THERE ARE LOTS OF THINGS IN THE SUMMER. YOU KNOW.
THE BEACH.
FIREWORKS.

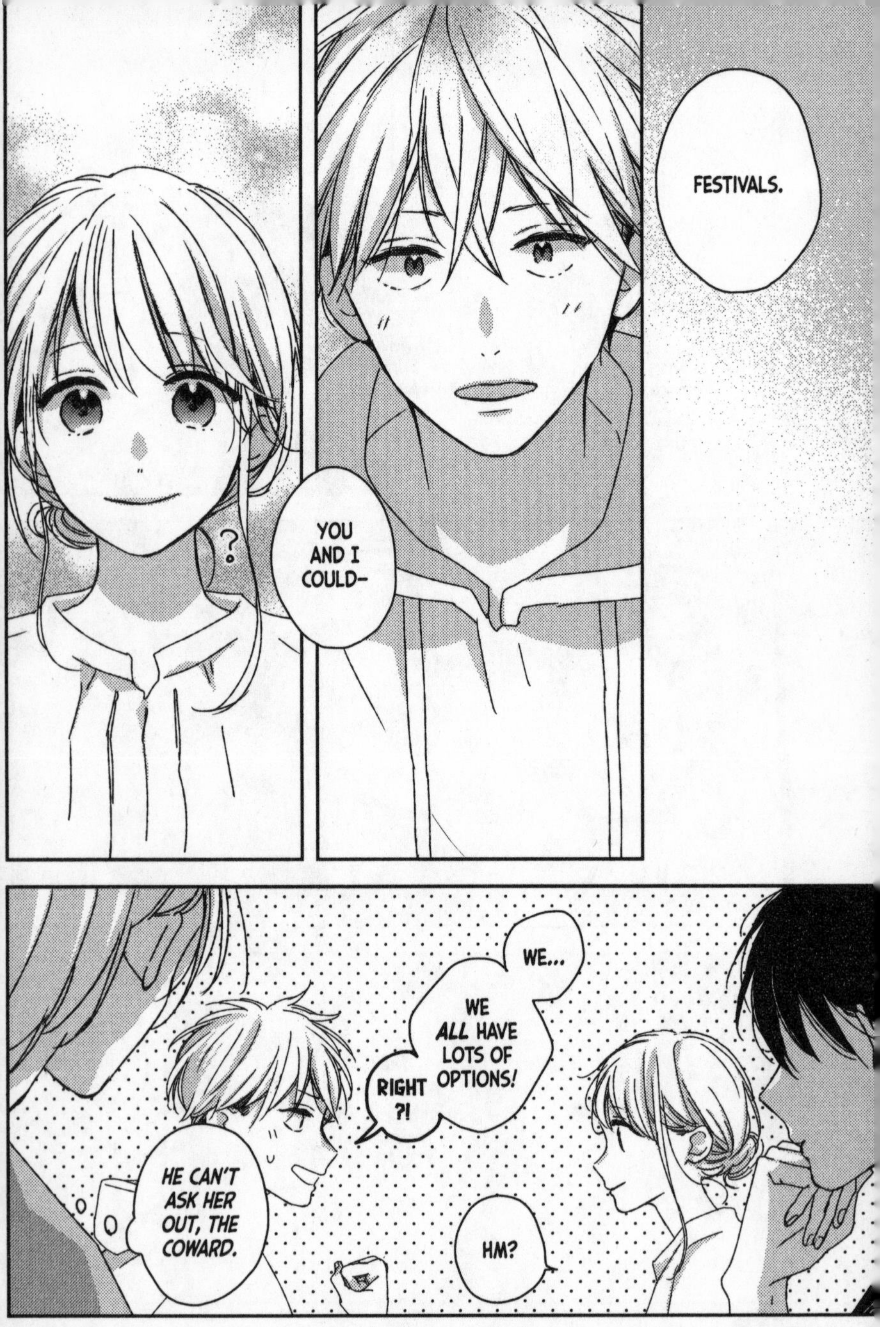
FESTIVALS.
YOU AND I COULD-
?
WE...
WE *ALL* HAVE LOTS OF OPTIONS!
RIGHT ?!
HM?
HE CAN'T ASK HER OUT, THE COWARD.

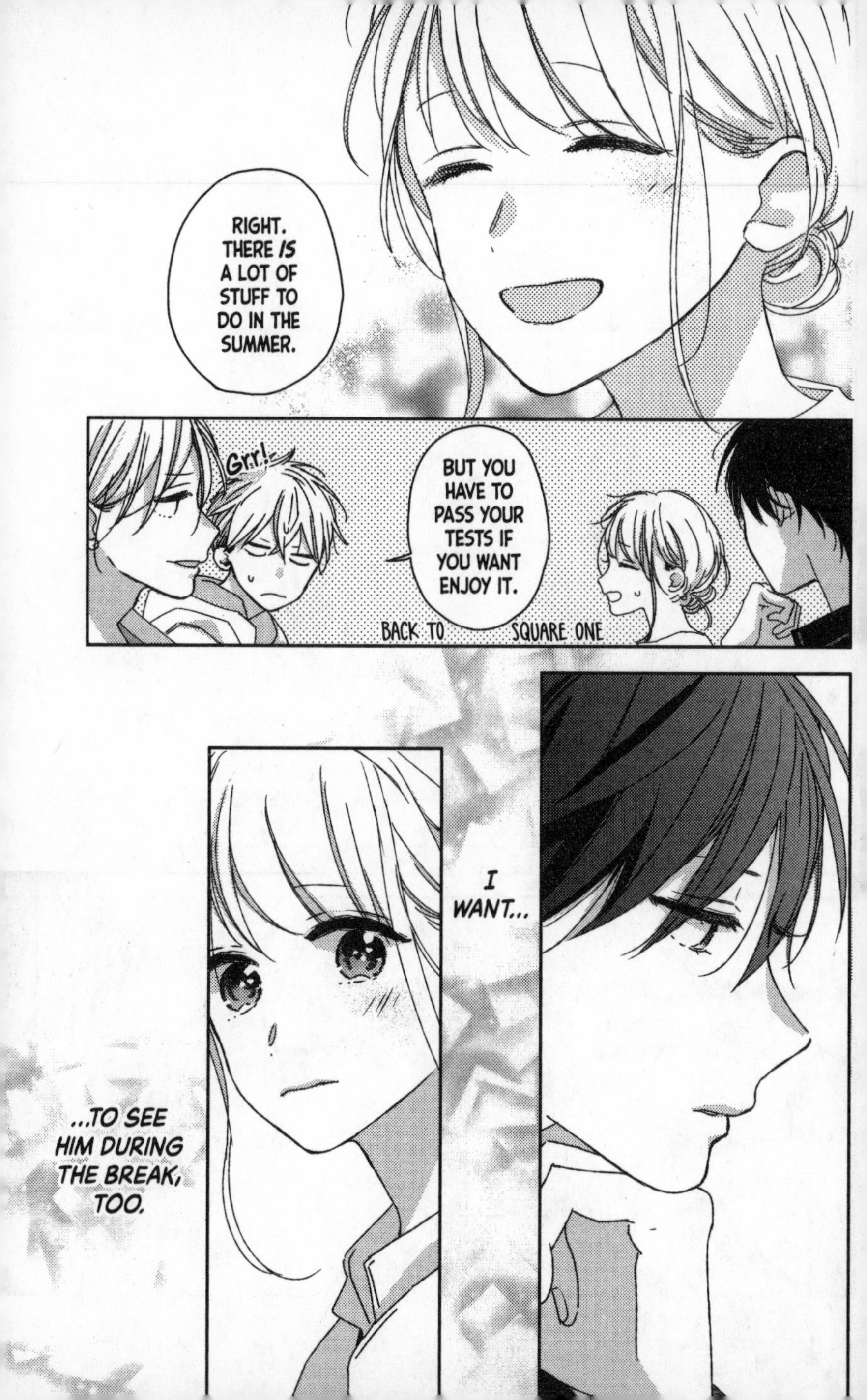
RIGHT. THERE IS A LOT OF STUFF TO DO IN THE SUMMER.
BUT YOU HAVE TO PASS YOUR TESTS IF YOU WANT ENJOY IT.
Grr!
BACK TO SQUARE ONE
I WANT...
...TO SEE HIM DURING THE BREAK, TOO.

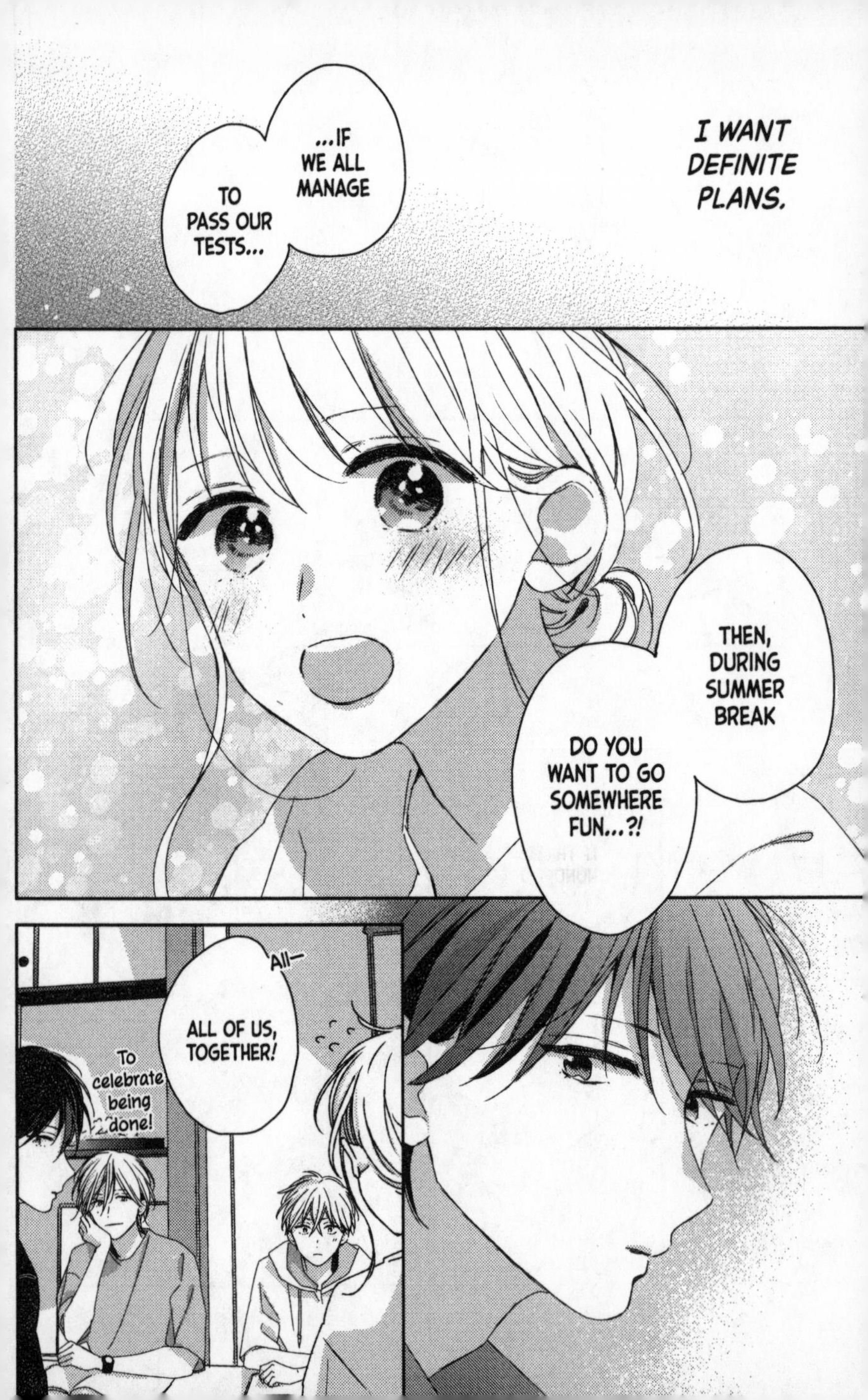
I WANT DEFINITE PLANS.
...IF WE ALL MANAGE TO PASS OUR TESTS...
THEN, DURING SUMMER BREAK DO YOU WANT TO GO SOMEWHERE FUN...?!
All—
ALL OF US, TOGETHER!
To celebrate being done!

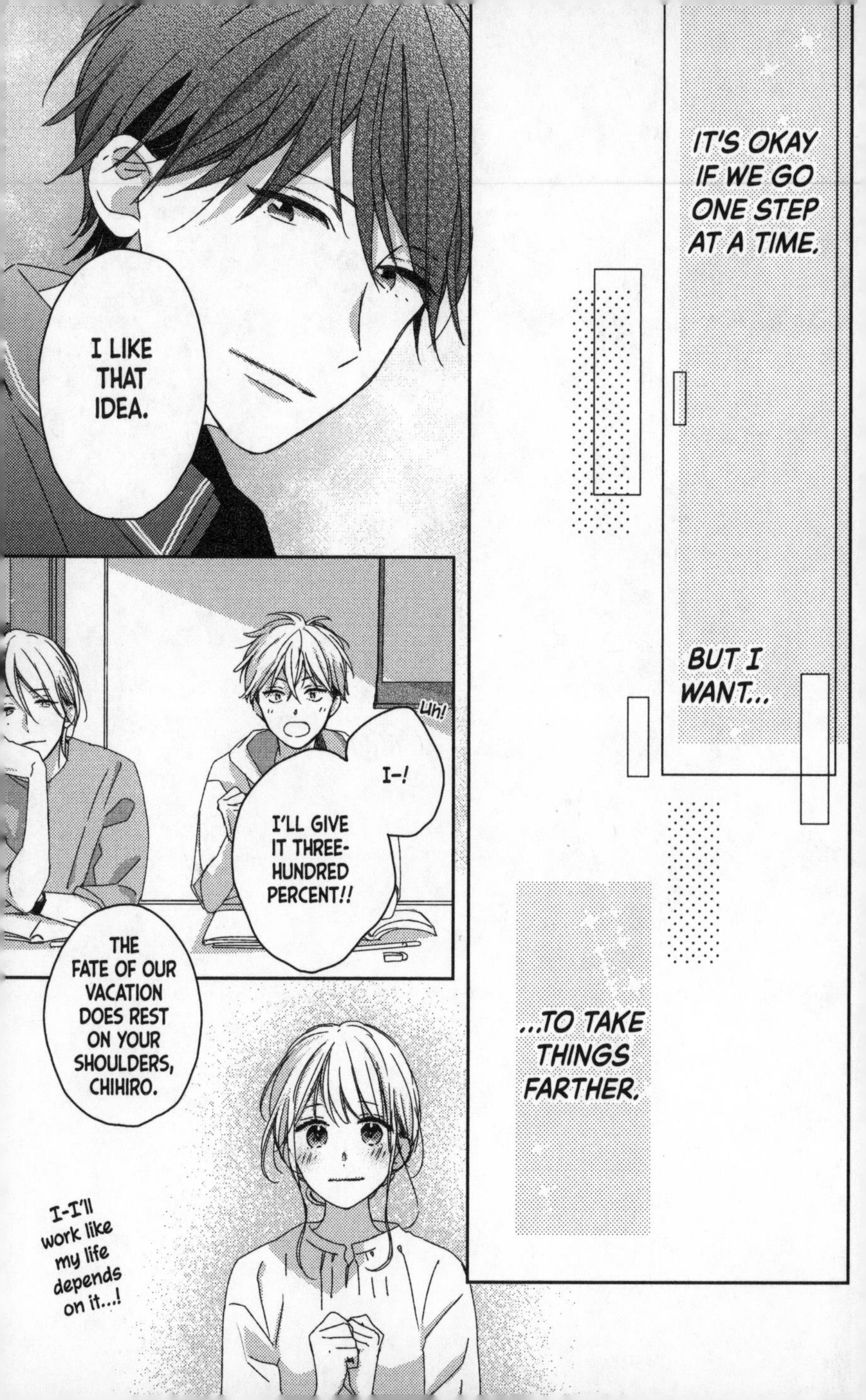
IT'S OKAY IF WE GO ONE STEP AT A TIME.
BUT I WANT...
...TO TAKE THINGS FARTHER.
I LIKE THAT IDEA.
Uh!
I-!
I'LL GIVE IT THREE-HUNDRED PERCENT!!
THE FATE OF OUR VACATION DOES REST ON YOUR SHOULDERS, CHIHIRO.
I-I'll work like my life depends on it...!

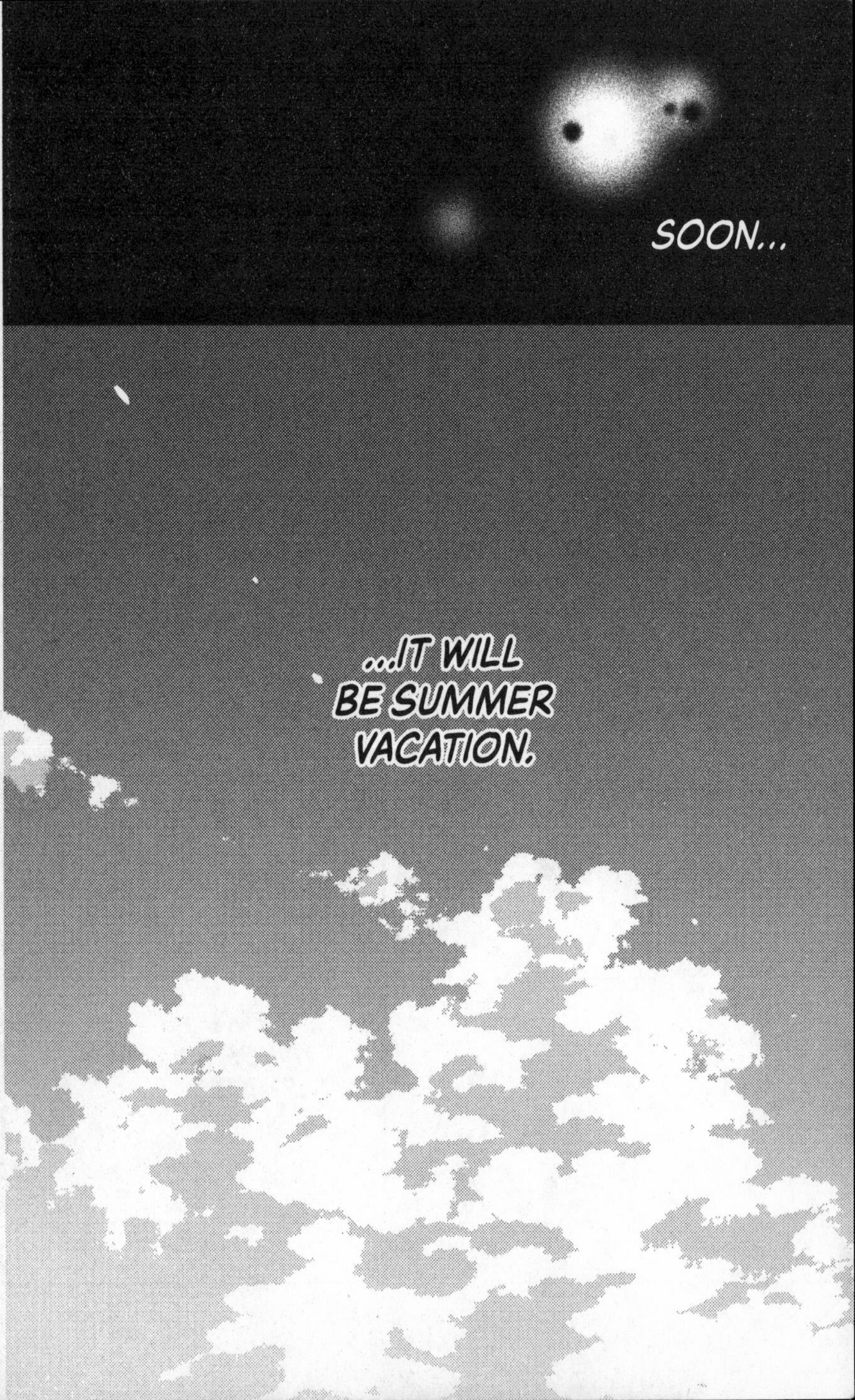
SOON...
...IT WILL BE SUMMER VACATION.

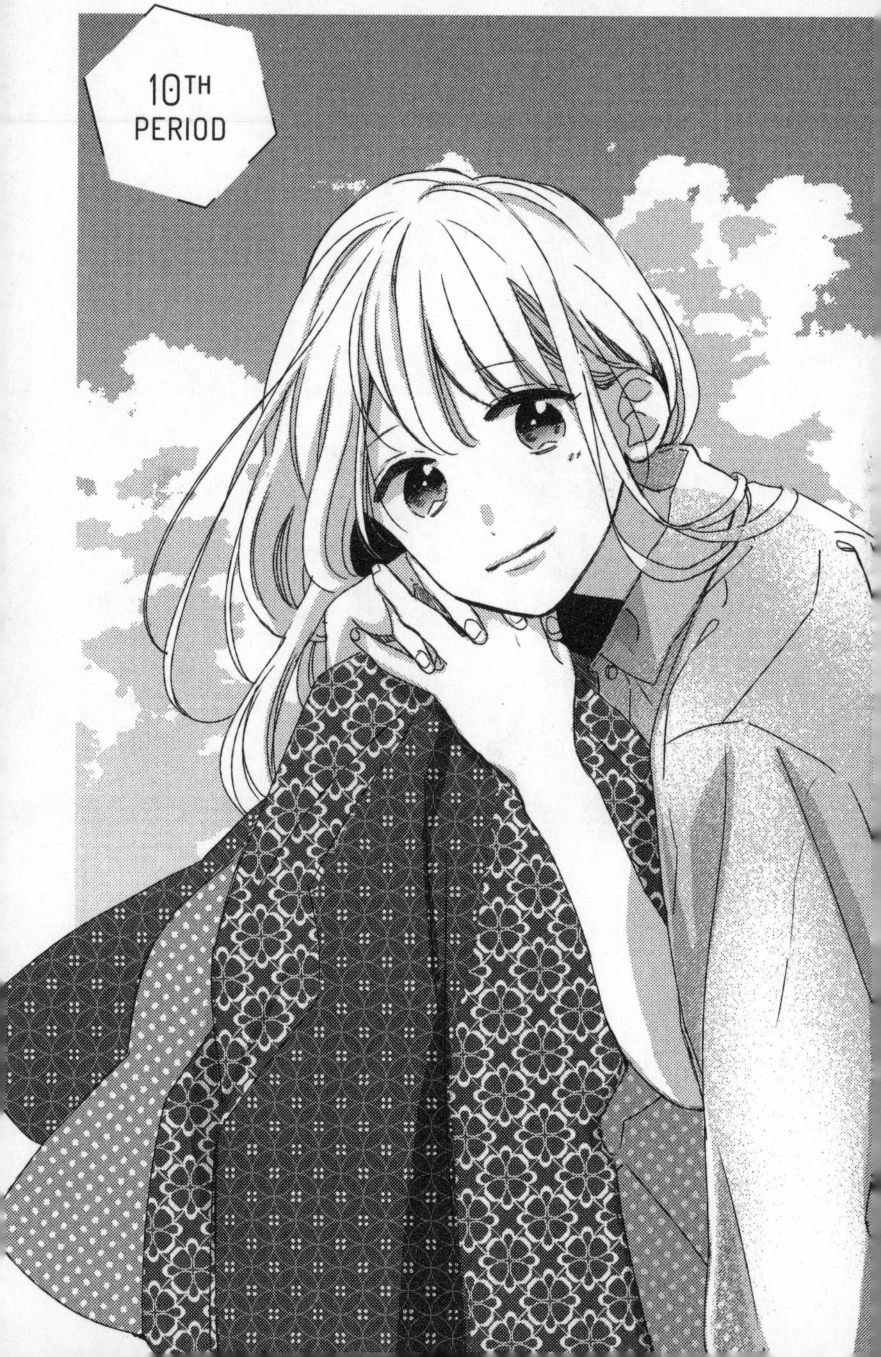
10TH
PERIOD

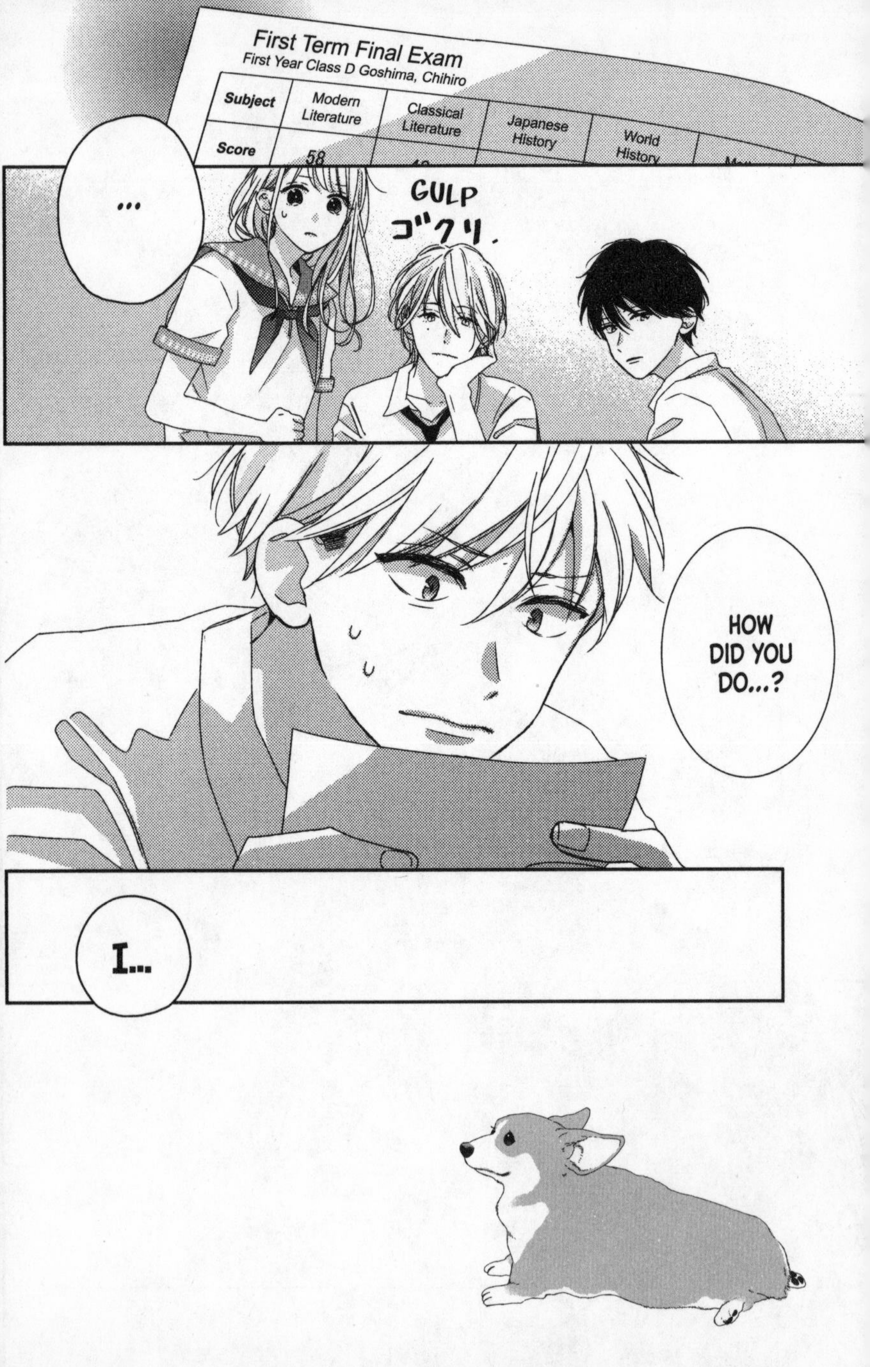
First Term Final Exam
First Year Class D Goshima, Chihiro
Subject
Modern Literature
Classical Literature
Japanese History
World History
Score
58
...
GULP
ゴクリ
HOW DID YOU DO...?
I...

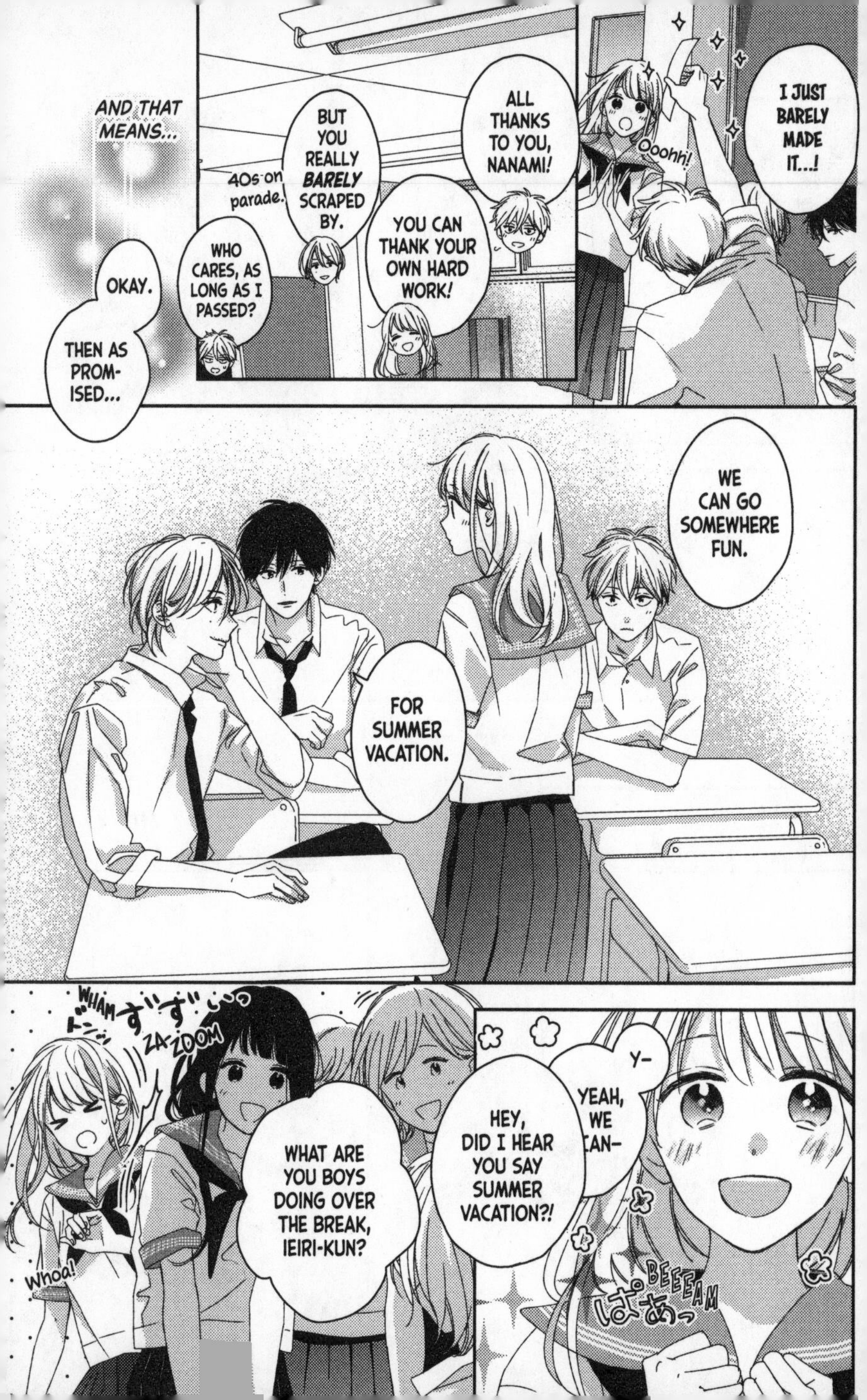
I JUST BARELY MADE IT...!
Ooohh!
ALL THANKS TO YOU, NANAMI!
BUT YOU REALLY *BARELY* SCRAPED BY.
40s on parade.
YOU CAN THANK YOUR OWN HARD WORK!
WHO CARES, AS LONG AS I PASSED?
AND THAT MEANS...
OKAY.
THEN AS PROMISED...
WE CAN GO SOMEWHERE FUN.
FOR SUMMER VACATION.
Y-
YEAH, WE CAN-
BEEEEAM
ぱあっ
HEY, DID I HEAR YOU SAY SUMMER VACATION?!
WHAT ARE YOU BOYS DOING OVER THE BREAK, IEIRI-KUN?
WHAM
ZA-ZDOM
Whoa!

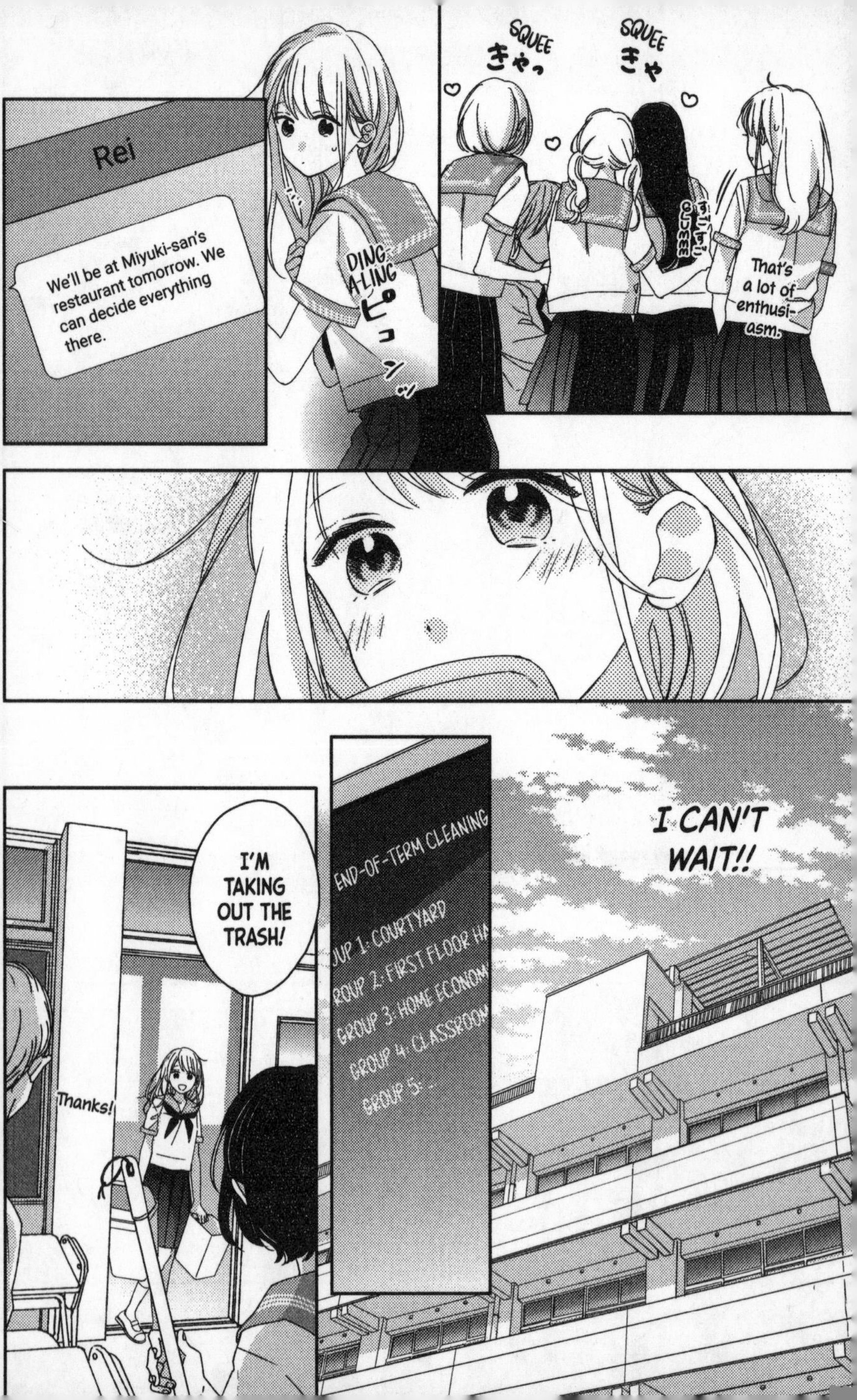
SQUEE
きゃっ
SQUEE
きゃ
That's a lot of enthusi-asm.
Rei
We'll be at Miyuki-san's restaurant tomorrow. We can decide everything there.
DING-A-LING
ピコンッ
I CAN'T WAIT!!
END-OF-TERM CLEANING
...UP 1: COURTYARD
GROUP 2: FIRST FLOOR HA...
GROUP 3: HOME ECONOM...
GROUP 4: CLASSROOM
GROUP 5: ...
I'M TAKING OUT THE TRASH!
Thanks!

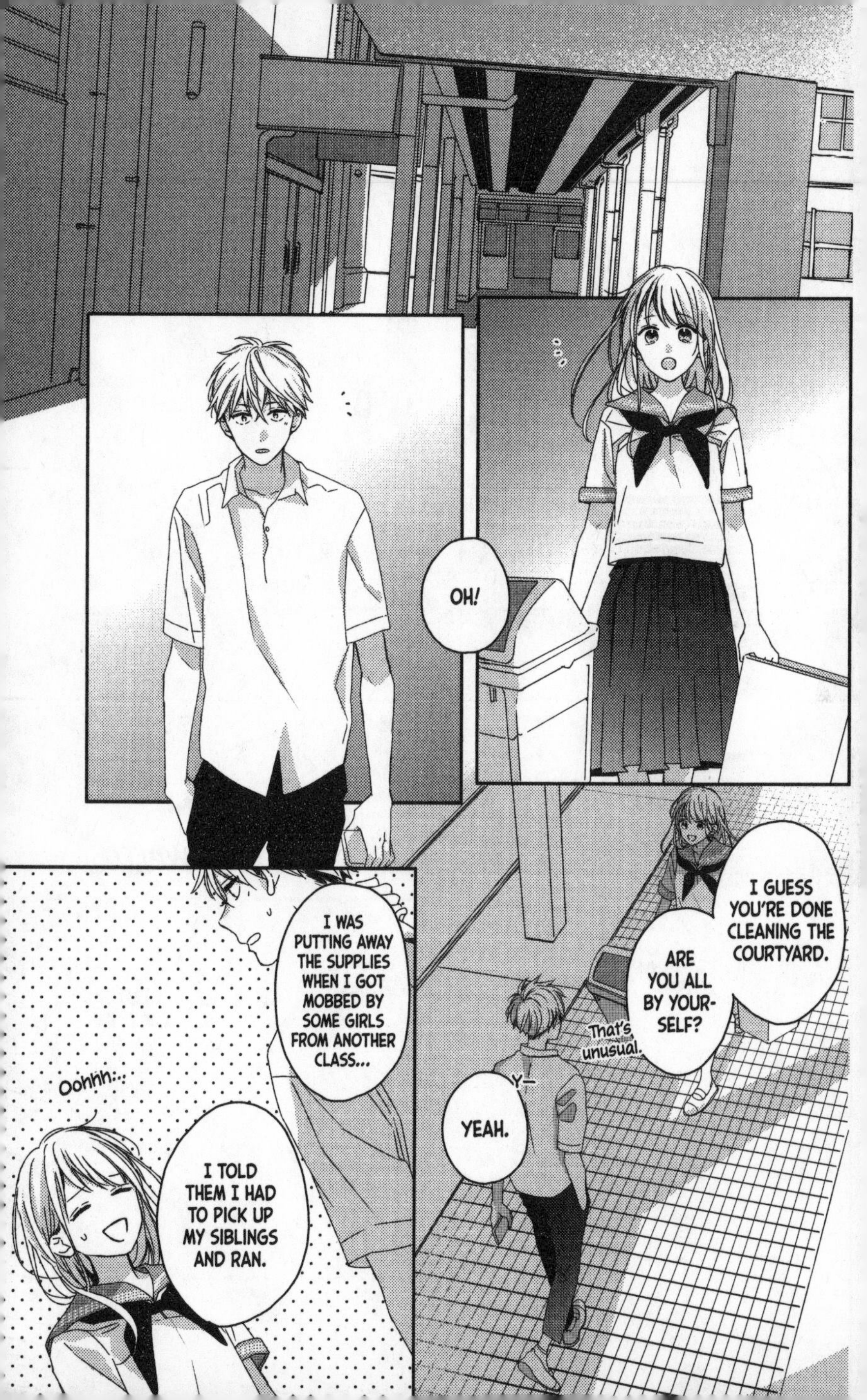
OH!
I GUESS YOU'RE DONE CLEANING THE COURTYARD.
ARE YOU ALL BY YOUR-SELF?
That's unusual.
Y—
YEAH.
I WAS PUTTING AWAY THE SUPPLIES WHEN I GOT MOBBED BY SOME GIRLS FROM ANOTHER CLASS...
Oohhh...
I TOLD THEM I HAD TO PICK UP MY SIBLINGS AND RAN.

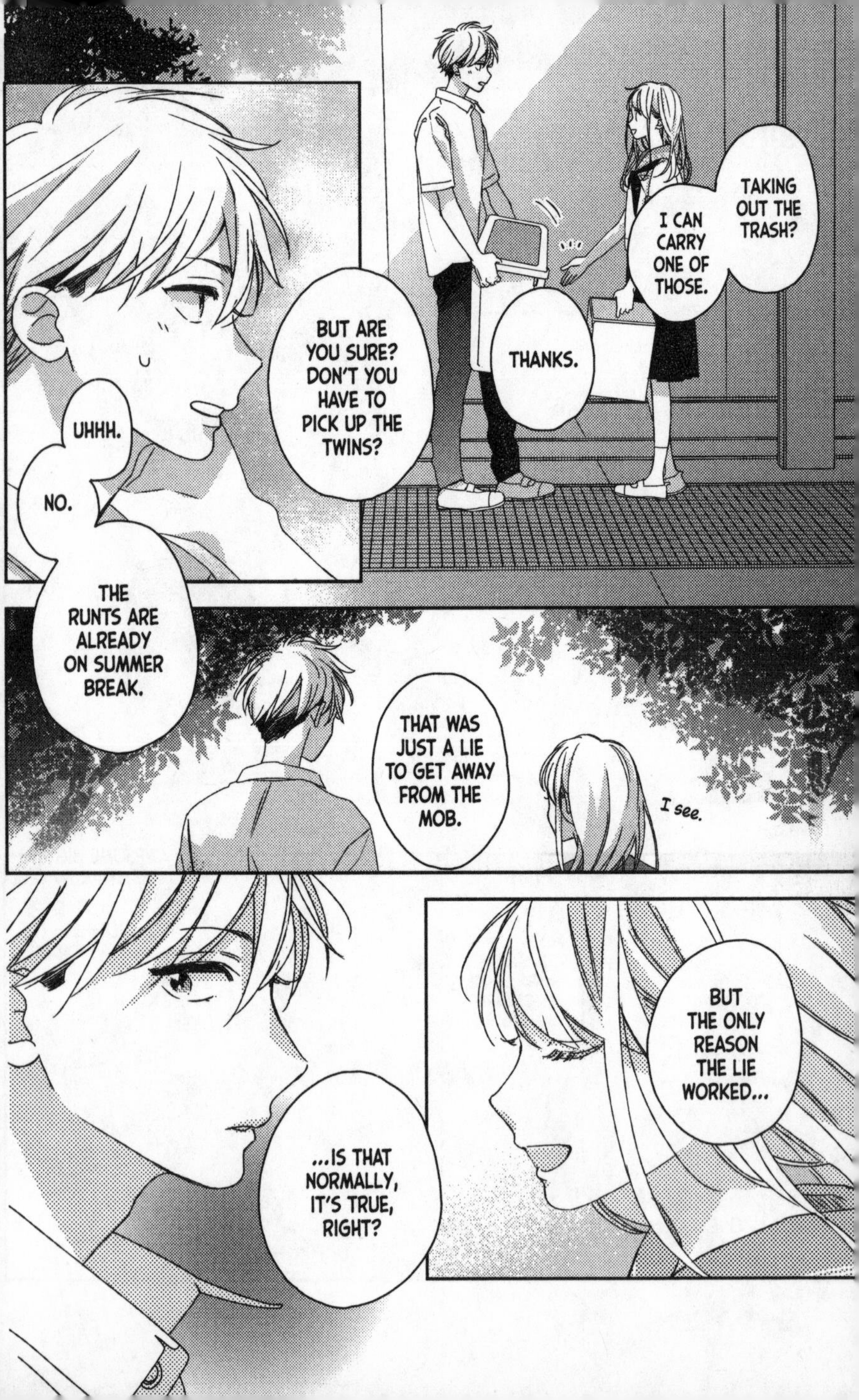
TAKING OUT THE TRASH?
I CAN CARRY ONE OF THOSE.
THANKS.
BUT ARE YOU SURE? DON'T YOU HAVE TO PICK UP THE TWINS?
UHHH.
NO.
THE RUNTS ARE ALREADY ON SUMMER BREAK.
I see.
THAT WAS JUST A LIE TO GET AWAY FROM THE MOB.
BUT THE ONLY REASON THE LIE WORKED...
...IS THAT NORMALLY, IT'S TRUE, RIGHT?

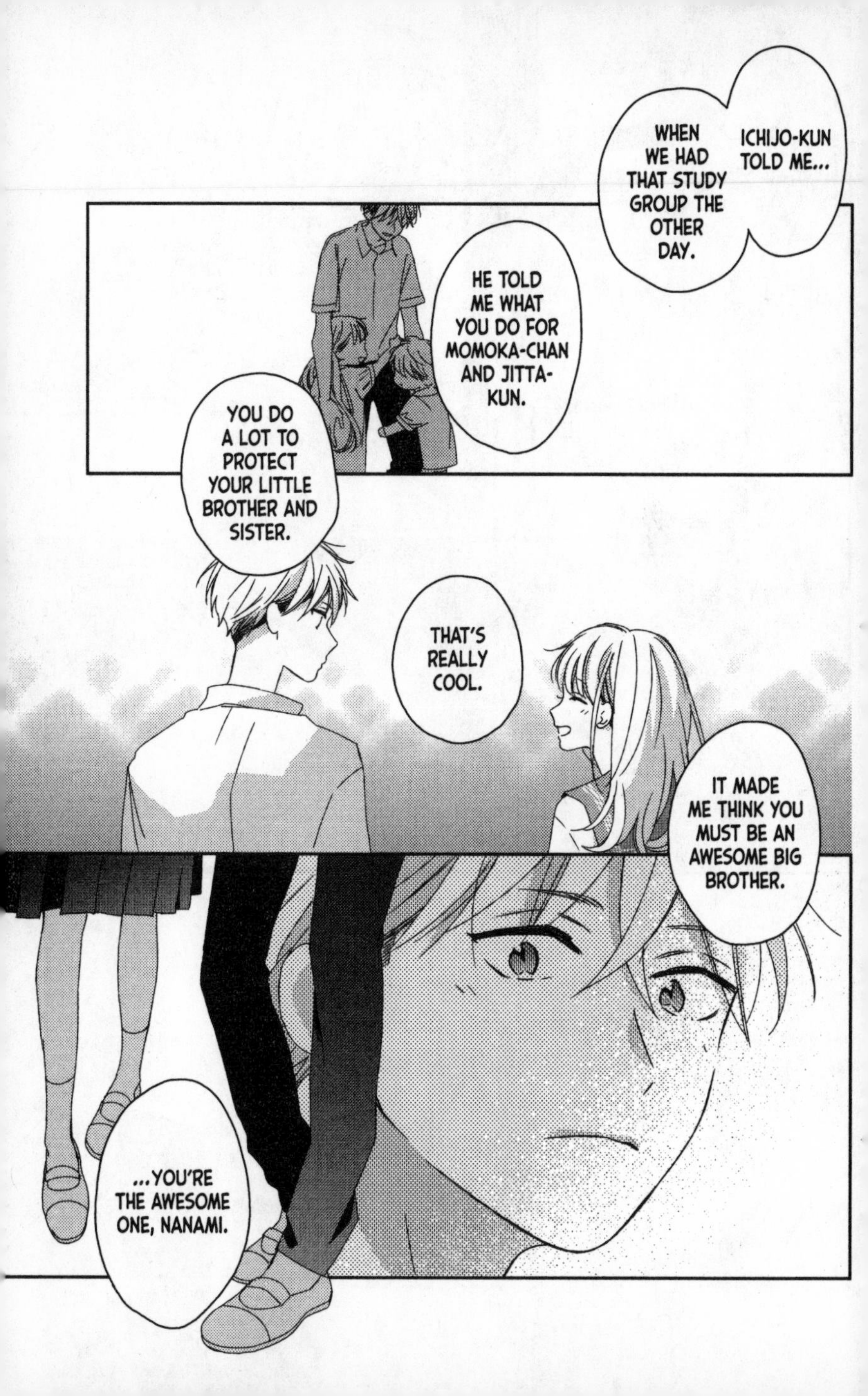
ICHIJO-KUN TOLD ME...
WHEN WE HAD THAT STUDY GROUP THE OTHER DAY.
HE TOLD ME WHAT YOU DO FOR MOMOKA-CHAN AND JITTA-KUN.
YOU DO A LOT TO PROTECT YOUR LITTLE BROTHER AND SISTER.
THAT'S REALLY COOL.
IT MADE ME THINK YOU MUST BE AN AWESOME BIG BROTHER.
...YOU'RE THE AWESOME ONE, NANAMI.

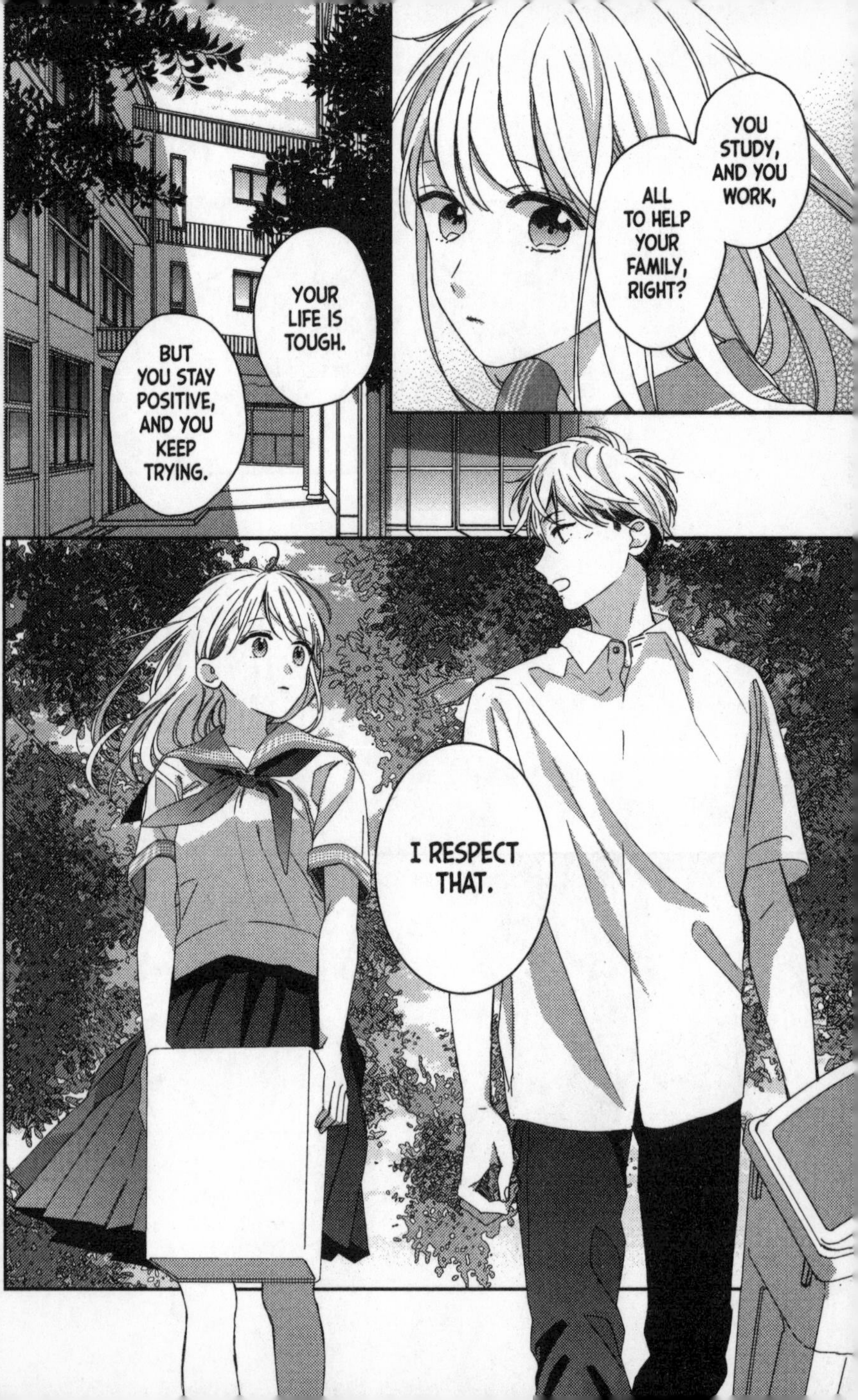
YOU STUDY, AND YOU WORK,
ALL TO HELP YOUR FAMILY, RIGHT?
YOUR LIFE IS TOUGH.
BUT YOU STAY POSITIVE, AND YOU KEEP TRYING.
I RESPECT THAT.

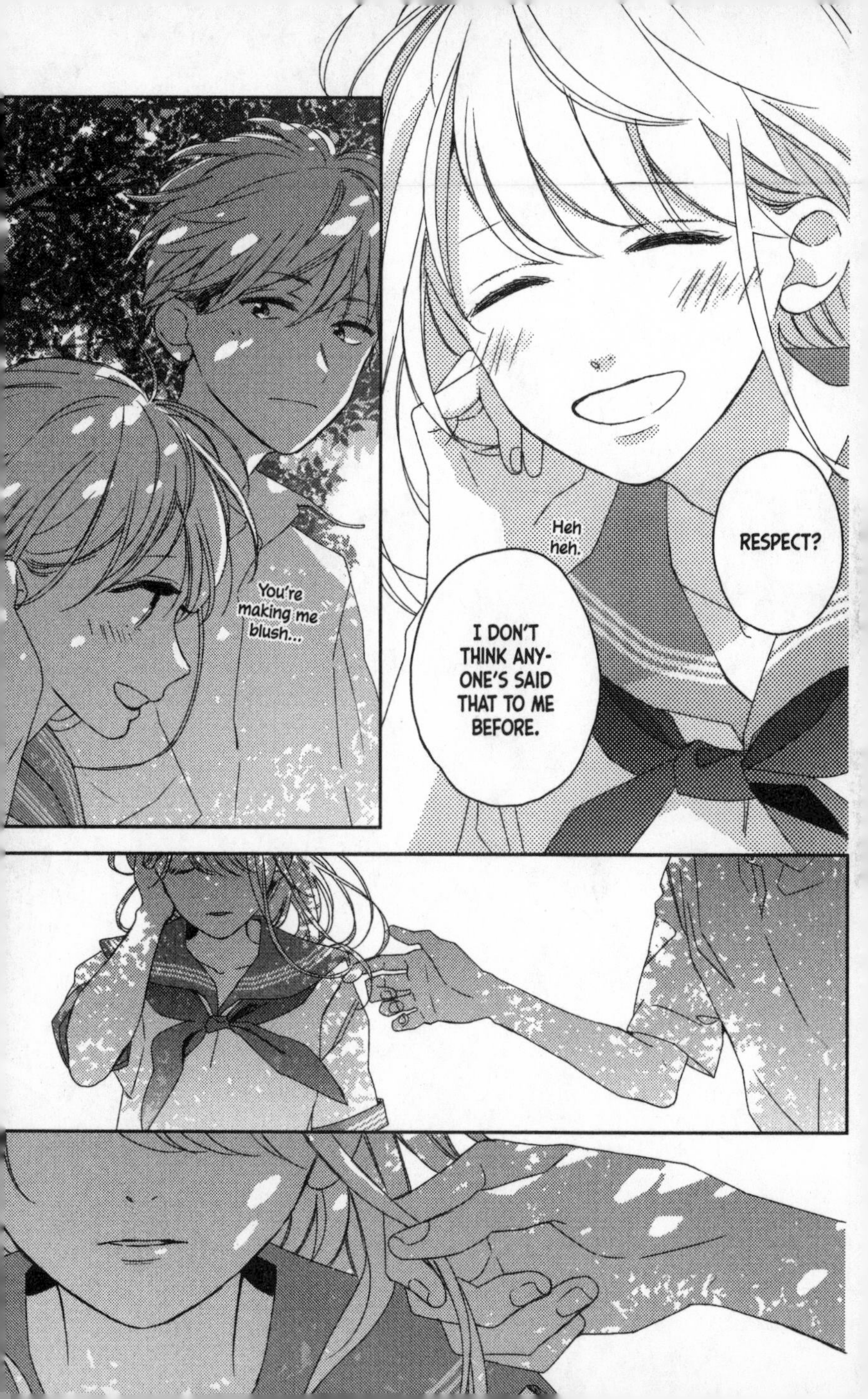
RESPECT?
Heh heh.
I DON'T THINK ANY-ONE'S SAID THAT TO ME BEFORE.
You're making me blush...

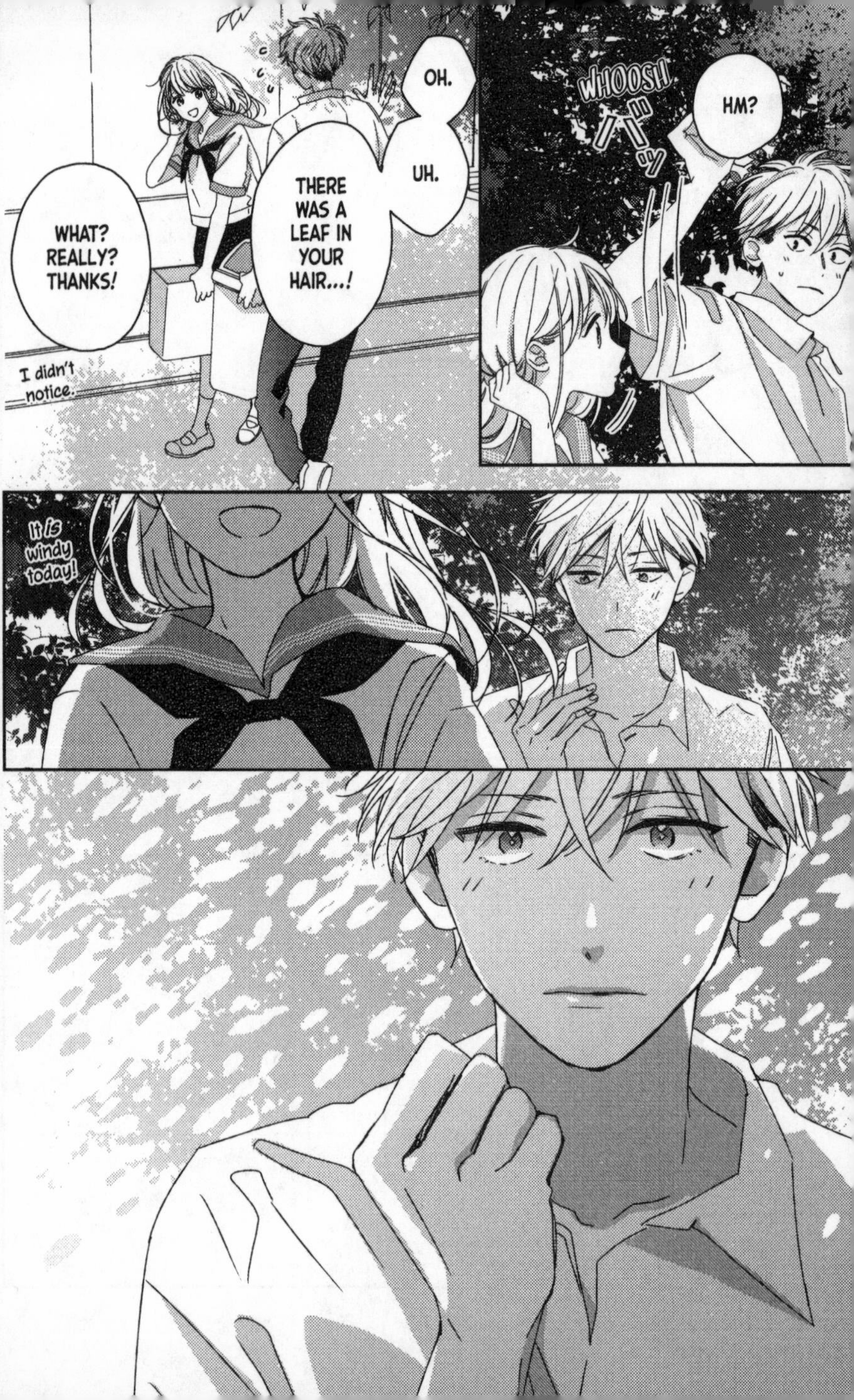
HM?
WHOOSH
バッ
OH.
UH.
THERE WAS A LEAF IN YOUR HAIR...!
WHAT? REALLY? THANKS!
I didn't notice.
It is windy today!

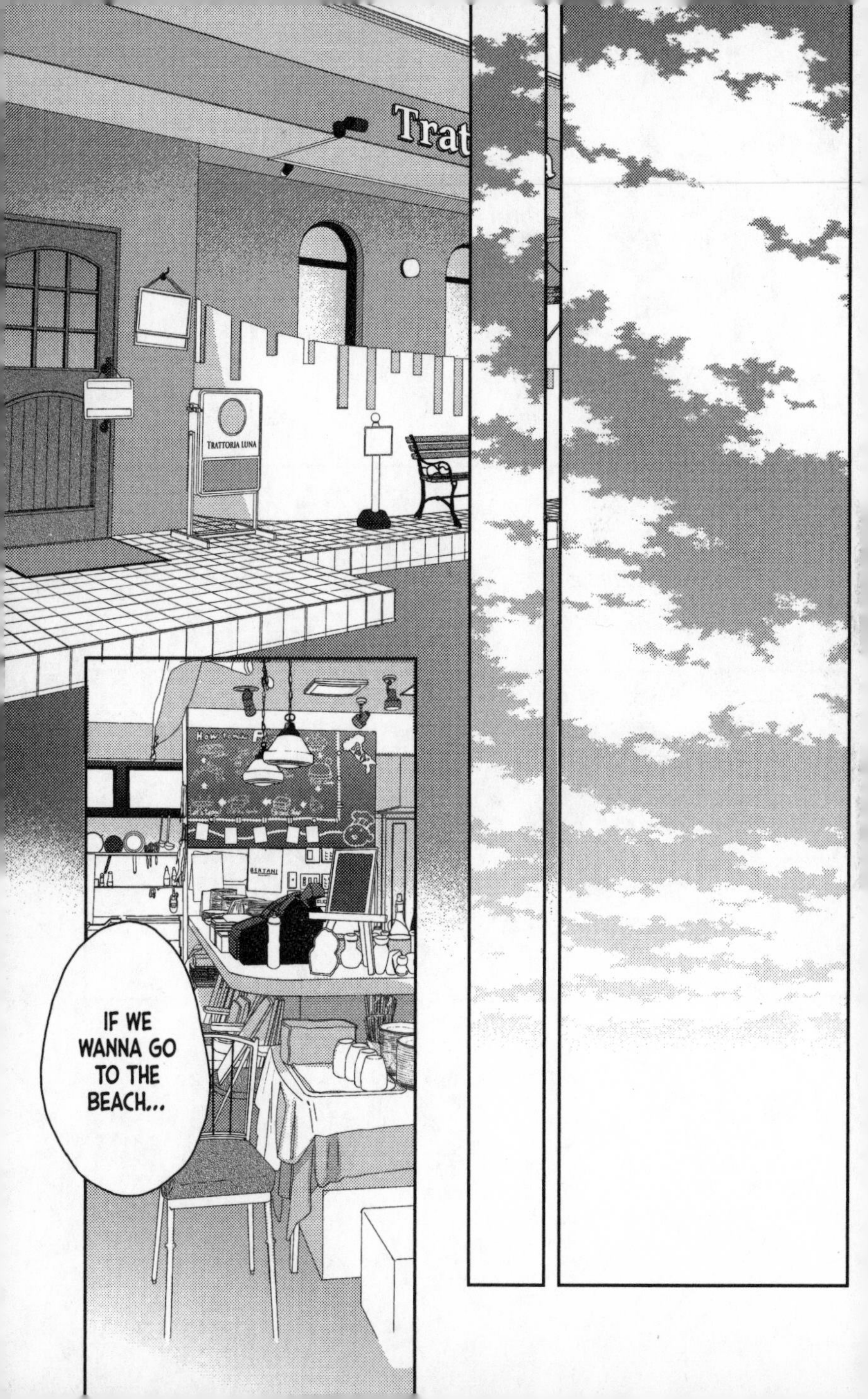
TRATTORIA LUNA
IF WE WANNA GO TO THE BEACH...

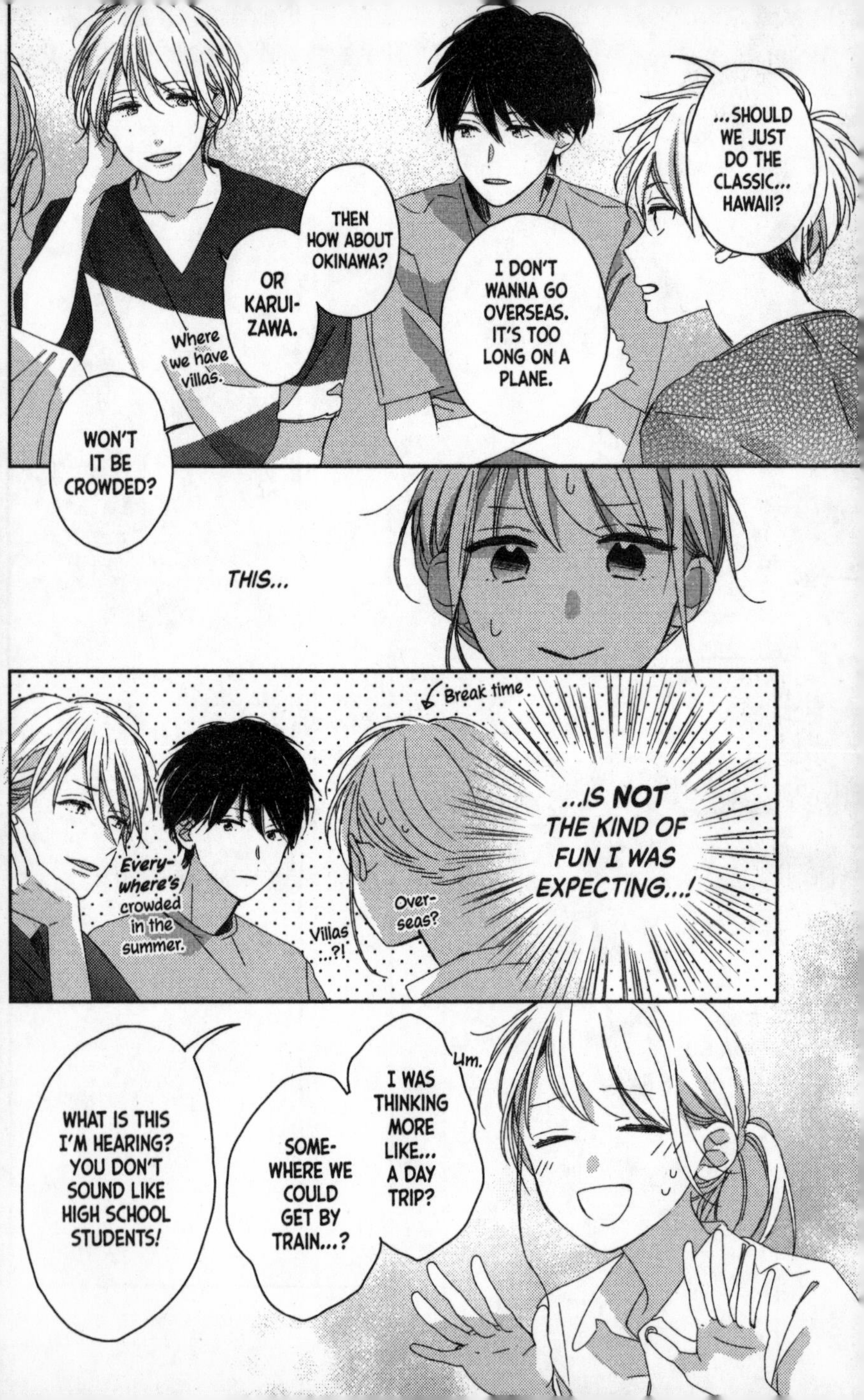
...SHOULD WE JUST DO THE CLASSIC... HAWAII?
I DON'T WANNA GO OVERSEAS. IT'S TOO LONG ON A PLANE.
THEN HOW ABOUT OKINAWA?
OR KARUIZAWA.
Where we have villas.
WON'T IT BE CROWDED?
THIS...
Break time
...IS NOT THE KIND OF FUN I WAS EXPECTING...!
Overseas?
Villas...?!
Everywhere's crowded in the summer.
Um.
I WAS THINKING MORE LIKE... A DAY TRIP?
SOMEWHERE WE COULD GET BY TRAIN...?
WHAT IS THIS I'M HEARING? YOU DON'T SOUND LIKE HIGH SCHOOL STUDENTS!

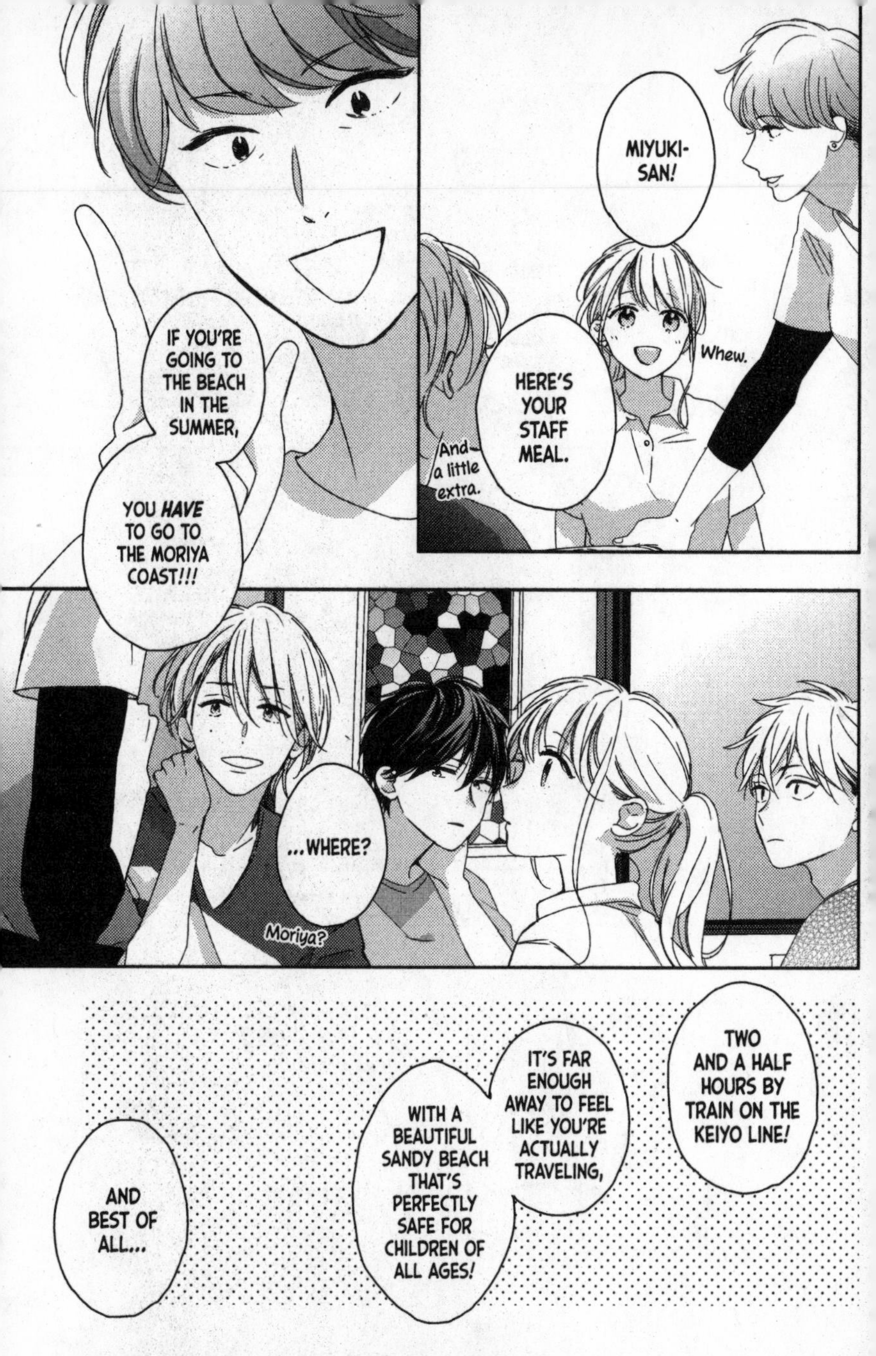
MIYUKI-SAN!
Whew.
HERE'S YOUR STAFF MEAL.
And— a little extra.
IF YOU'RE GOING TO THE BEACH IN THE SUMMER,
YOU ***HAVE*** TO GO TO THE MORIYA COAST!!!
...WHERE?
Moriya?
TWO AND A HALF HOURS BY TRAIN ON THE KEIYO LINE!
IT'S FAR ENOUGH AWAY TO FEEL LIKE YOU'RE ACTUALLY TRAVELING,
WITH A BEAUTIFUL SANDY BEACH THAT'S PERFECTLY SAFE FOR CHILDREN OF ALL AGES!
AND BEST OF ALL...

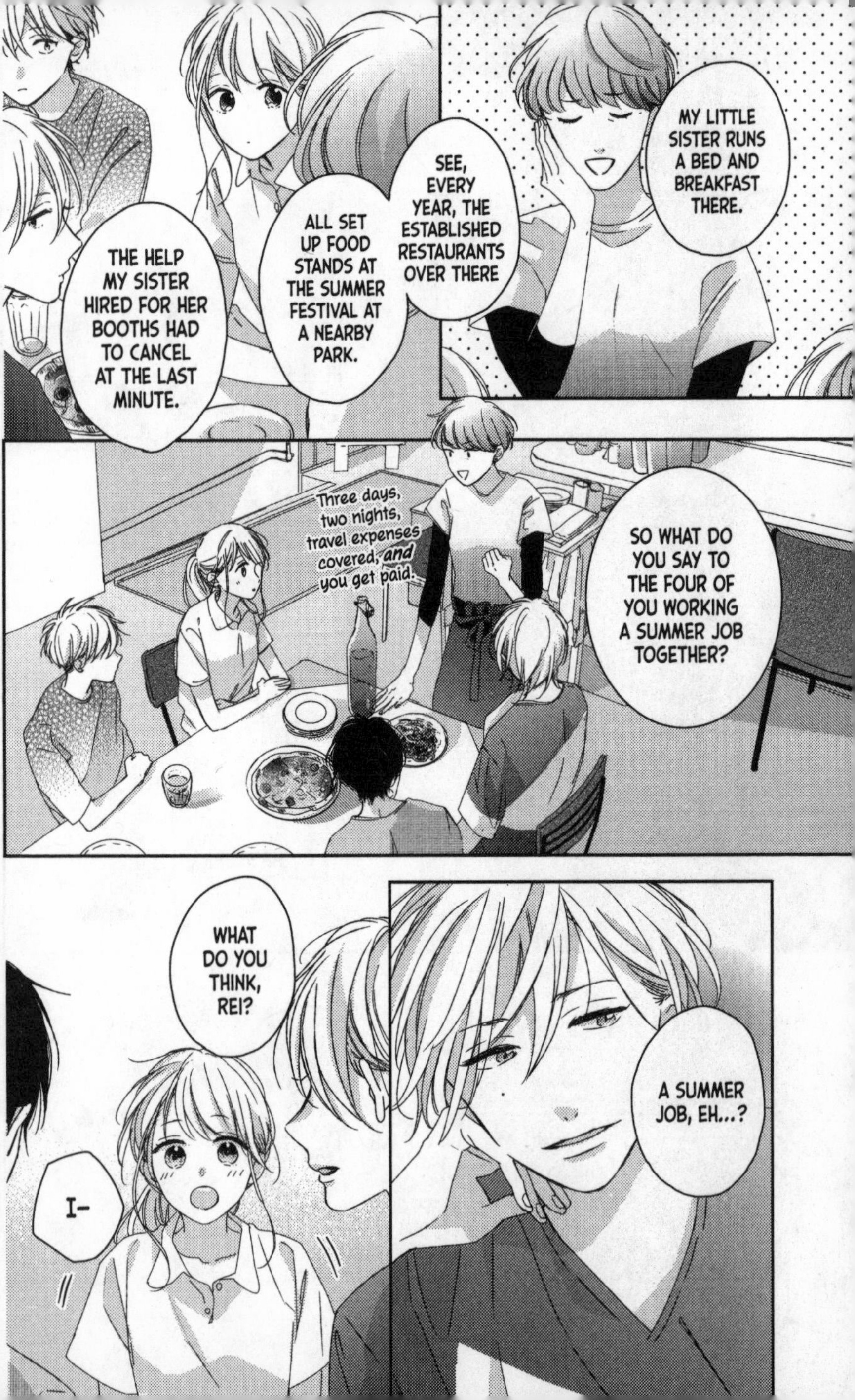
MY LITTLE SISTER RUNS A BED AND BREAKFAST THERE.
SEE, EVERY YEAR, THE ESTABLISHED RESTAURANTS OVER THERE
ALL SET UP FOOD STANDS AT THE SUMMER FESTIVAL AT A NEARBY PARK.
THE HELP MY SISTER HIRED FOR HER BOOTHS HAD TO CANCEL AT THE LAST MINUTE.
SO WHAT DO YOU SAY TO THE FOUR OF YOU WORKING A SUMMER JOB TOGETHER?
Three days, two nights, travel expenses covered, and you get paid.
A SUMMER JOB, EH...?
WHAT DO YOU THINK, REI?
I-

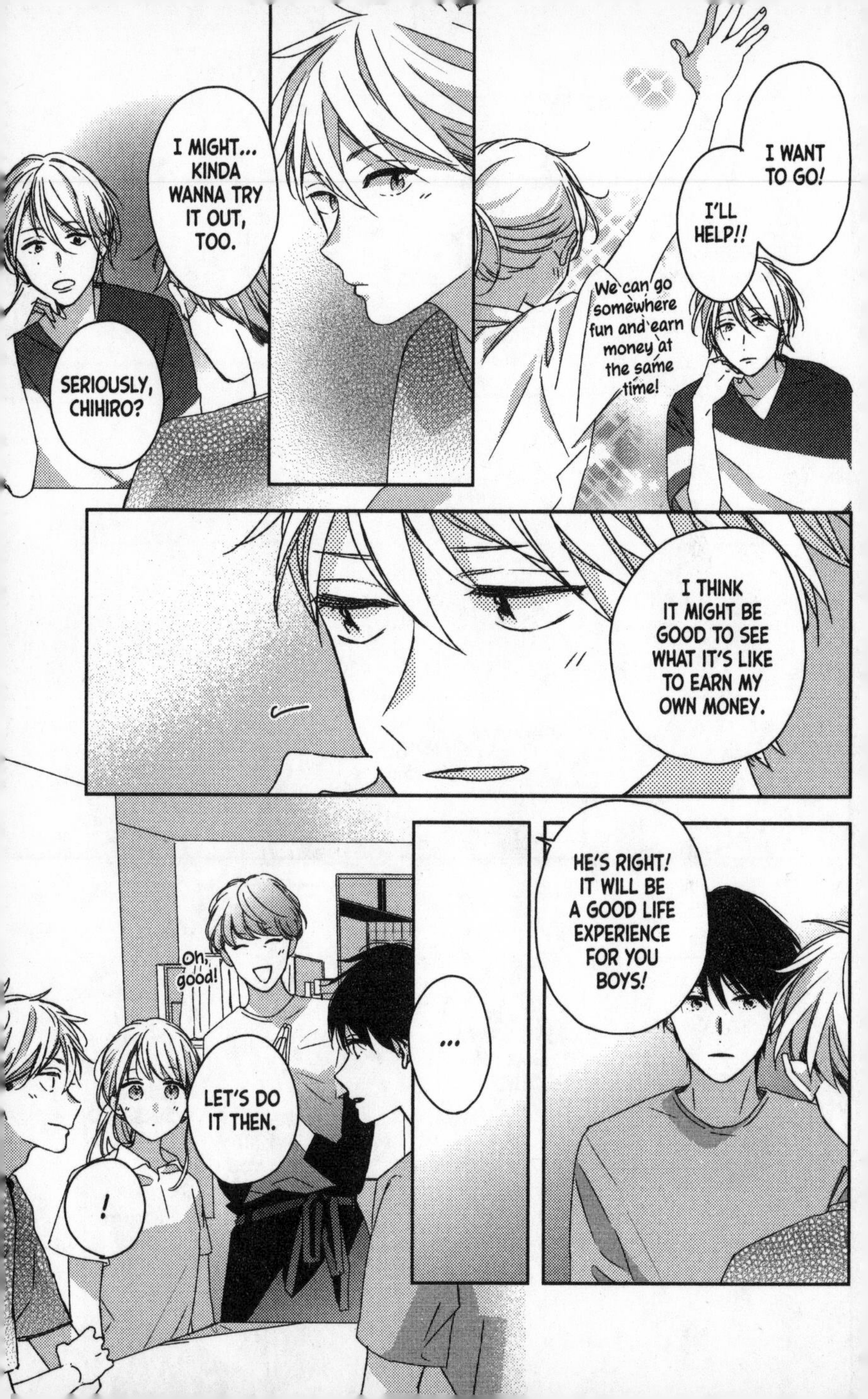
I WANT TO GO!
I'LL HELP!!
We can go somewhere fun and earn money at the same time!
I MIGHT... KINDA WANNA TRY IT OUT, TOO.
SERIOUSLY, CHIHIRO?
I THINK IT MIGHT BE GOOD TO SEE WHAT IT'S LIKE TO EARN MY OWN MONEY.
HE'S RIGHT! IT WILL BE A GOOD LIFE EXPERIENCE FOR YOU BOYS!
...
Oh, good!
LET'S DO IT THEN.
!

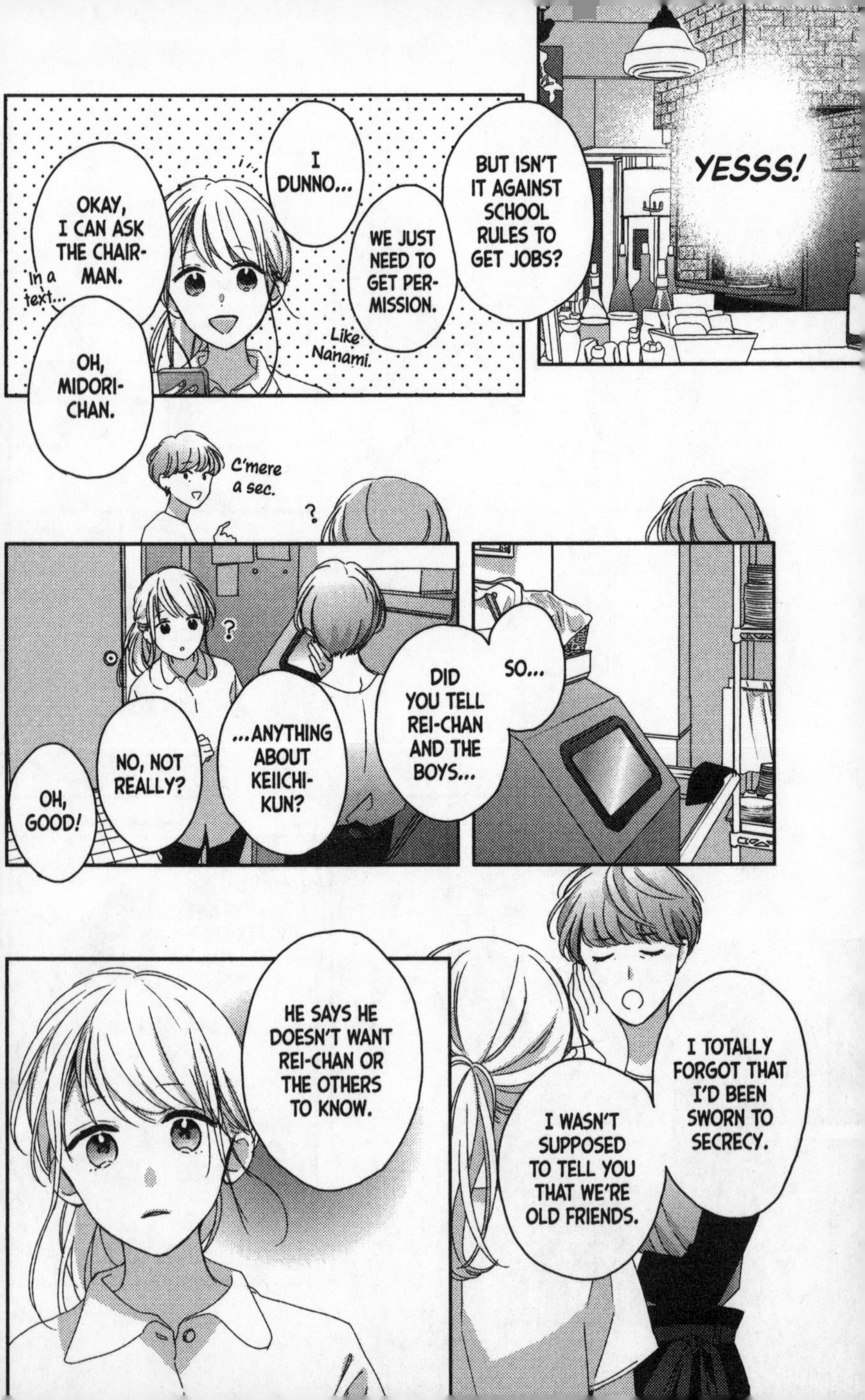
YESSS!
BUT ISN'T IT AGAINST SCHOOL RULES TO GET JOBS?
I DUNNO...
WE JUST NEED TO GET PERMISSION.
Like Nanami.
OKAY, I CAN ASK THE CHAIRMAN.
In a text...
OH, MIDORI-CHAN.
C'mere a sec.
?
SO...
DID YOU TELL REI-CHAN AND THE BOYS...
...ANYTHING ABOUT KEIICHI-KUN?
?
NO, NOT REALLY?
OH, GOOD!
I TOTALLY FORGOT THAT I'D BEEN SWORN TO SECRECY.
I WASN'T SUPPOSED TO TELL YOU THAT WE'RE OLD FRIENDS.
HE SAYS HE DOESN'T WANT REI-CHAN OR THE OTHERS TO KNOW.

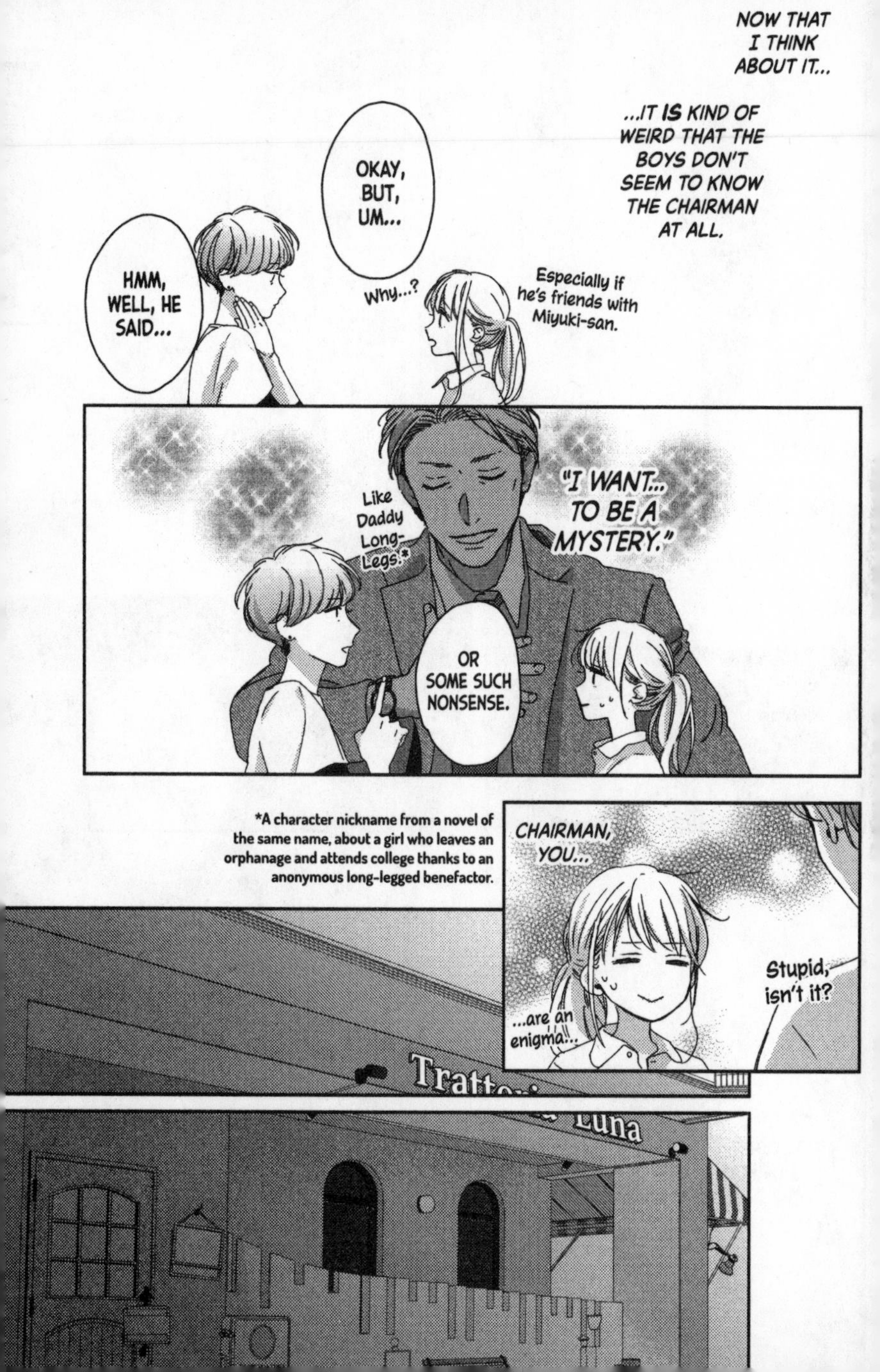
NOW THAT I THINK ABOUT IT...
...IT **IS** KIND OF WEIRD THAT THE BOYS DON'T SEEM TO KNOW THE CHAIRMAN AT ALL.
Especially if he's friends with Miyuki-san.
Why...?
OKAY, BUT, UM...
HMM, WELL, HE SAID...
"I WANT... TO BE A MYSTERY."
Like Daddy Long-Legs.*
OR SOME SUCH NONSENSE.
CHAIRMAN, YOU...
...are an enigma...
Stupid, isn't it?

*A character nickname from a novel of the same name, about a girl who leaves an orphanage and attends college thanks to an anonymous long-legged benefactor.

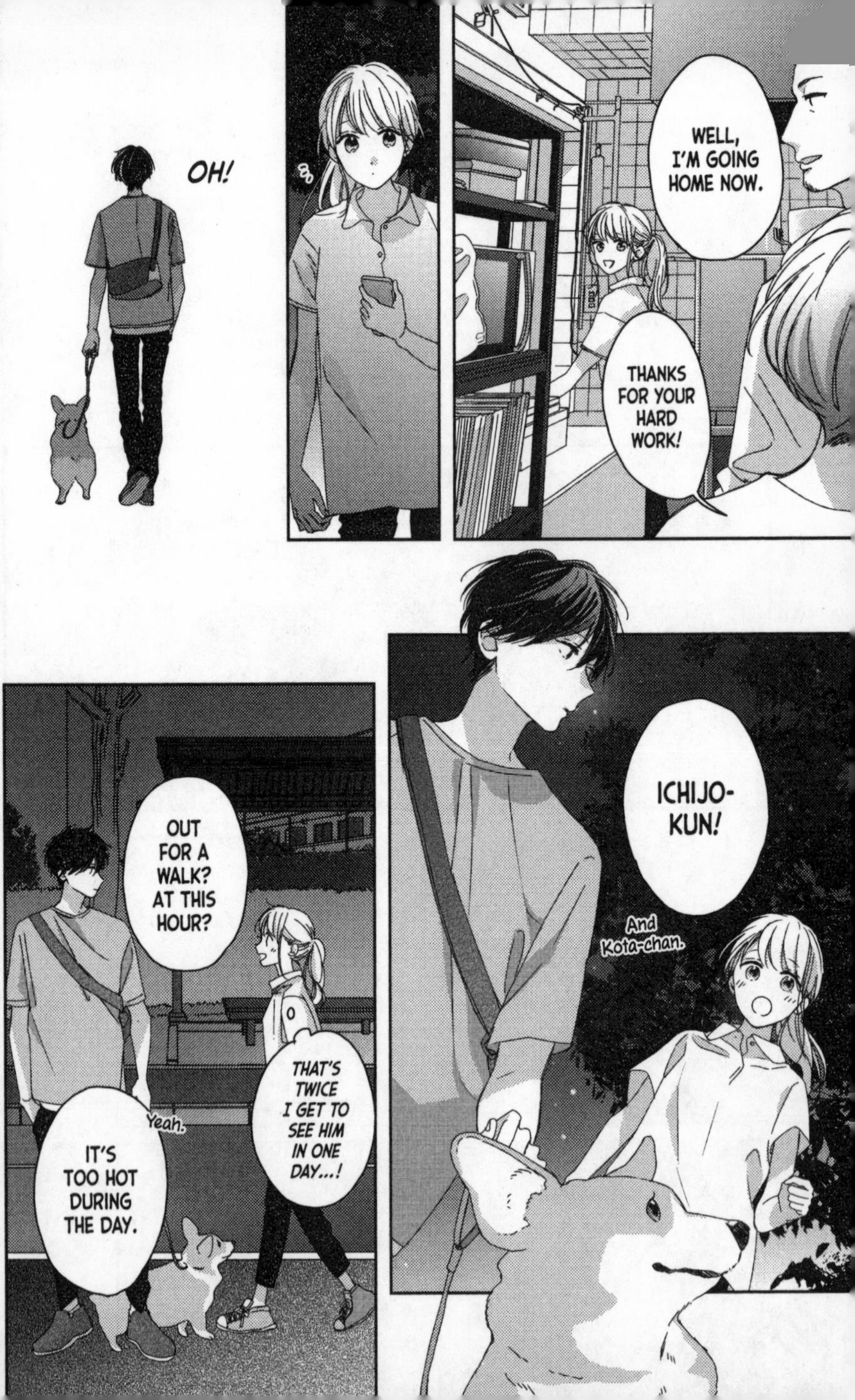

WELL, I'M GOING HOME NOW.
THANKS FOR YOUR HARD WORK!
OH!
ICHIJO-KUN!
And Kota-chan.
OUT FOR A WALK? AT THIS HOUR?
THAT'S TWICE I GET TO SEE HIM IN ONE DAY...!
Yeah.
IT'S TOO HOT DURING THE DAY.

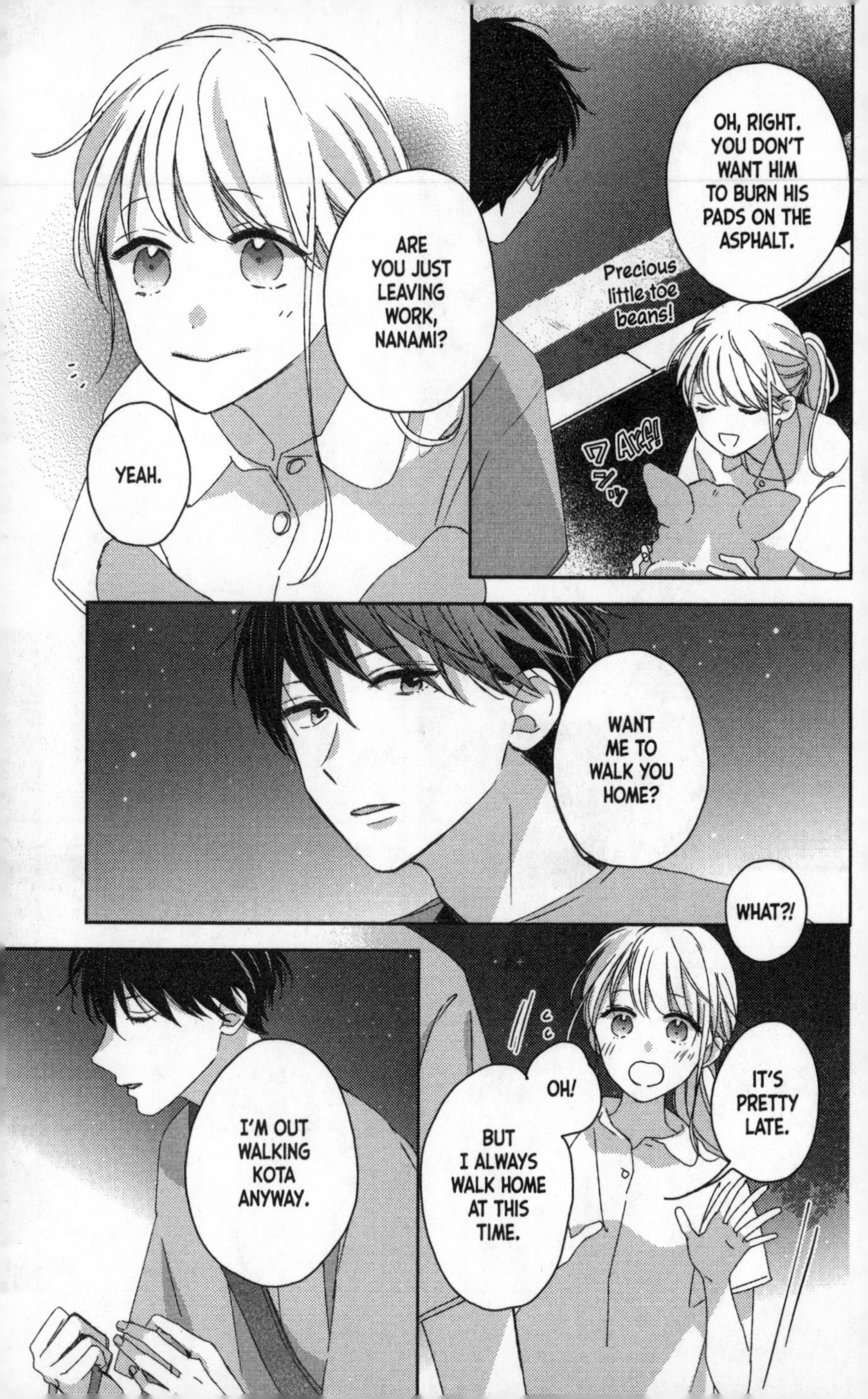
OH, RIGHT. YOU DON'T WANT HIM TO BURN HIS PADS ON THE ASPHALT.
Precious little toe beans!
Arf!
ARE YOU JUST LEAVING WORK, NANAMI?
YEAH.
WANT ME TO WALK YOU HOME?
WHAT?!
IT'S PRETTY LATE.
OH!
BUT I ALWAYS WALK HOME AT THIS TIME.
I'M OUT WALKING KOTA ANYWAY.

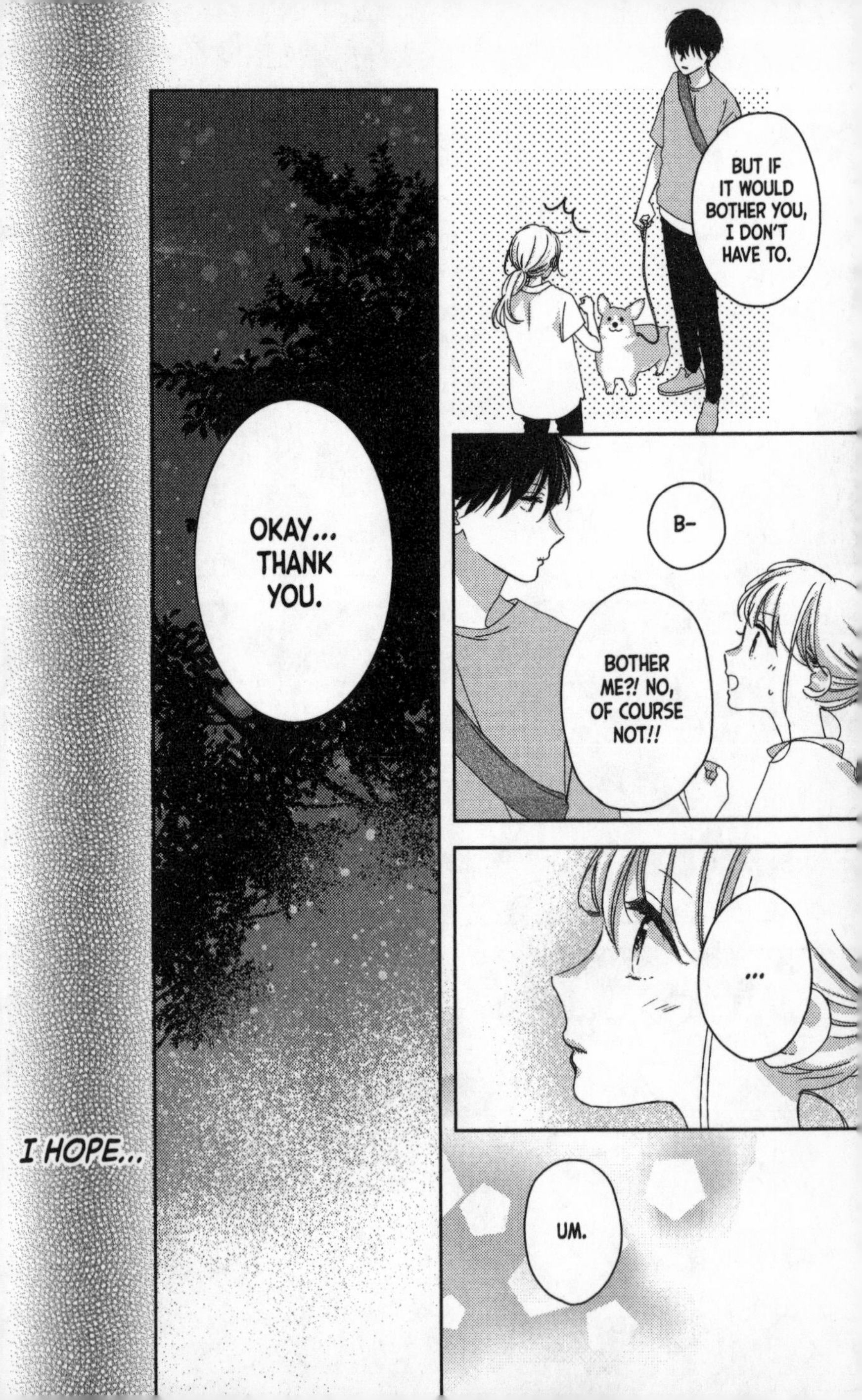
BUT IF IT WOULD BOTHER YOU, I DON'T HAVE TO.
B–
BOTHER ME?! NO, OF COURSE NOT!!
...
UM.
OKAY... THANK YOU.
I HOPE...

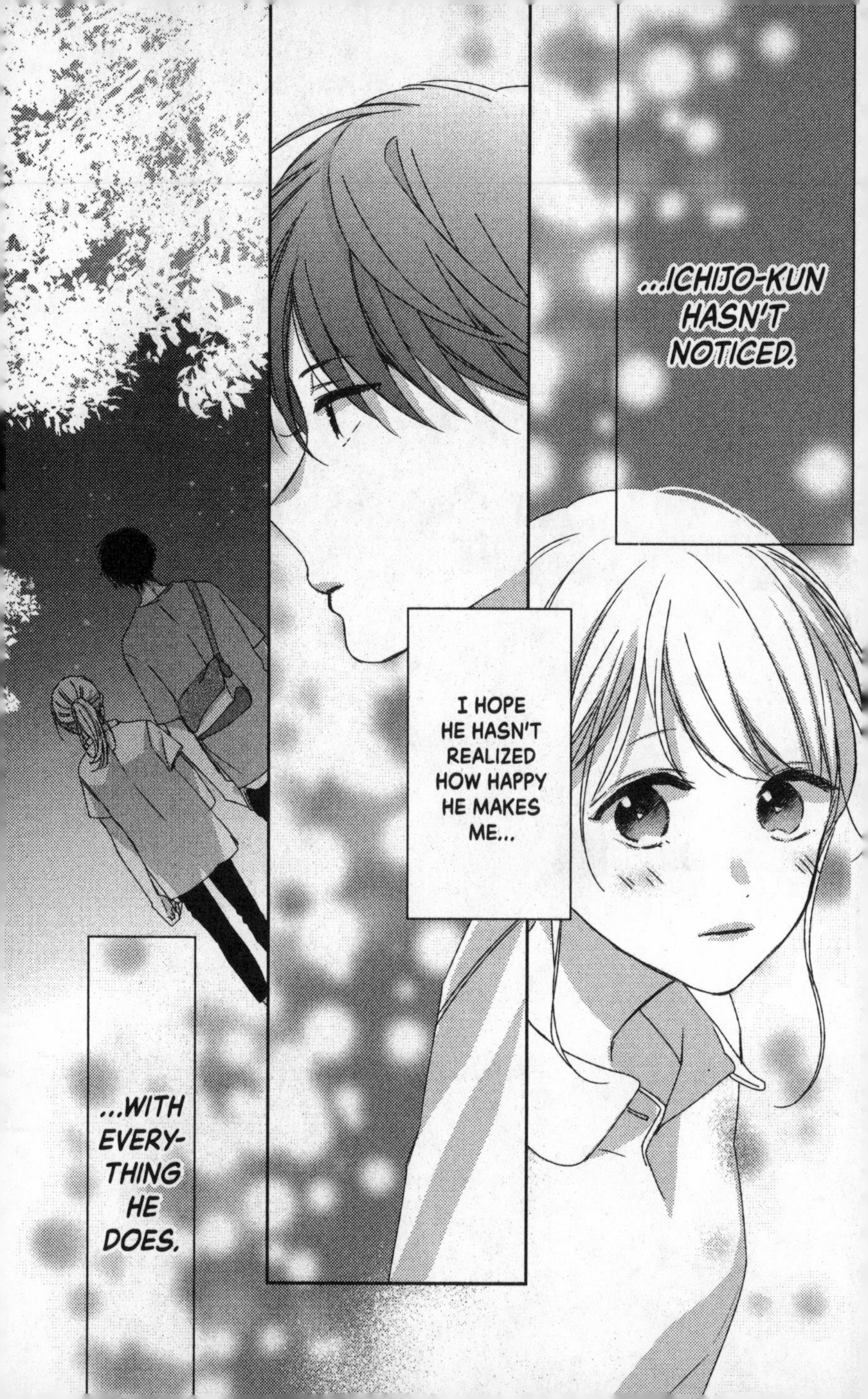
...ICHIJO-KUN HASN'T NOTICED.
I HOPE HE HASN'T REALIZED HOW HAPPY HE MAKES ME...
...WITH EVERY-THING HE DOES.

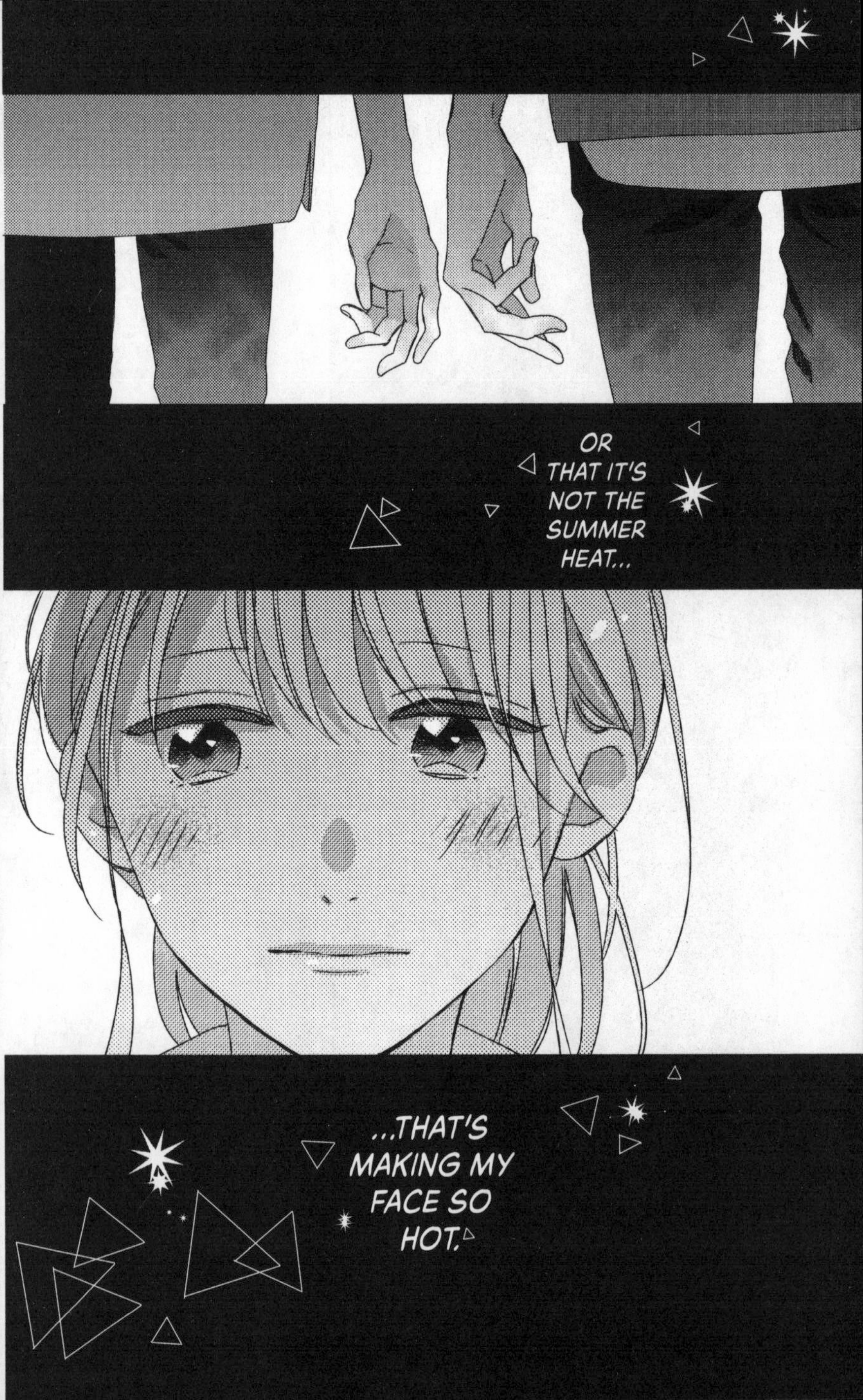
OR THAT IT'S NOT THE SUMMER HEAT...
...THAT'S MAKING MY FACE SO HOT.

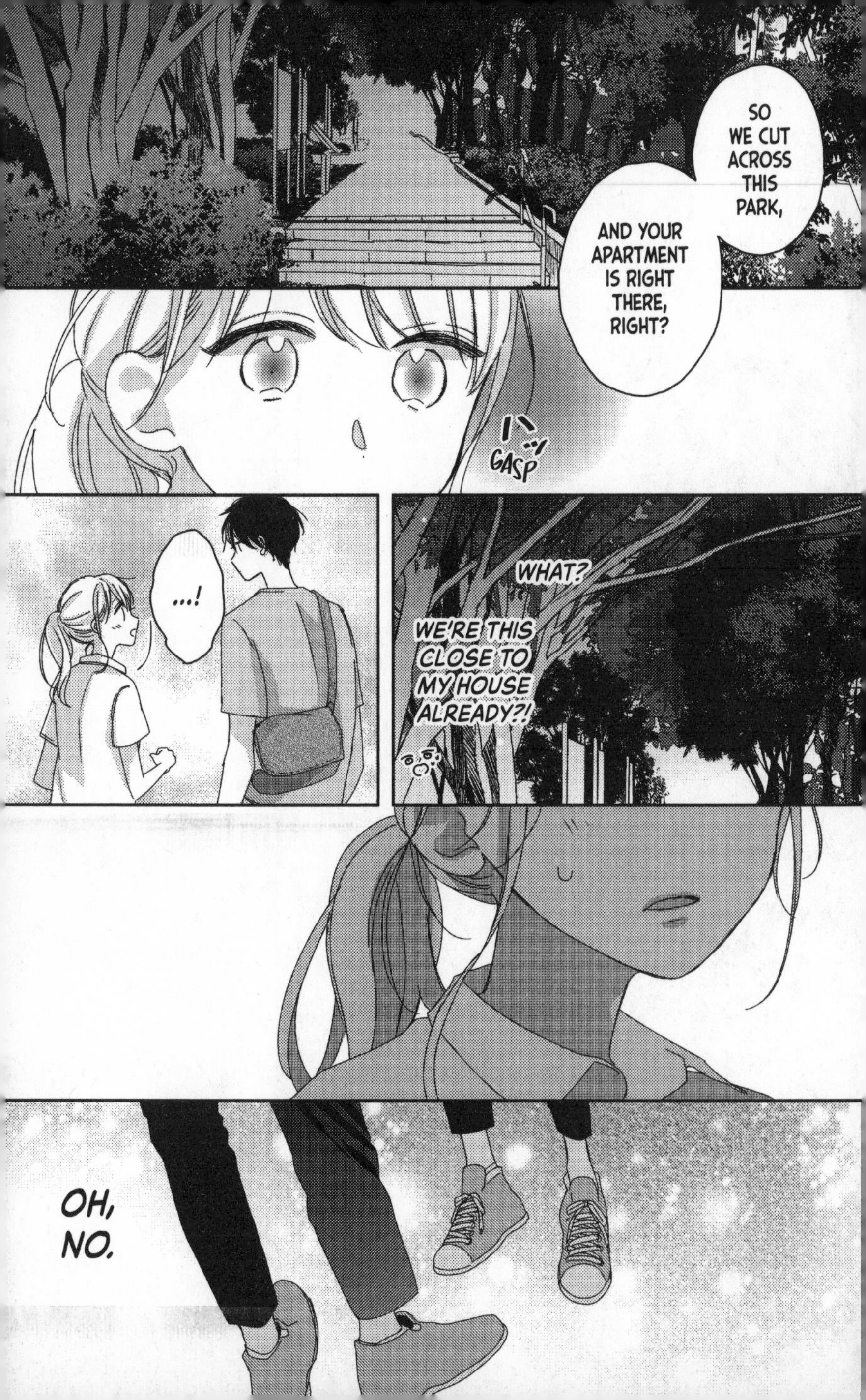
SO WE CUT ACROSS THIS PARK,
AND YOUR APARTMENT IS RIGHT THERE, RIGHT?
GASP
WHAT?
WE'RE THIS CLOSE TO MY HOUSE ALREADY?!
...!
OH, NO.

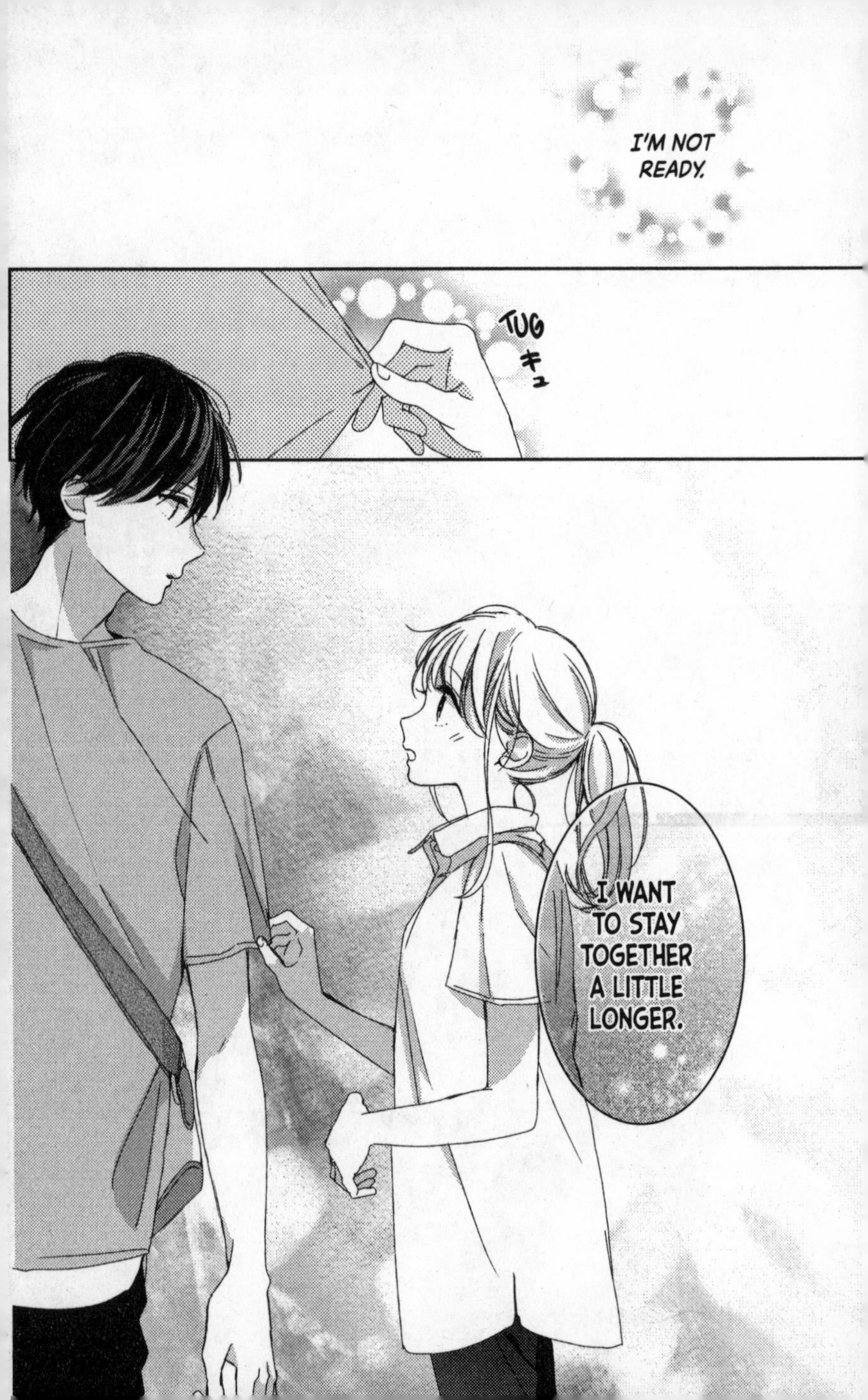
I'M NOT READY.
TUG
キュ
I WANT TO STAY TOGETHER A LITTLE LONGER.

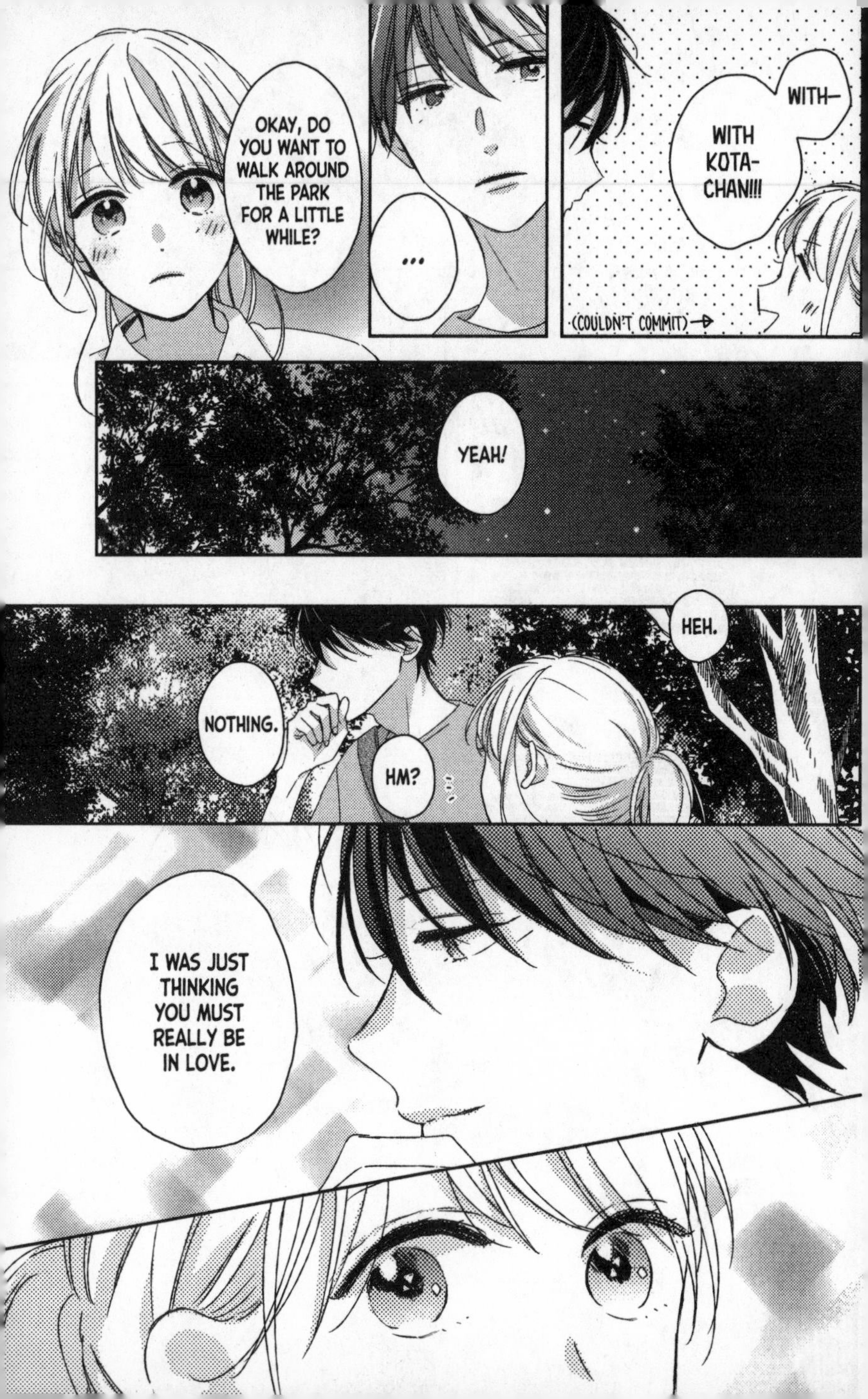
WITH—
WITH KOTA-CHAN!!!
(COULDN'T COMMIT)
...
OKAY, DO YOU WANT TO WALK AROUND THE PARK FOR A LITTLE WHILE?
YEAH!
HEH.
HM?
NOTHING.
I WAS JUST THINKING YOU MUST REALLY BE IN LOVE.

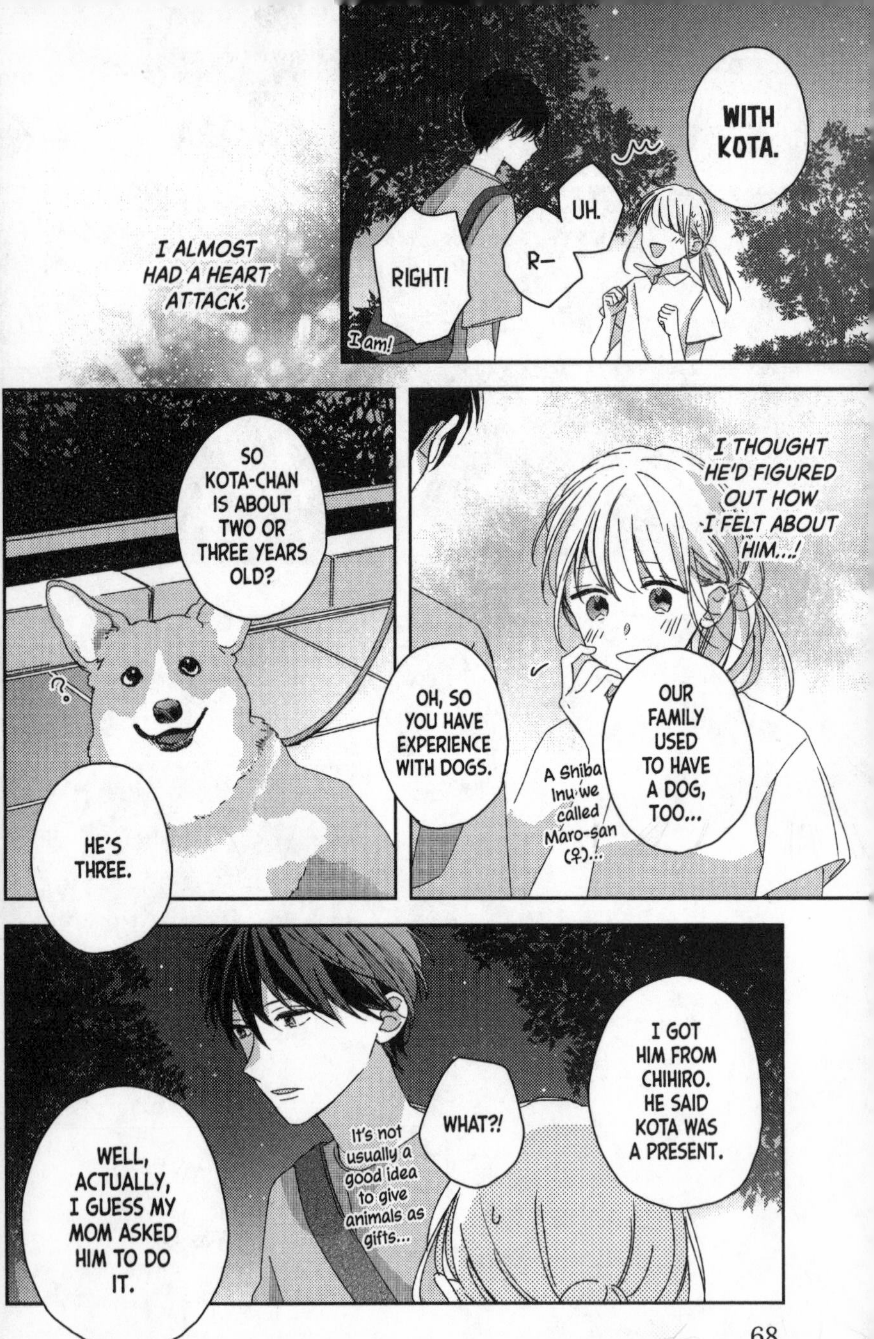
WITH KOTA.
UH.
R—
RIGHT!
I am!
I ALMOST HAD A HEART ATTACK.
I THOUGHT HE'D FIGURED OUT HOW I FELT ABOUT HIM...!
OUR FAMILY USED TO HAVE A DOG, TOO...
A Shiba Inu we called Maro-san (♀)...
OH, SO YOU HAVE EXPERIENCE WITH DOGS.
SO KOTA-CHAN IS ABOUT TWO OR THREE YEARS OLD?
?
HE'S THREE.
I GOT HIM FROM CHIHIRO. HE SAID KOTA WAS A PRESENT.
WHAT?!
It's not usually a good idea to give animals as gifts...
WELL, ACTUALLY, I GUESS MY MOM ASKED HIM TO DO IT.

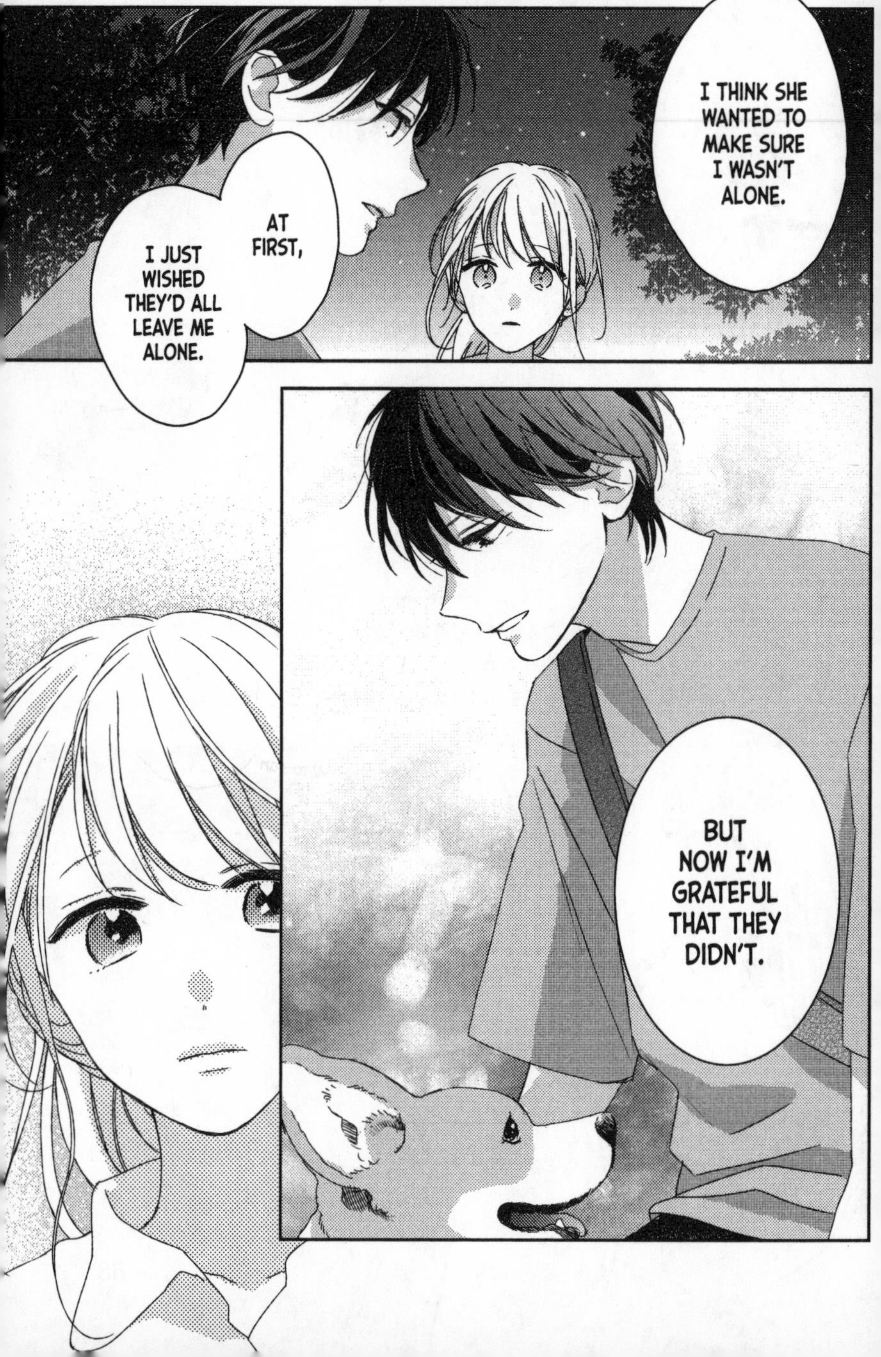
I THINK SHE WANTED TO MAKE SURE I WASN'T ALONE.
AT FIRST, I JUST WISHED THEY'D ALL LEAVE ME ALONE.
BUT NOW I'M GRATEFUL THAT THEY DIDN'T.

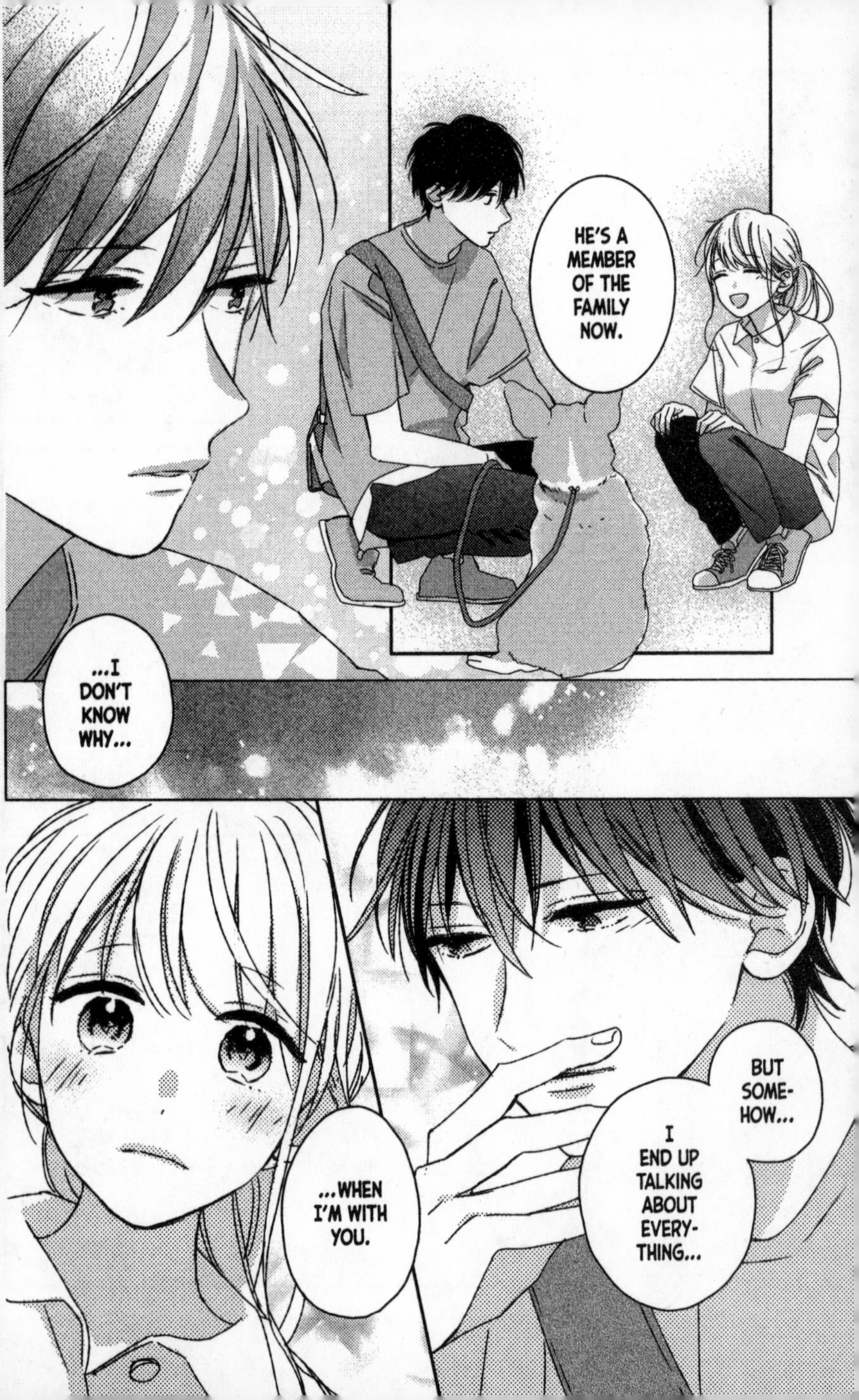
HE'S A MEMBER OF THE FAMILY NOW.
...I DON'T KNOW WHY...
BUT SOME-HOW...
I END UP TALKING ABOUT EVERY-THING...
...WHEN I'M WITH YOU.

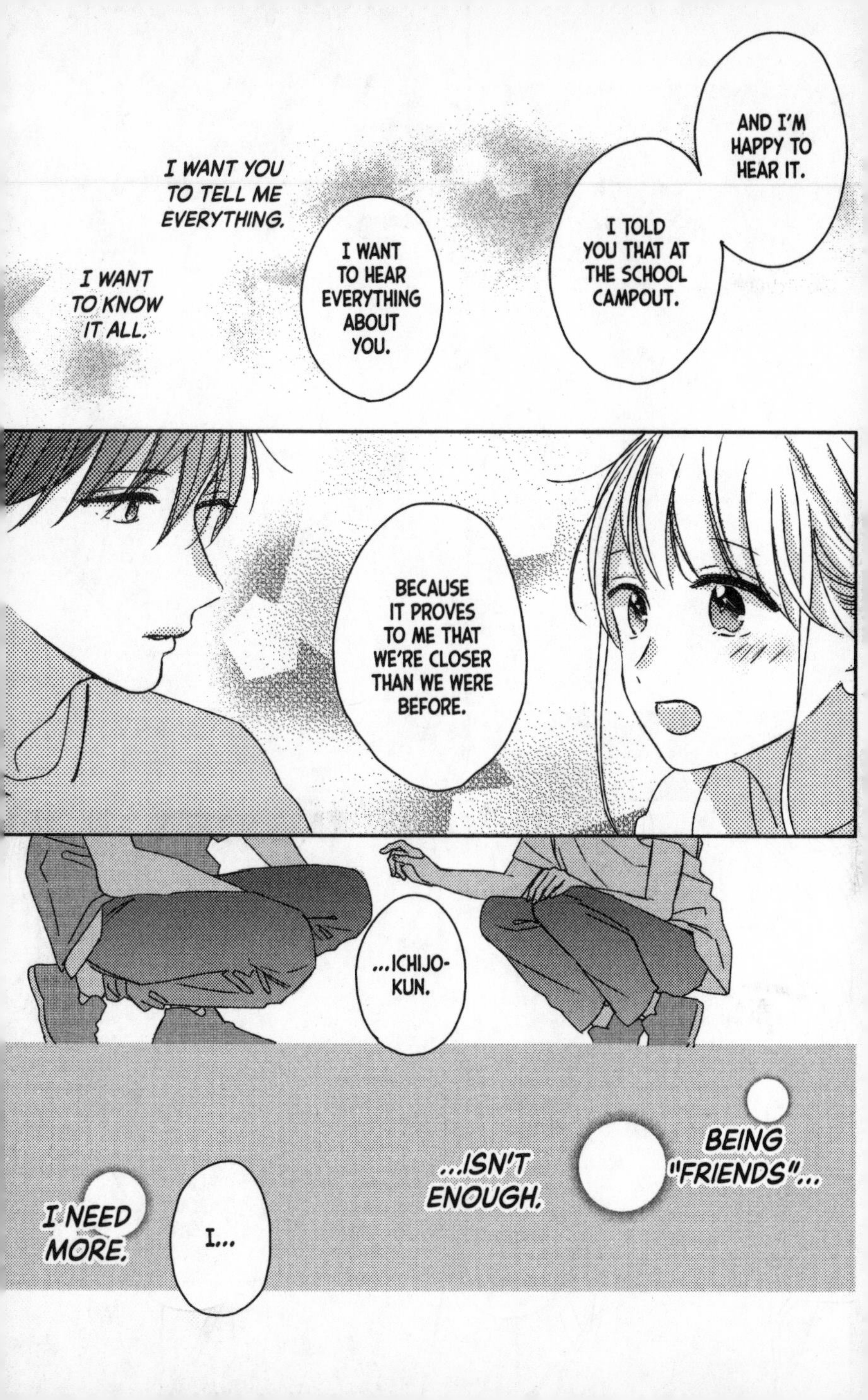
AND I'M HAPPY TO HEAR IT.
I TOLD YOU THAT AT THE SCHOOL CAMPOUT.
I WANT TO HEAR EVERYTHING ABOUT YOU.
I WANT YOU TO TELL ME EVERYTHING.
I WANT TO KNOW IT ALL.
BECAUSE IT PROVES TO ME THAT WE'RE CLOSER THAN WE WERE BEFORE.
...ICHIJO-KUN.
BEING "FRIENDS"...
...ISN'T ENOUGH.
I...
I NEED MORE.

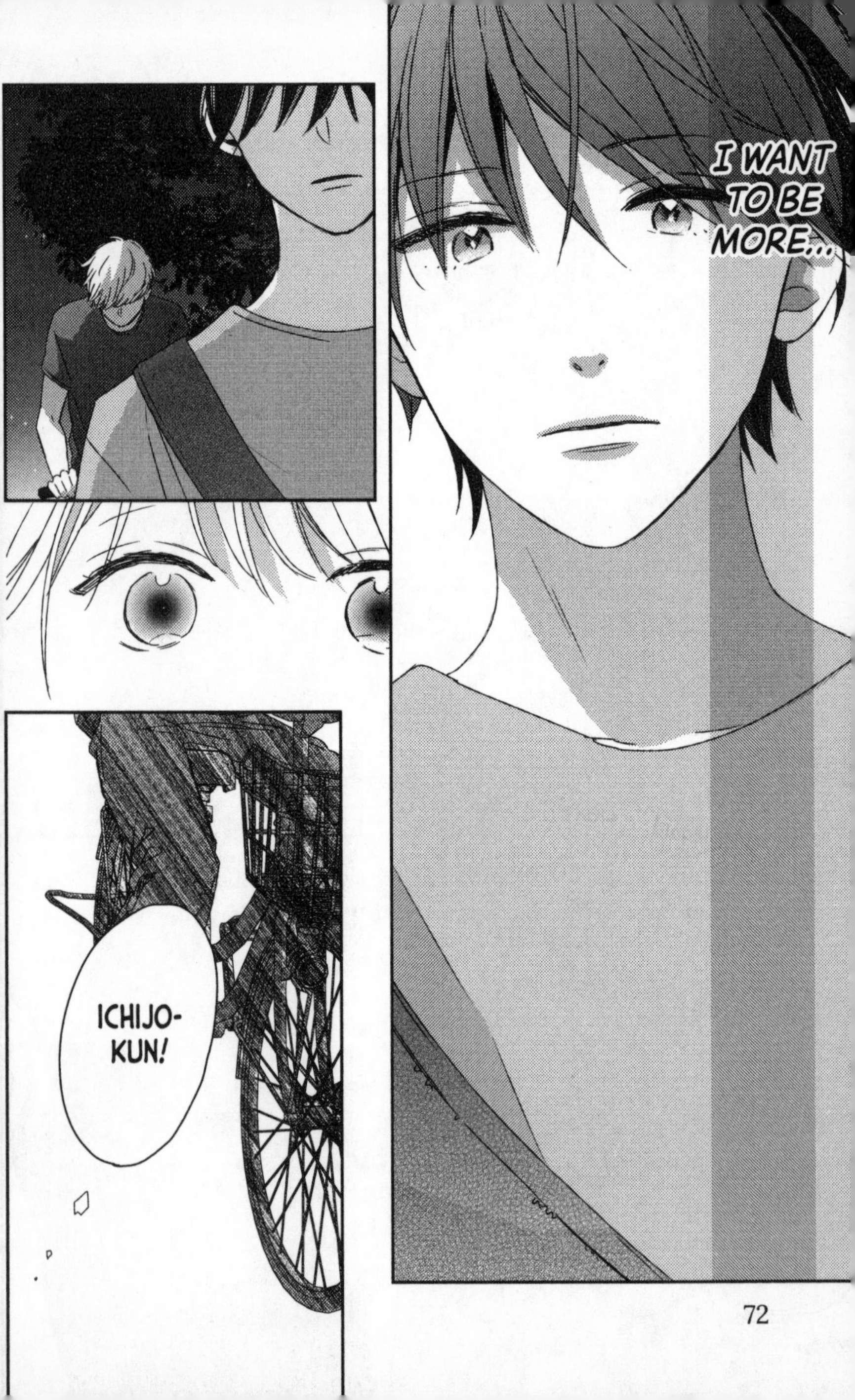
I WANT TO BE MORE...
ICHIJO-KUN!

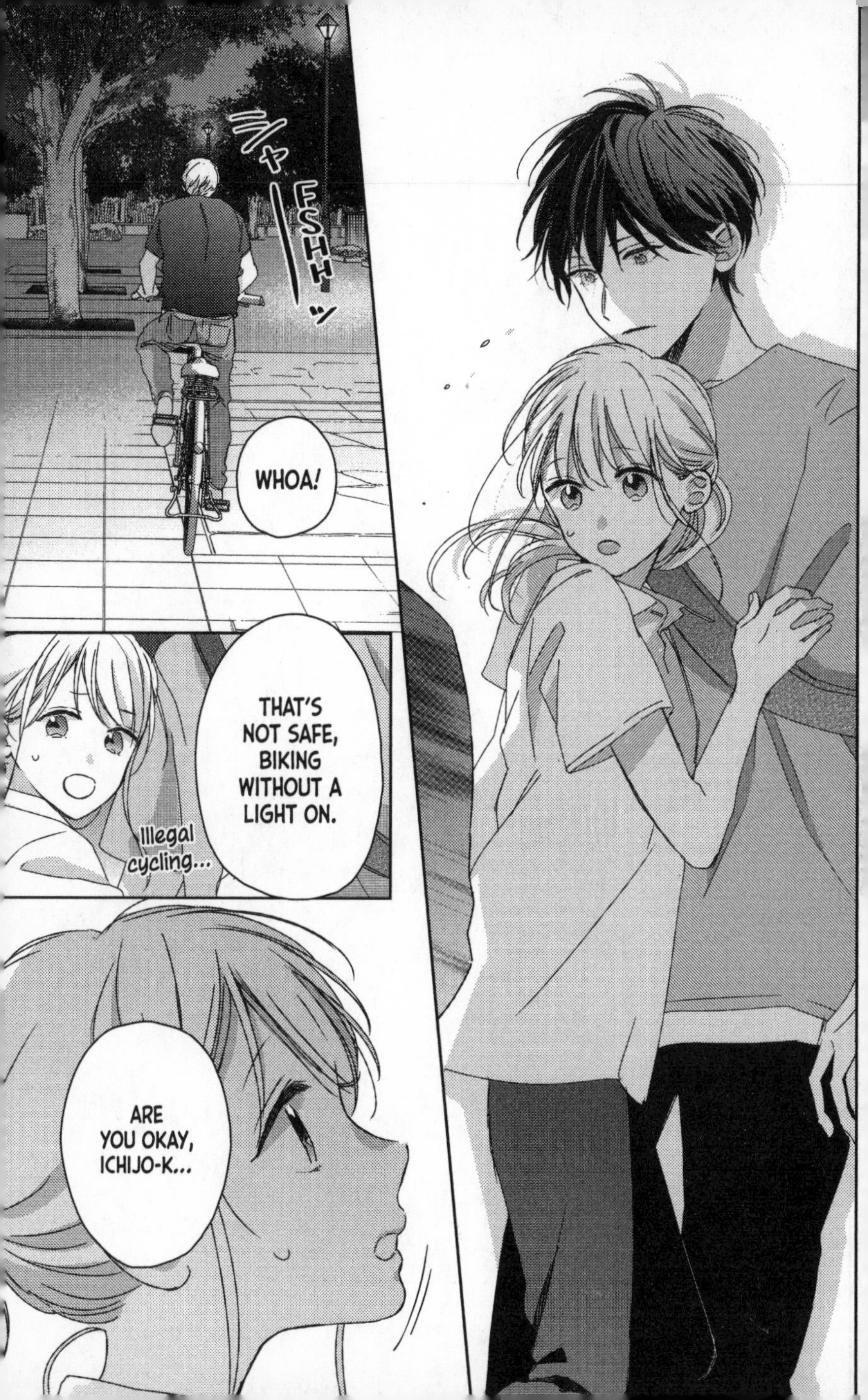
FSHH
WHOA!
THAT'S NOT SAFE, BIKING WITHOUT A LIGHT ON.
Illegal cycling...
ARE YOU OKAY, ICHIJO-K...

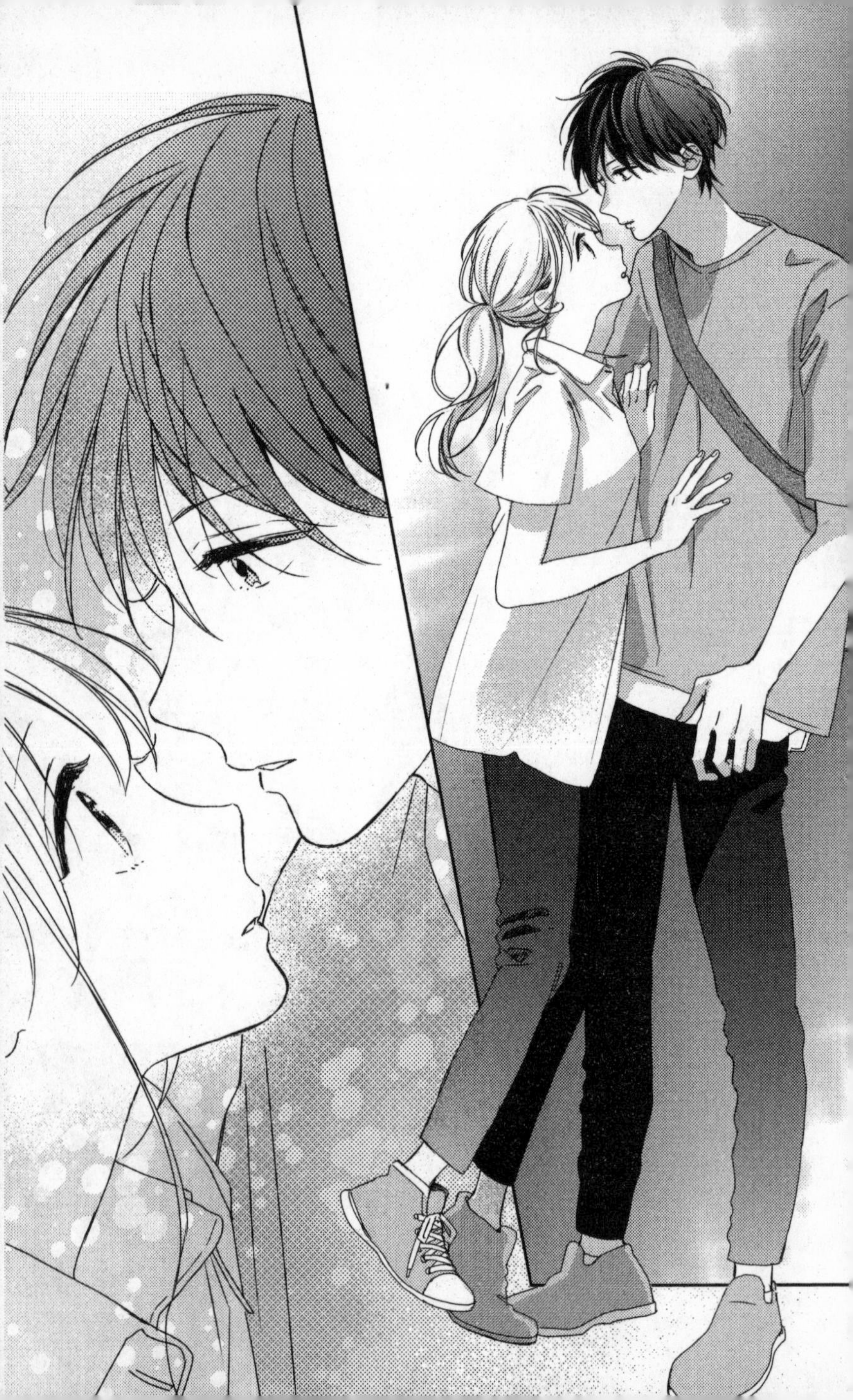

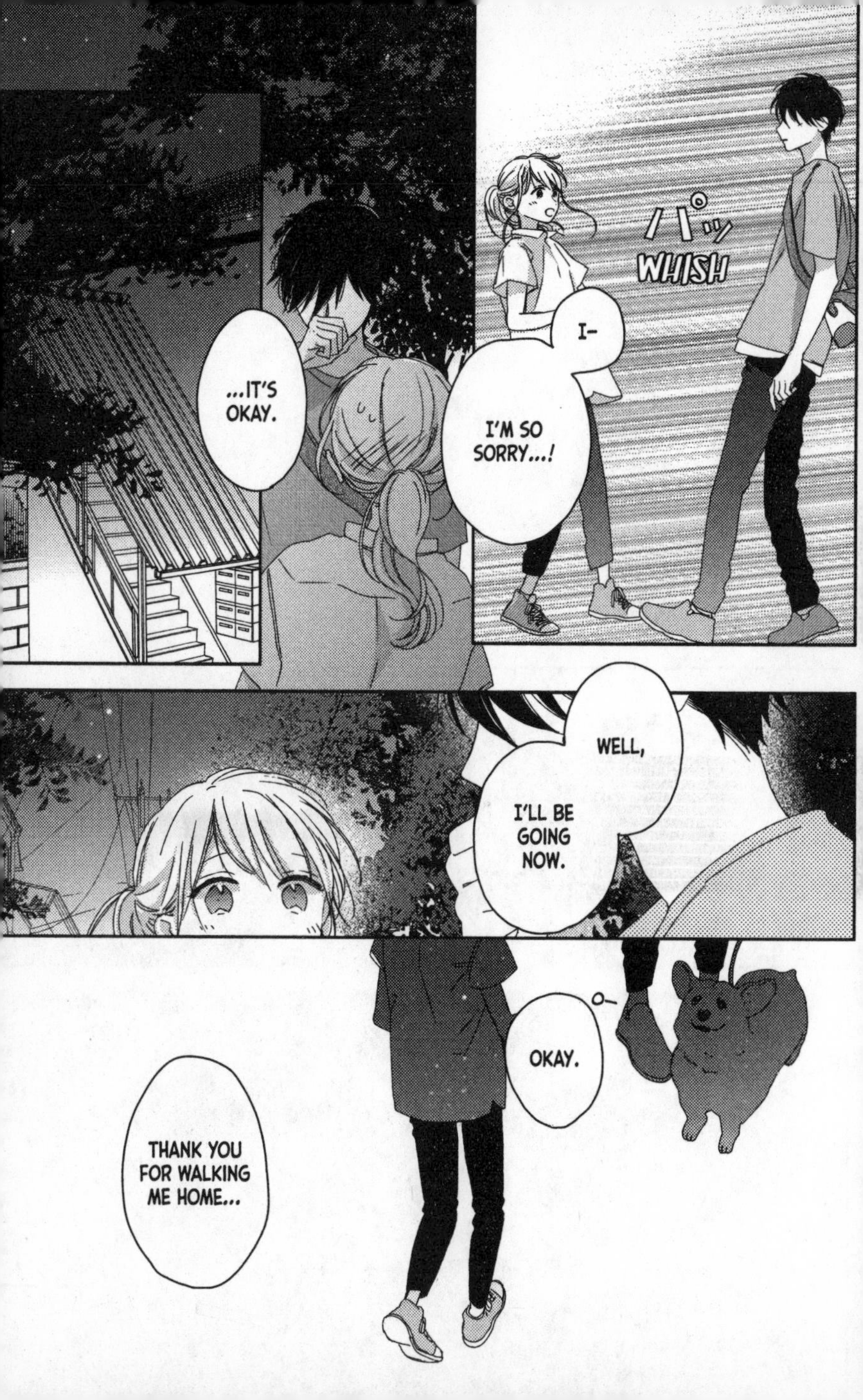
パッ
WHISH
I-
I'M SO SORRY...!
...IT'S OKAY.
WELL,
I'LL BE GOING NOW.
O-
OKAY.
THANK YOU FOR WALKING ME HOME...

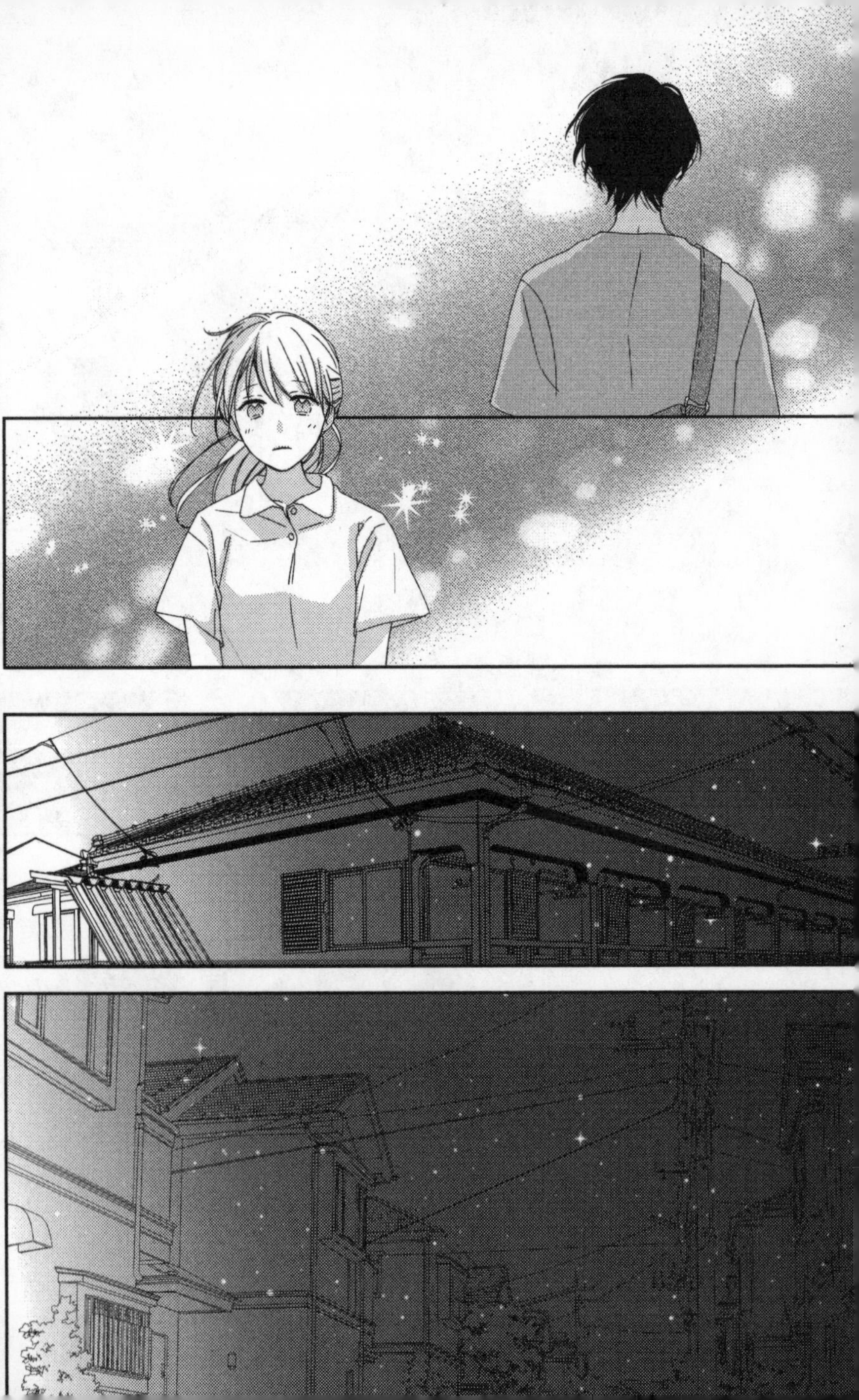

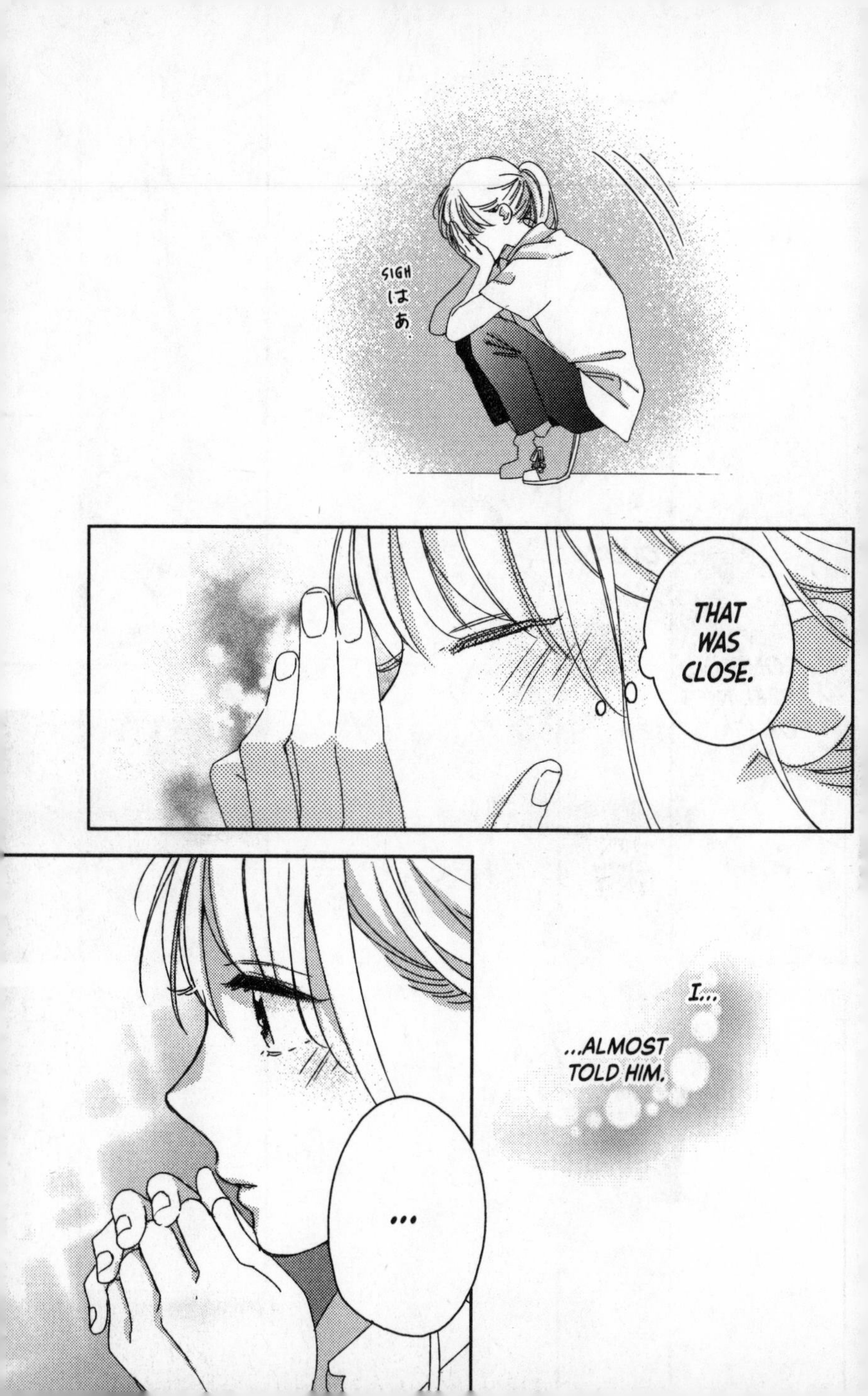
SIGH
はあ.
THAT WAS CLOSE.
I...
...ALMOST TOLD HIM.
...

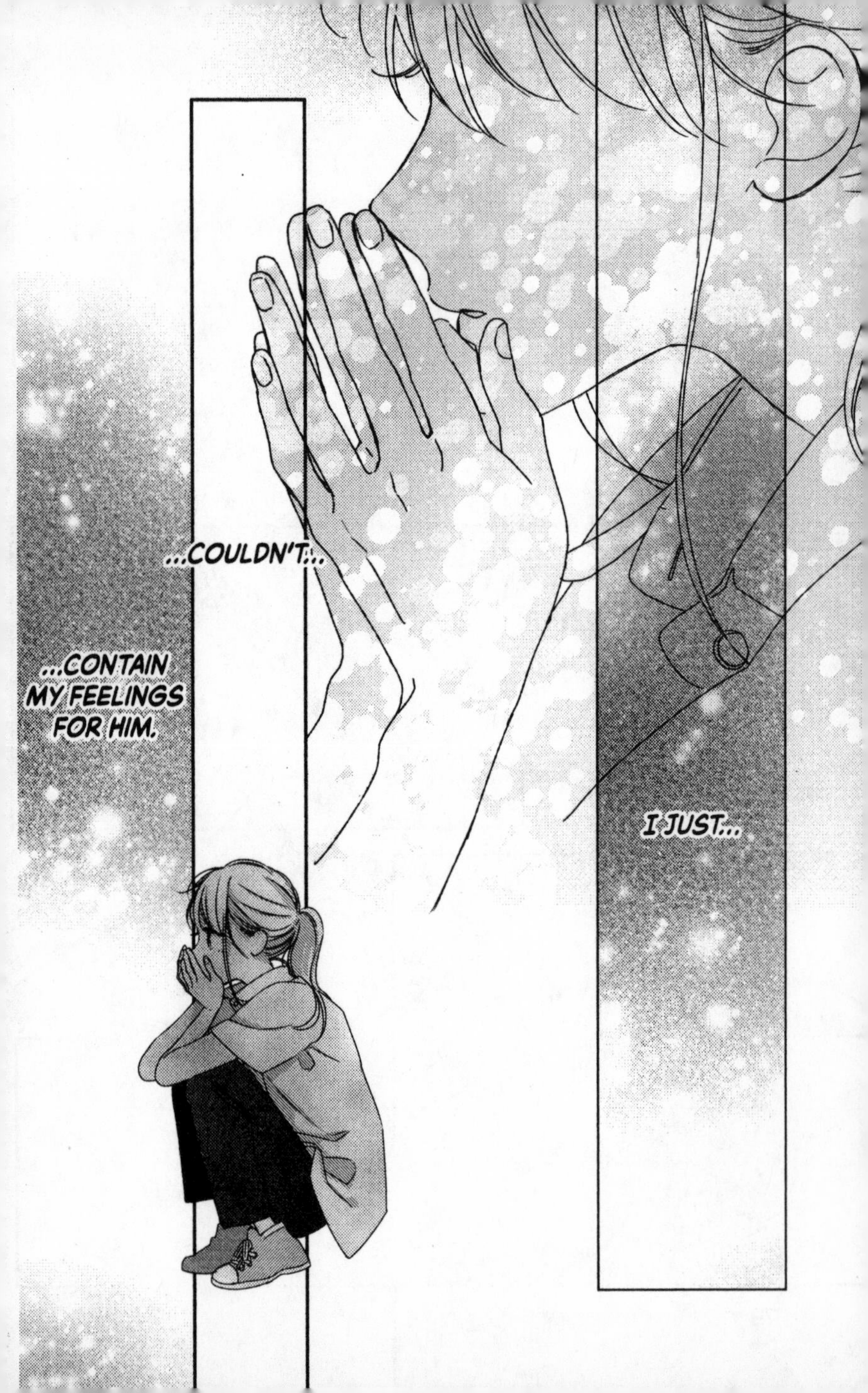
I JUST...
...COULDN'T...
...CONTAIN MY FEELINGS FOR HIM.

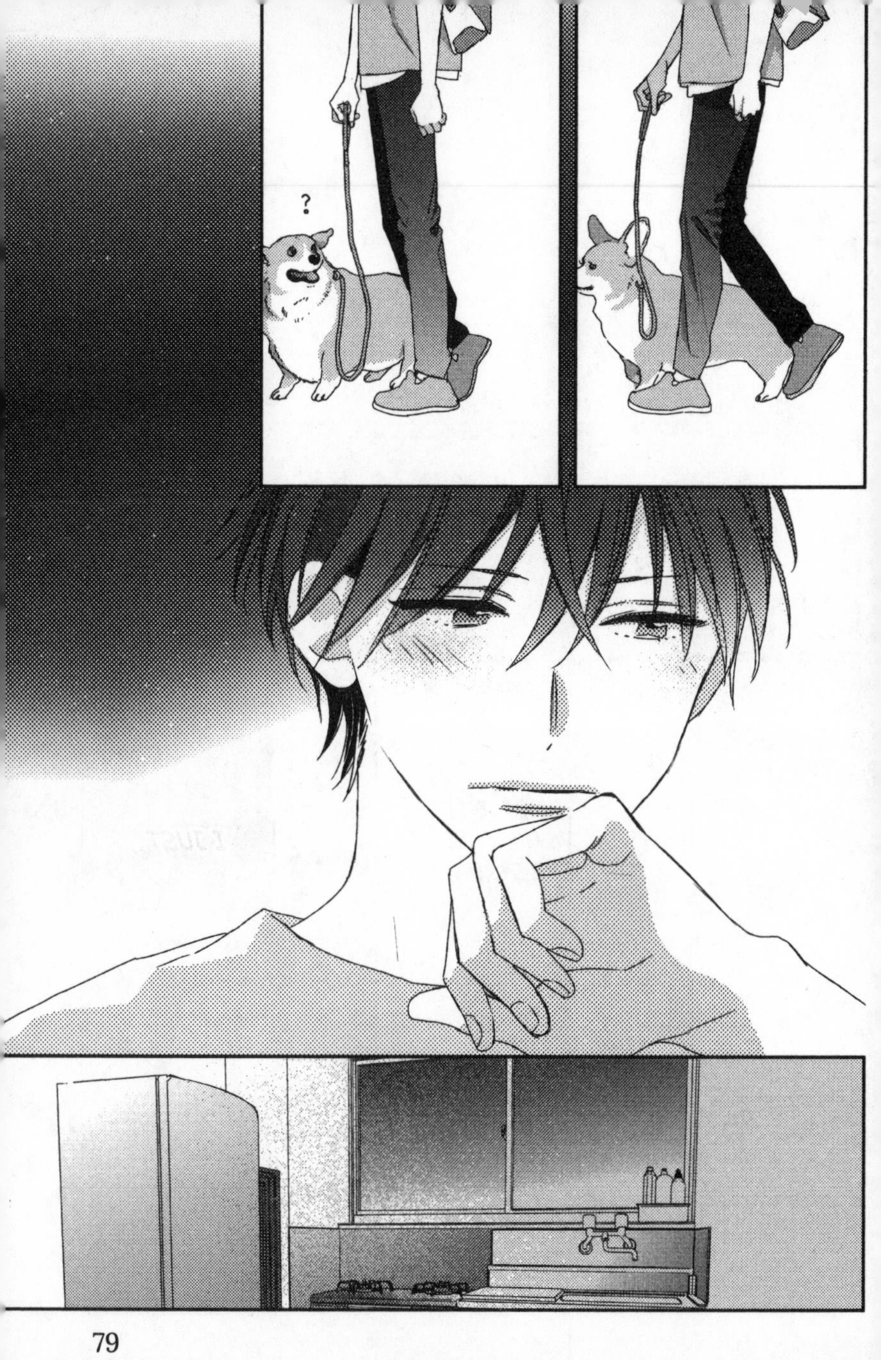
?

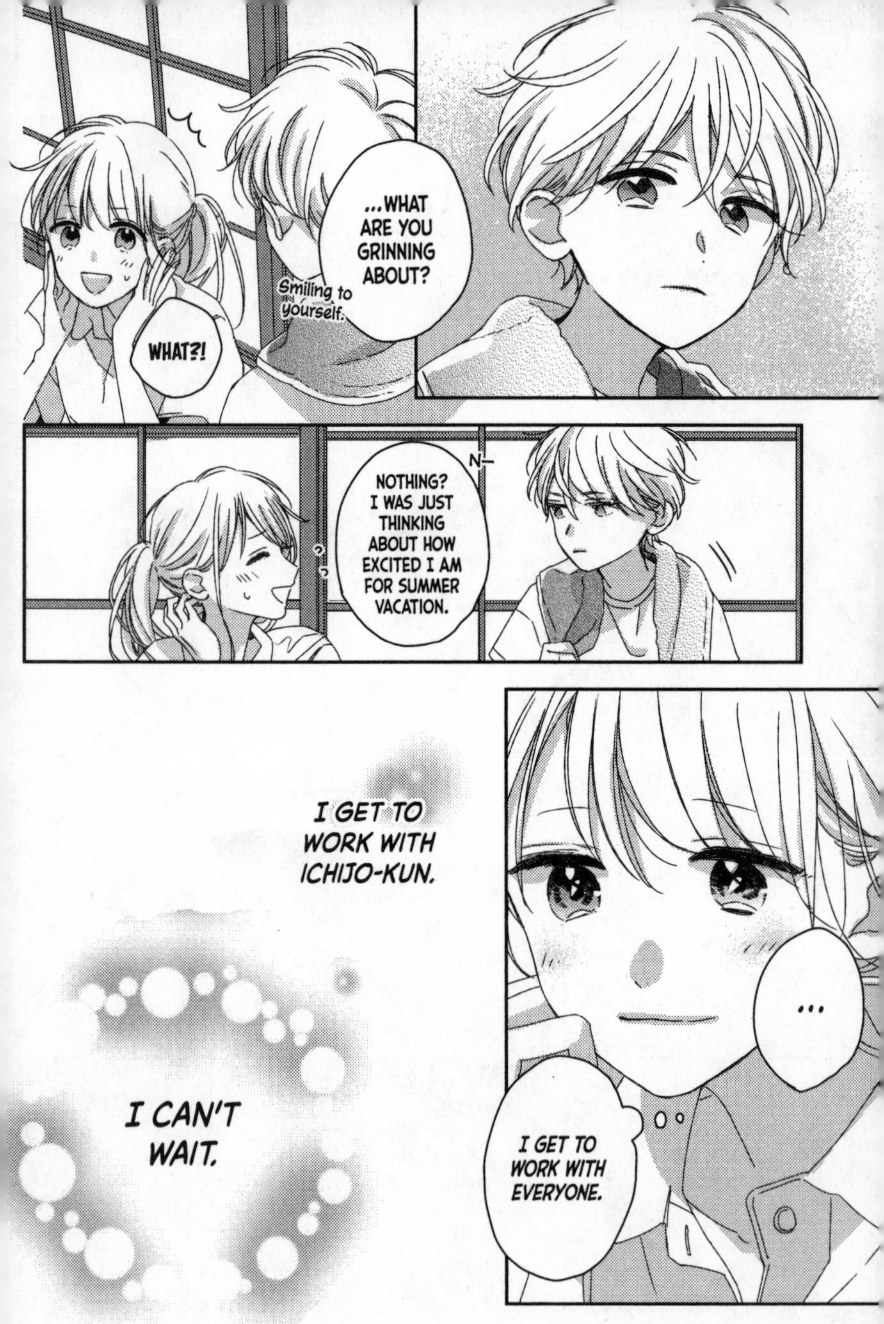
...WHAT ARE YOU GRINNING ABOUT?
Smiling to yourself.
WHAT?!
N—
NOTHING? I WAS JUST THINKING ABOUT HOW EXCITED I AM FOR SUMMER VACATION.
...
I GET TO WORK WITH EVERYONE.
I GET TO WORK WITH ICHIJO-KUN.
I CAN'T WAIT.

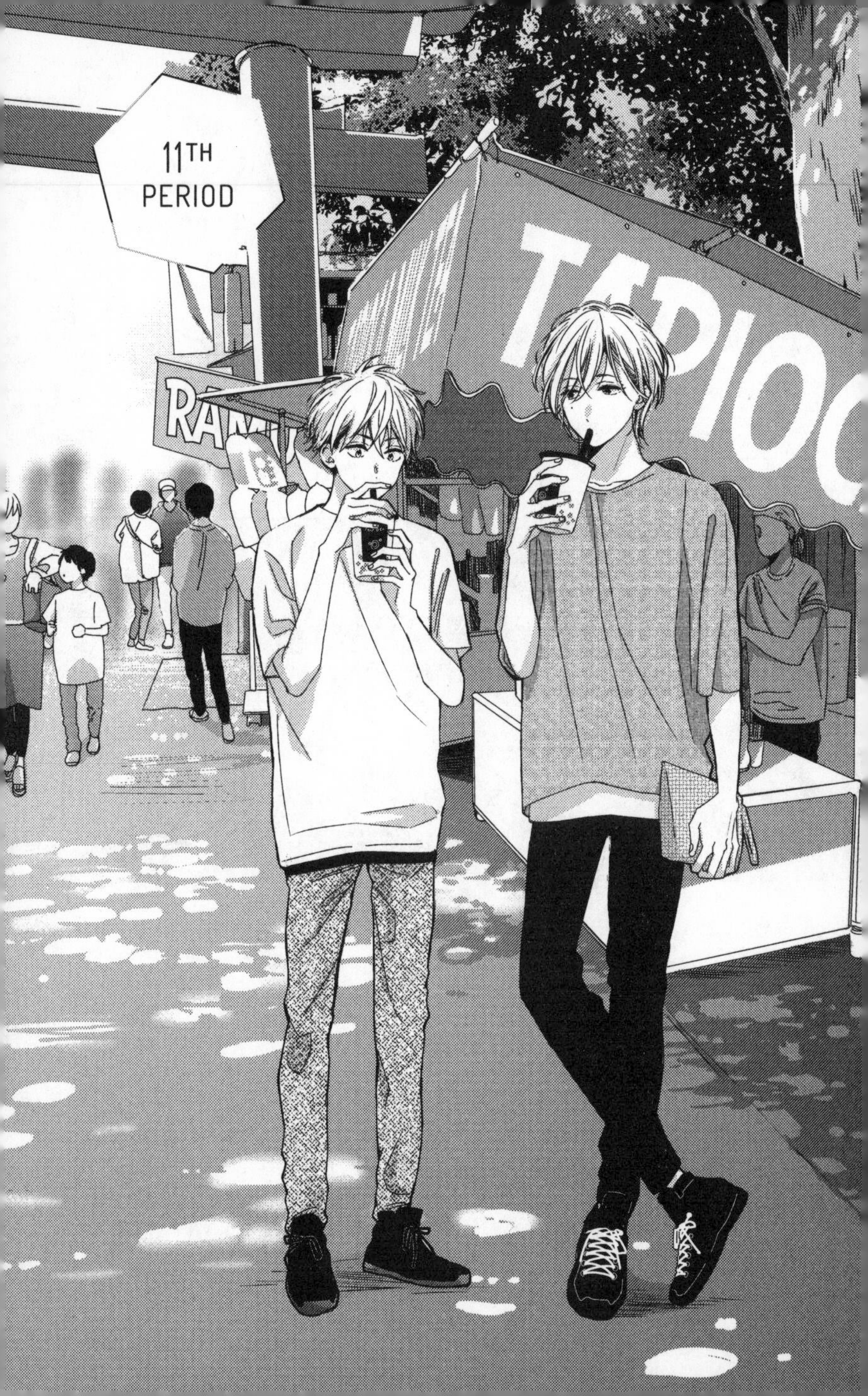
11TH
PERIOD
TAPIOC
RAM

SUMMER VACATION HAS BEGUN.

AND AS PROM- ISED...

森谷 Moriya
もりや

THANK YOU VERY MUCH FOR PICKING UP *THOSE NOT-SO-SWEET BOYS!* VOLUME THREE, THE VOLUME OF... "ARE THE RELATIONSHIPS CHANGING...?!"

PERSONALLY, I HAD FUN DRAWING YUKATA!

I MADE MY OWN CLIP STUDIO BRUSH FOR THE MORNING GLORY PATTERN ON MIDORI'S YUKATA.

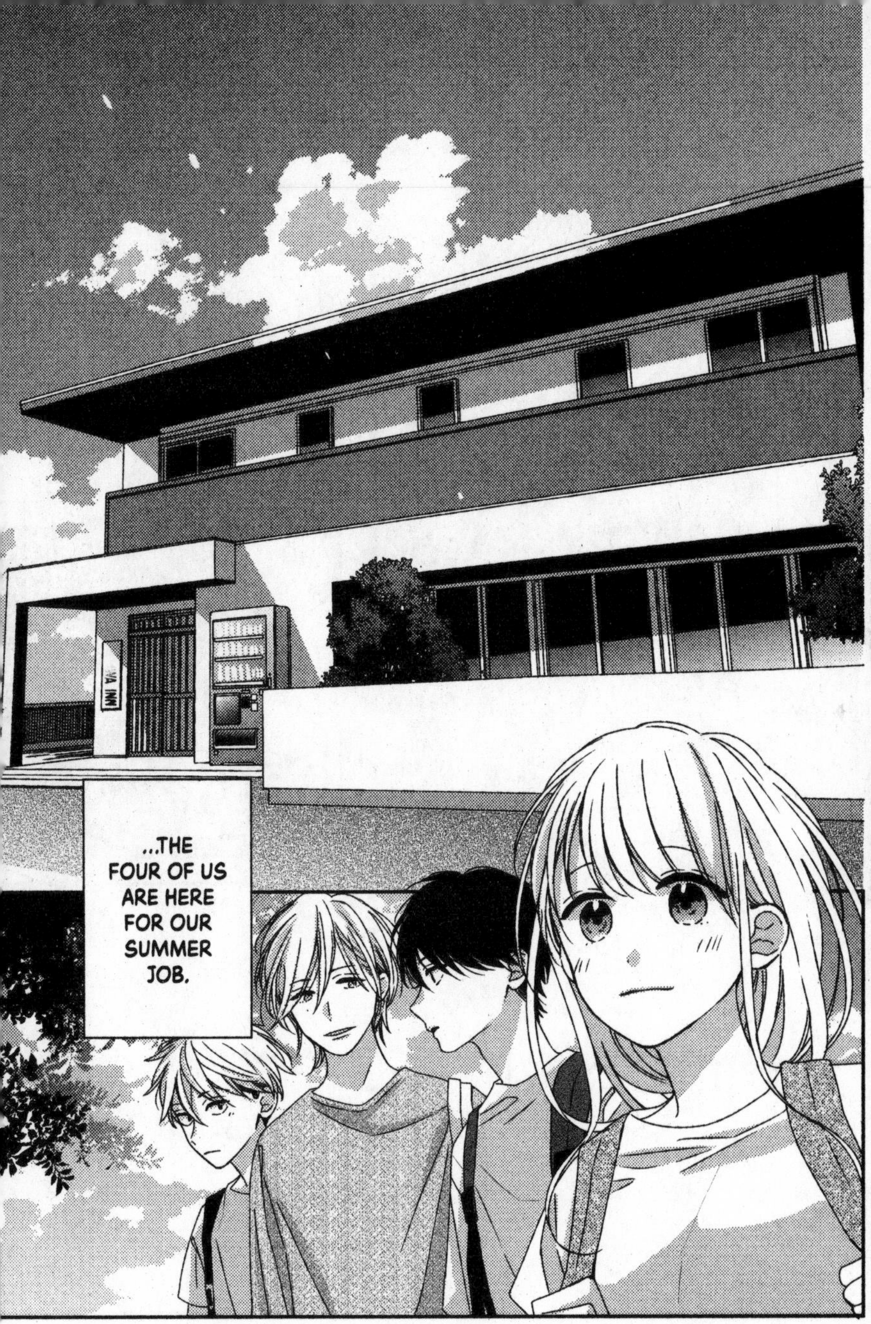

A INN
...THE FOUR OF US ARE HERE FOR OUR SUMMER JOB.

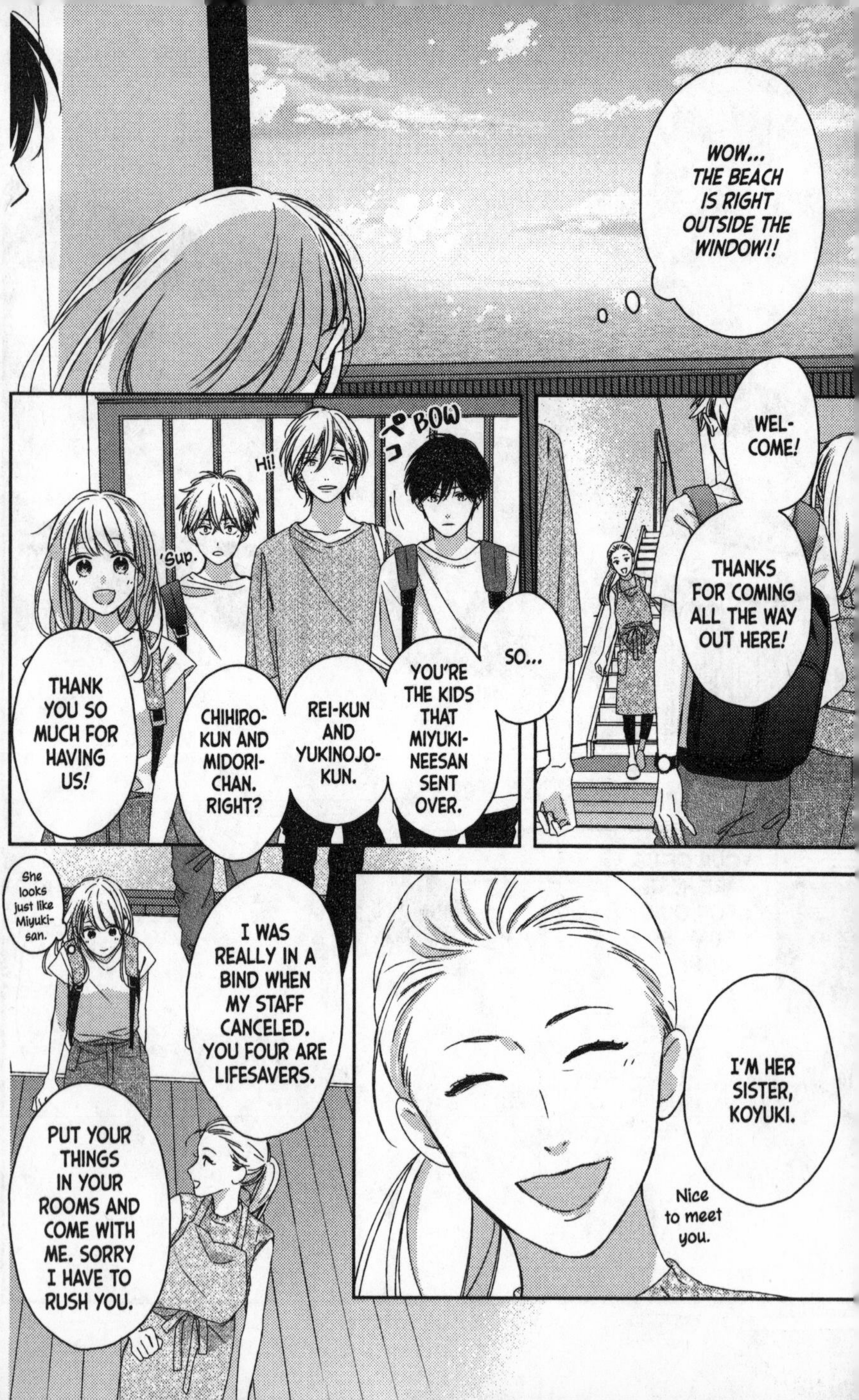
WOW... THE BEACH IS RIGHT OUTSIDE THE WINDOW!!
WEL-COME!
THANKS FOR COMING ALL THE WAY OUT HERE!
BOW
Hi!
SO...
YOU'RE THE KIDS THAT MIYUKI-NEESAN SENT OVER.
REI-KUN AND YUKINOJO-KUN.
'Sup.
CHIHIRO-KUN AND MIDORI-CHAN. RIGHT?
THANK YOU SO MUCH FOR HAVING US!
I'M HER SISTER, KOYUKI.
Nice to meet you.
I WAS REALLY IN A BIND WHEN MY STAFF CANCELED. YOU FOUR ARE LIFESAVERS.
She looks just like Miyuki-san.
PUT YOUR THINGS IN YOUR ROOMS AND COME WITH ME. SORRY I HAVE TO RUSH YOU.

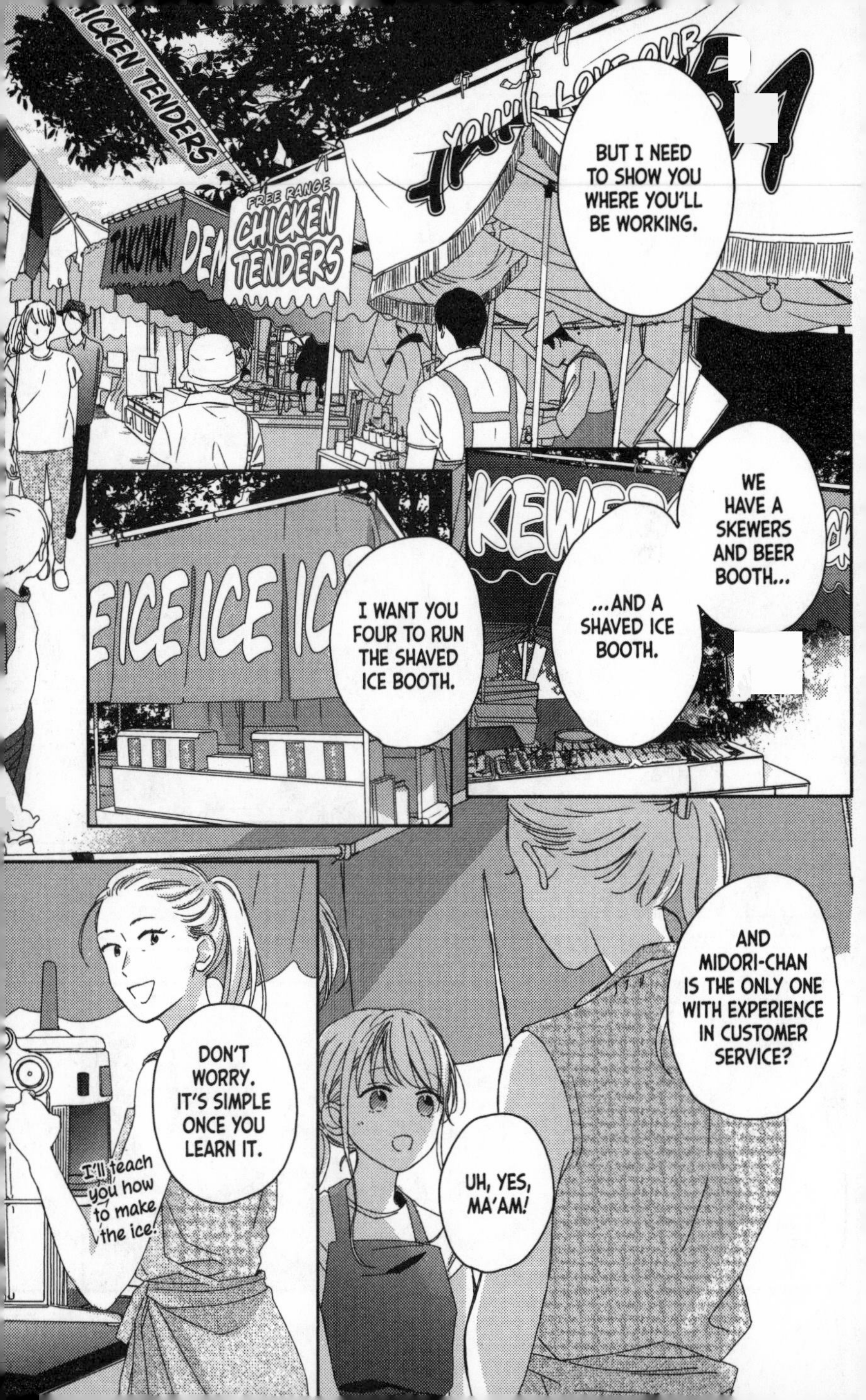
CHICKEN TENDERS
FREE RANGE CHICKEN TENDERS
TAKOYAKI
BUT I NEED TO SHOW YOU WHERE YOU'LL BE WORKING.
WE HAVE A SKEWERS AND BEER BOOTH...
...AND A SHAVED ICE BOOTH.
ICE ICE
I WANT YOU FOUR TO RUN THE SHAVED ICE BOOTH.
AND MIDORI-CHAN IS THE ONLY ONE WITH EXPERIENCE IN CUSTOMER SERVICE?
UH, YES, MA'AM!
DON'T WORRY. IT'S SIMPLE ONCE YOU LEARN IT.
I'll teach you how to make the ice.

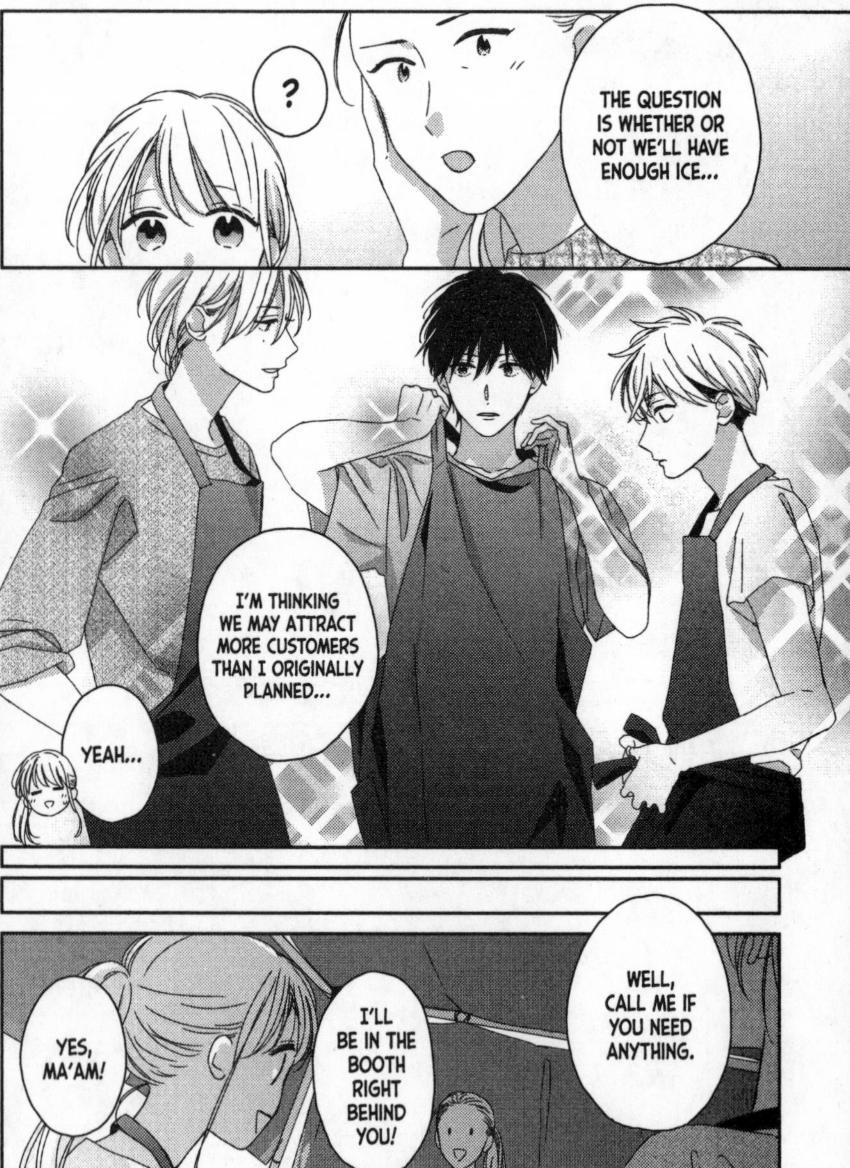
THE QUESTION IS WHETHER OR NOT WE'LL HAVE ENOUGH ICE...
?
I'M THINKING WE MAY ATTRACT MORE CUSTOMERS THAN I ORIGINALLY PLANNED...
YEAH...
WELL, CALL ME IF YOU NEED ANYTHING.
I'LL BE IN THE BOOTH RIGHT BEHIND YOU!
YES, MA'AM!

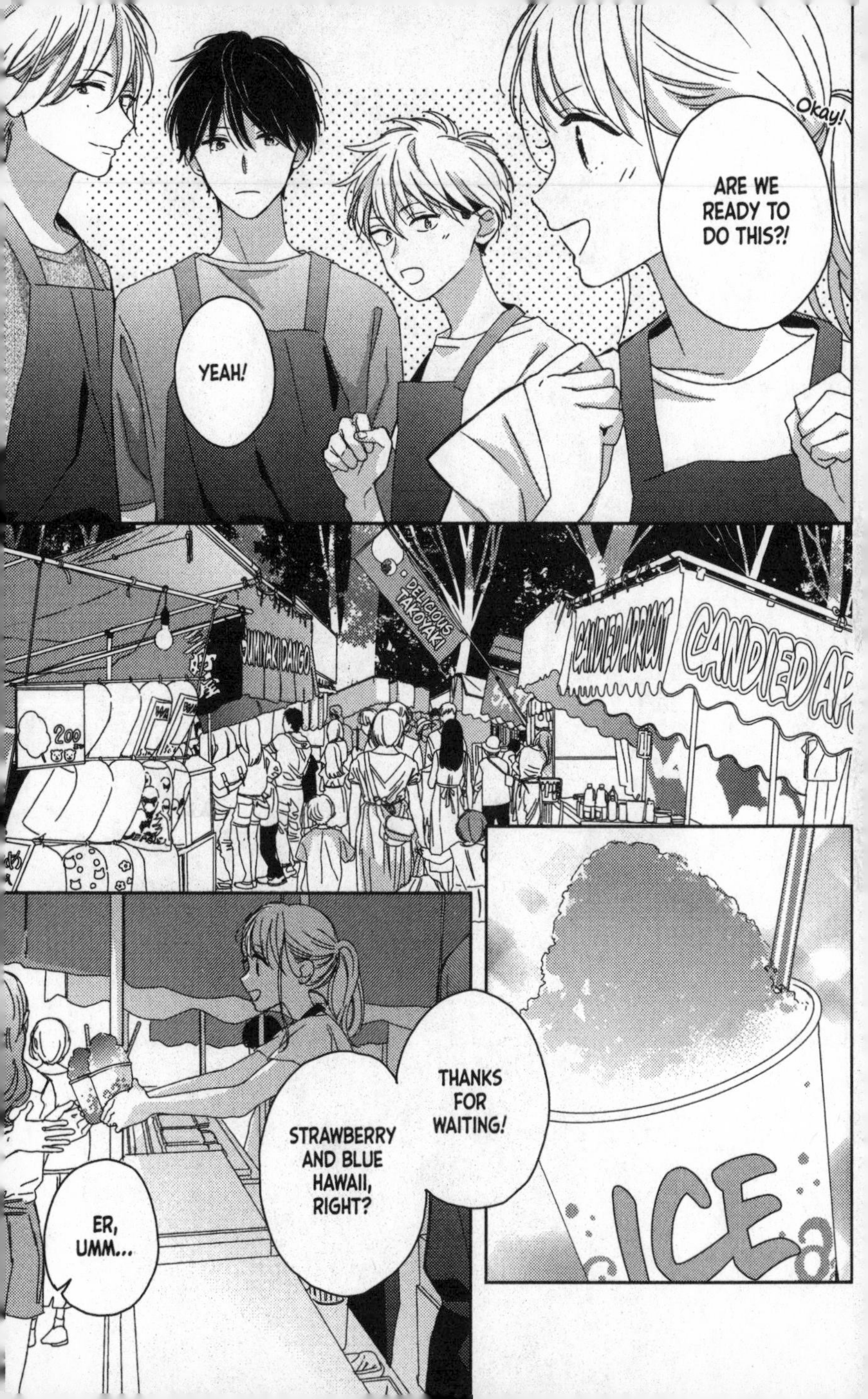
Okay!
ARE WE READY TO DO THIS?!
YEAH!
DELICIOUS TAKOYAKI
CANDIED APRICOT
200
ICE
THANKS FOR WAITING!
STRAWBERRY AND BLUE HAWAII, RIGHT?
ER, UMM...

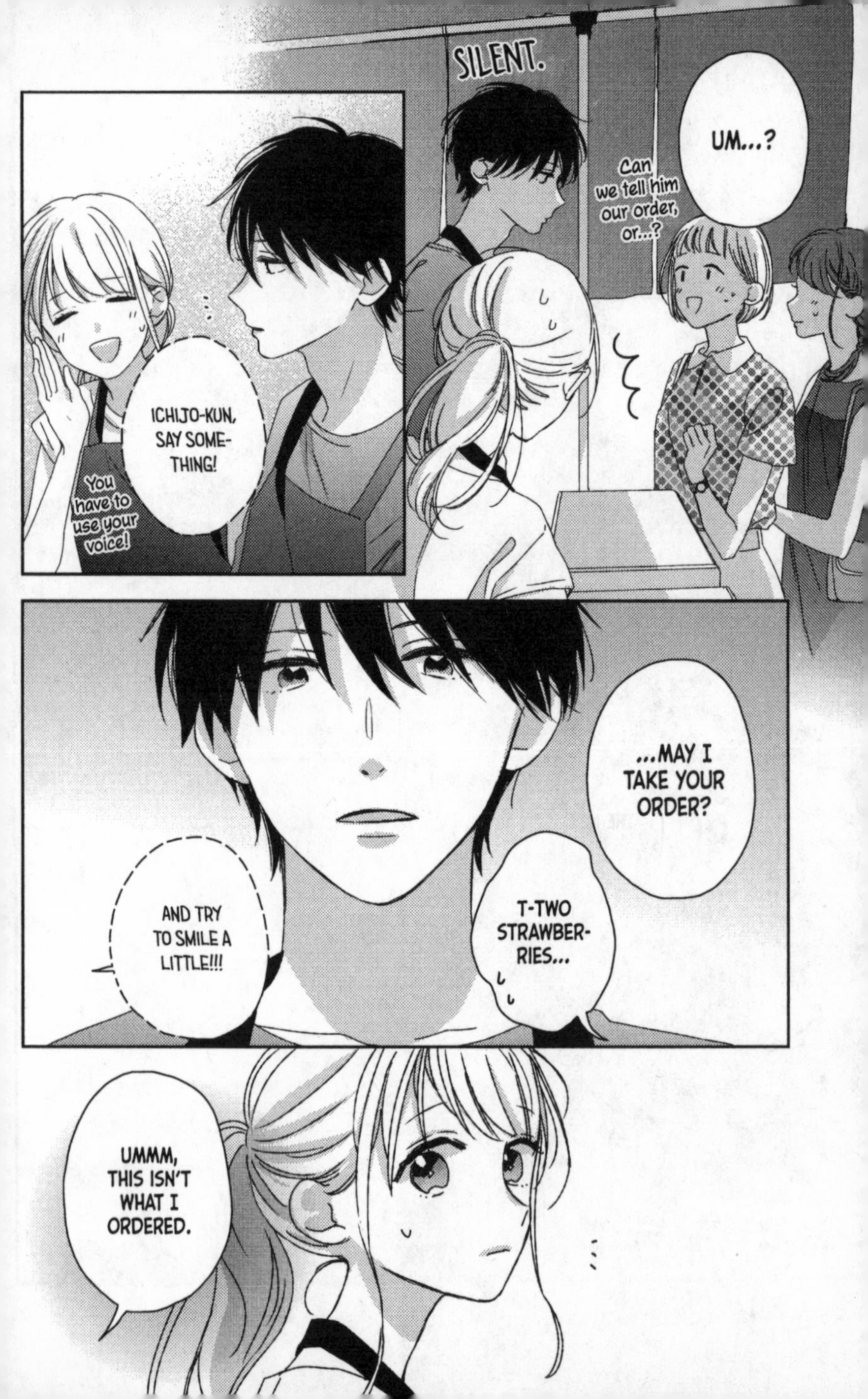
SILENT.
UM...?
Can we tell him our order, or...?
ICHIJO-KUN, SAY SOME-THING!
You have to use your voice!
...MAY I TAKE YOUR ORDER?
T-TWO STRAWBER-RIES...
AND TRY TO SMILE A LITTLE!!!
UMMM, THIS ISN'T WHAT I ORDERED.

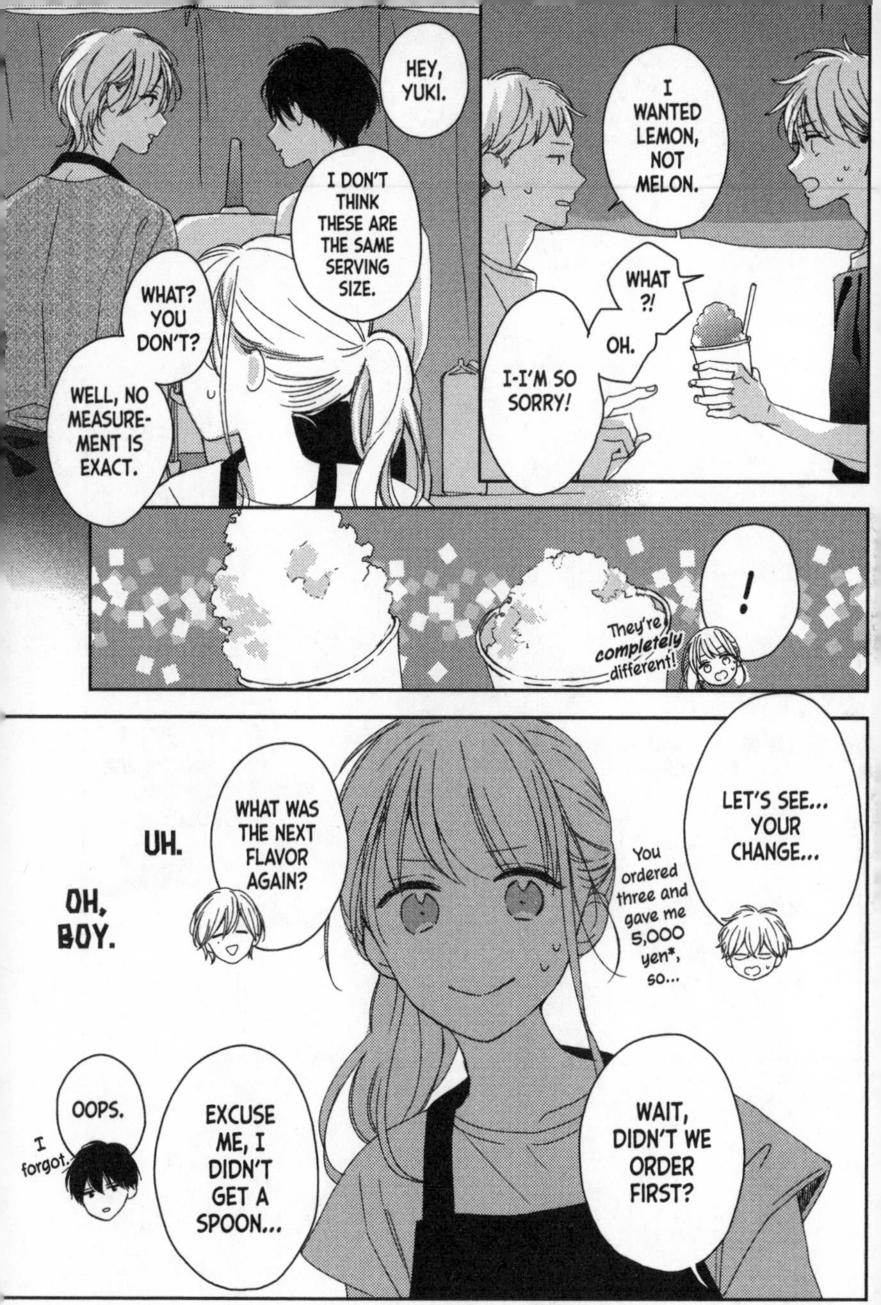
I WANTED LEMON, NOT MELON.
WHAT ?!
OH.
I-I'M SO SORRY!
HEY, YUKI.
I DON'T THINK THESE ARE THE SAME SERVING SIZE.
WHAT? YOU DON'T?
WELL, NO MEASUREMENT IS EXACT.
!
They're completely different!
LET'S SEE... YOUR CHANGE...
You ordered three and gave me 5,000 yen*, so...
WHAT WAS THE NEXT FLAVOR AGAIN?
UH.
OH, BOY.
WAIT, DIDN'T WE ORDER FIRST?
EXCUSE ME, I DIDN'T GET A SPOON...
OOPS.
I forgot.

*About $5

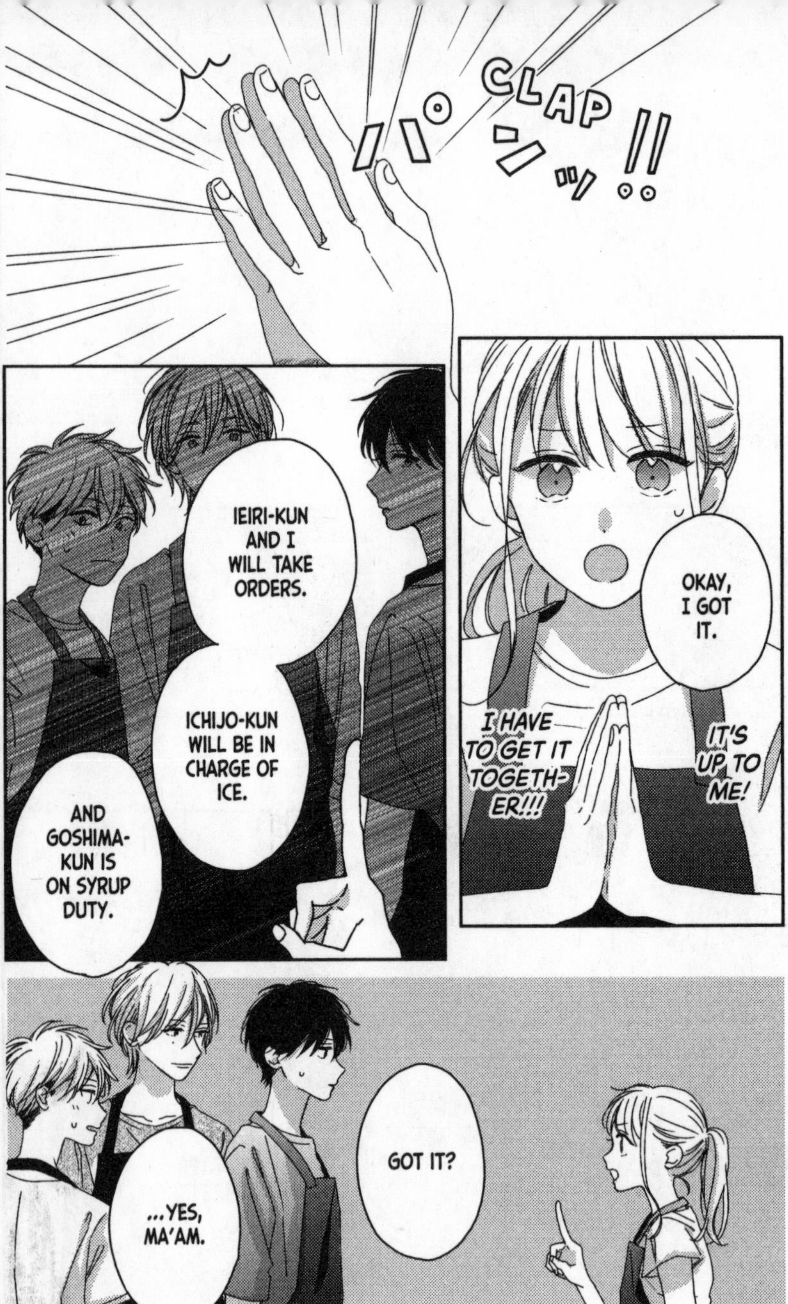
CLAP
パンッ!!
OKAY, I GOT IT.
IT'S UP TO ME!
I HAVE TO GET IT TOGETH-ER!!!
IEIRI-KUN AND I WILL TAKE ORDERS.
ICHIJO-KUN WILL BE IN CHARGE OF ICE.
AND GOSHIMA-KUN IS ON SYRUP DUTY.
GOT IT?
...YES, MA'AM.

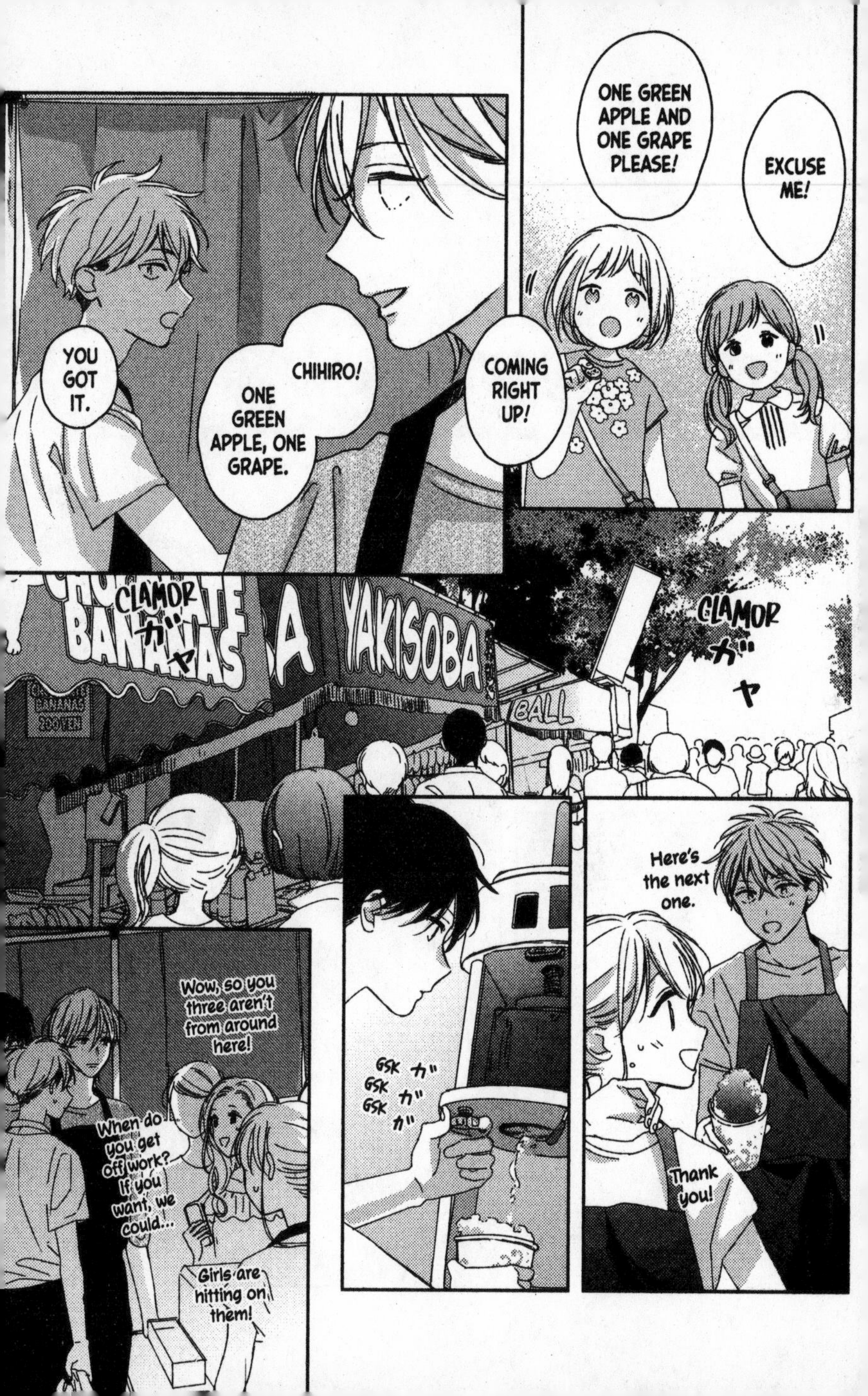
EXCUSE ME!
ONE GREEN APPLE AND ONE GRAPE PLEASE!
COMING RIGHT UP!
CHIHIRO!
ONE GREEN APPLE, ONE GRAPE.
YOU GOT IT.
CLAMOR ガヤ
YAKISOBA
BALL
BANANAS
CLAMOR ガヤ
Here's the next one.
Thank you!
GSK GSK GSK ガガガ
Wow, so you three aren't from around here!
When do you get off work? If you want, we could...
Girls are hitting on them!

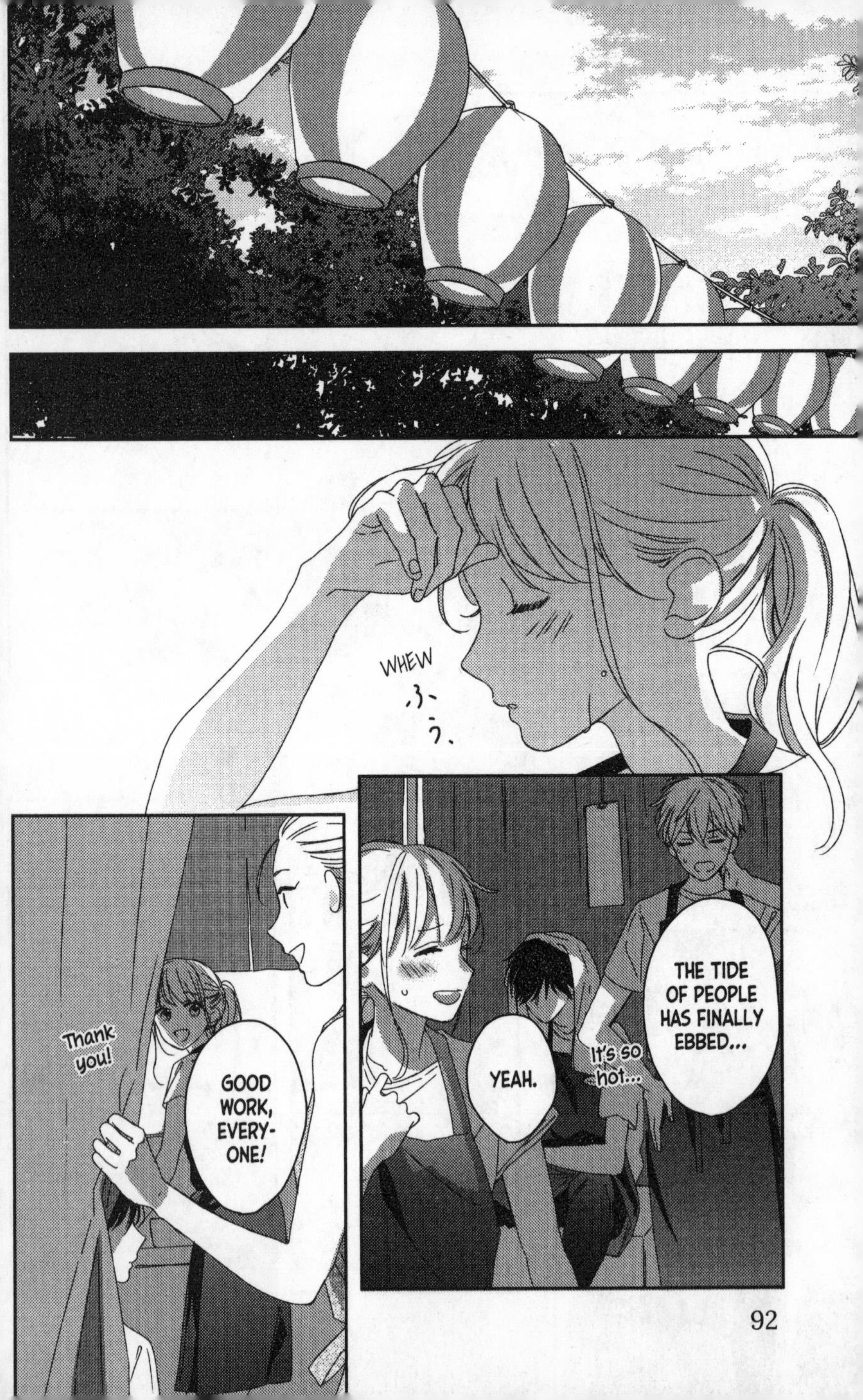
WHEW
ふぅ
THE TIDE OF PEOPLE HAS FINALLY EBBED...
It's so hot...
YEAH.
GOOD WORK, EVERY-ONE!
Thank you!

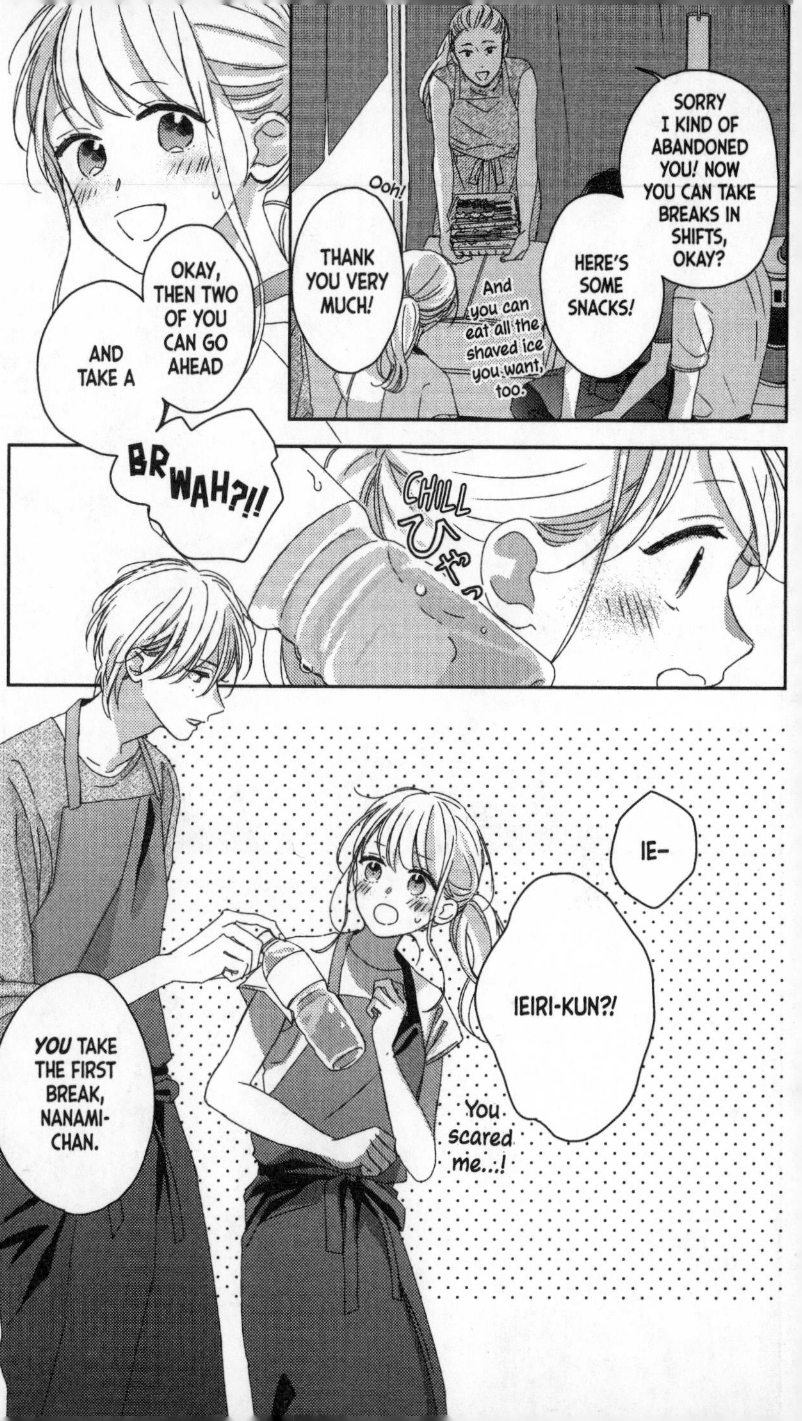
SORRY I KIND OF ABANDONED YOU! NOW YOU CAN TAKE BREAKS IN SHIFTS, OKAY?
HERE'S SOME SNACKS!
And you can eat all the shaved ice you want, too.
Ooh!
THANK YOU VERY MUCH!
OKAY, THEN TWO OF YOU CAN GO AHEAD
AND TAKE A
BRWAH?!!
CHILL
ひゃっ
IE-
IEIRI-KUN?!
You scared me...!
YOU TAKE THE FIRST BREAK, NANAMI-CHAN.

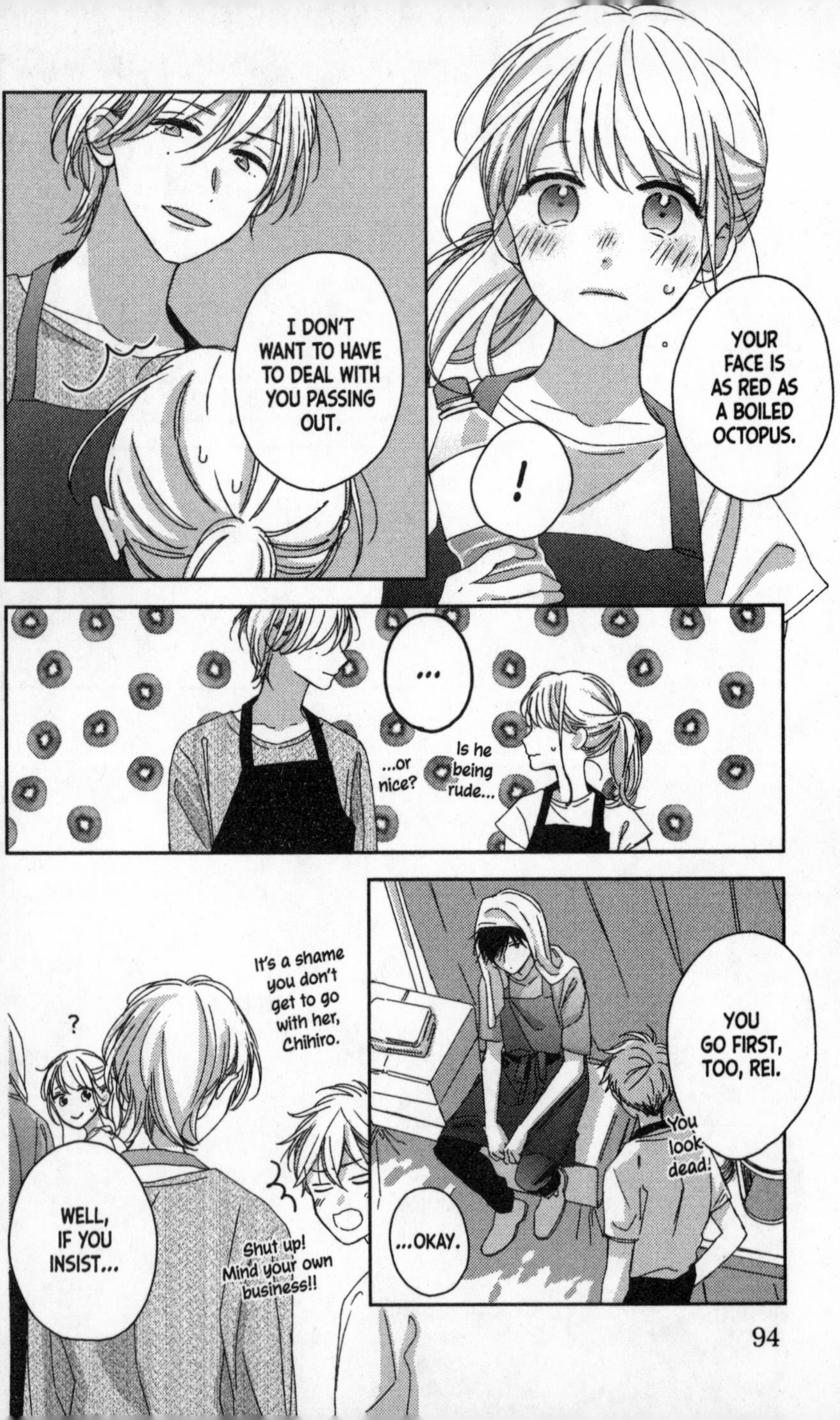
YOUR FACE IS AS RED AS A BOILED OCTOPUS.
!
I DON'T WANT TO HAVE TO DEAL WITH YOU PASSING OUT.
...
Is he being rude...
...or nice?
YOU GO FIRST, TOO, REI.
You look dead!
...OKAY.
It's a shame you don't get to go with her, Chihiro.
?
WELL, IF YOU INSIST...
Shut up! Mind your own business!!

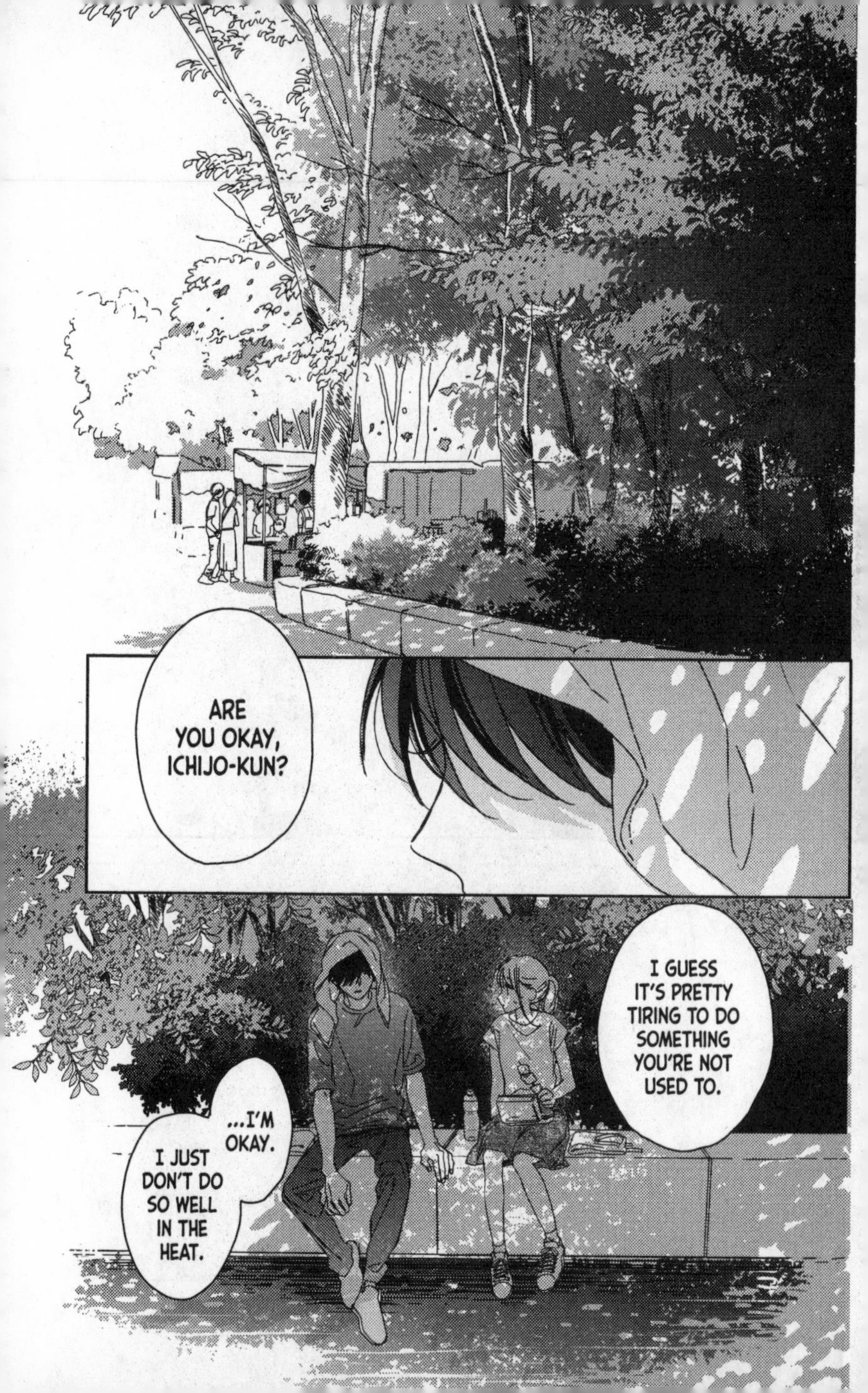
ARE YOU OKAY, ICHIJO-KUN?
I GUESS IT'S PRETTY TIRING TO DO SOMETHING YOU'RE NOT USED TO.
...I'M OKAY.
I JUST DON'T DO SO WELL IN THE HEAT.

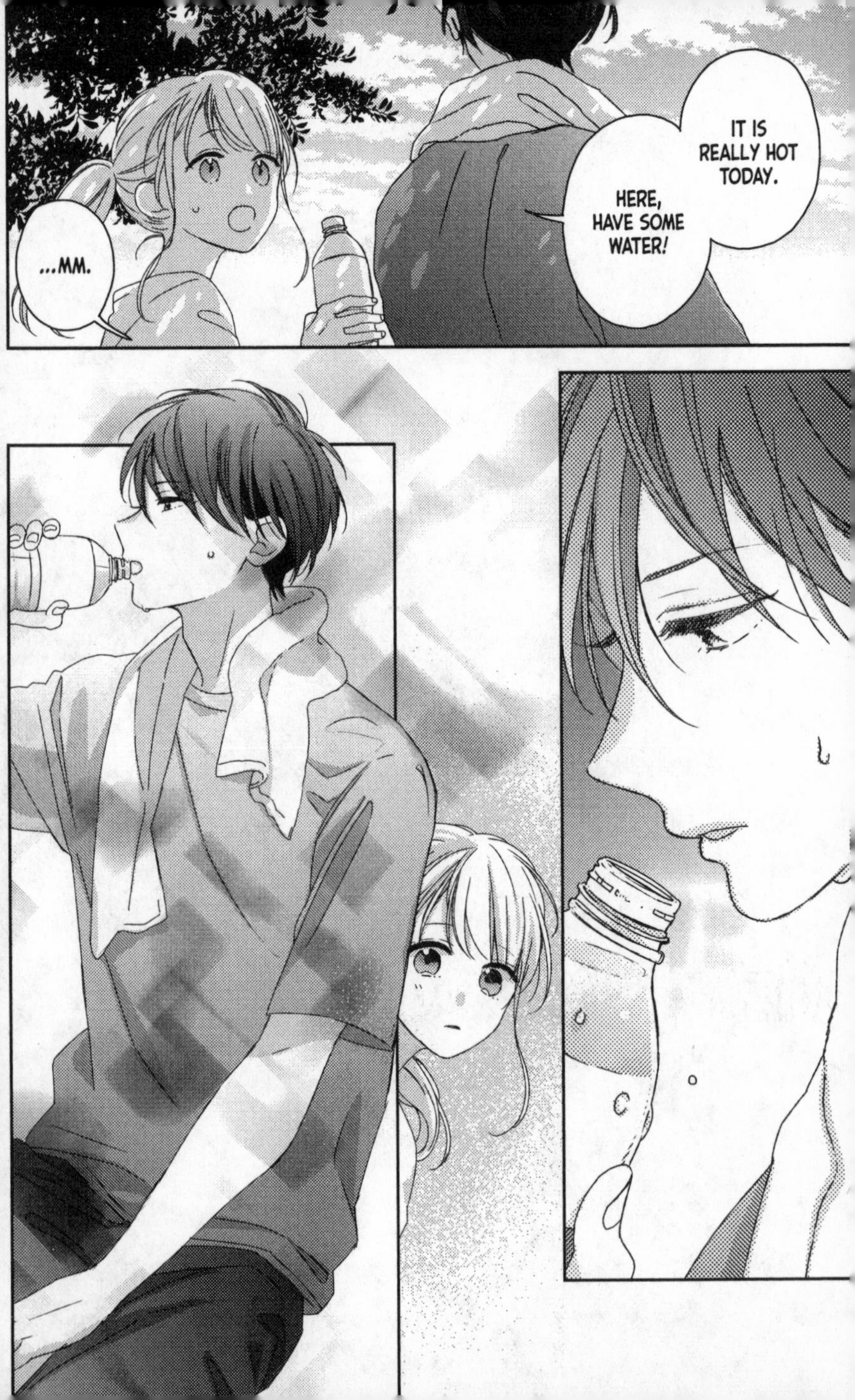
IT IS REALLY HOT TODAY.
HERE, HAVE SOME WATER!
...MM.

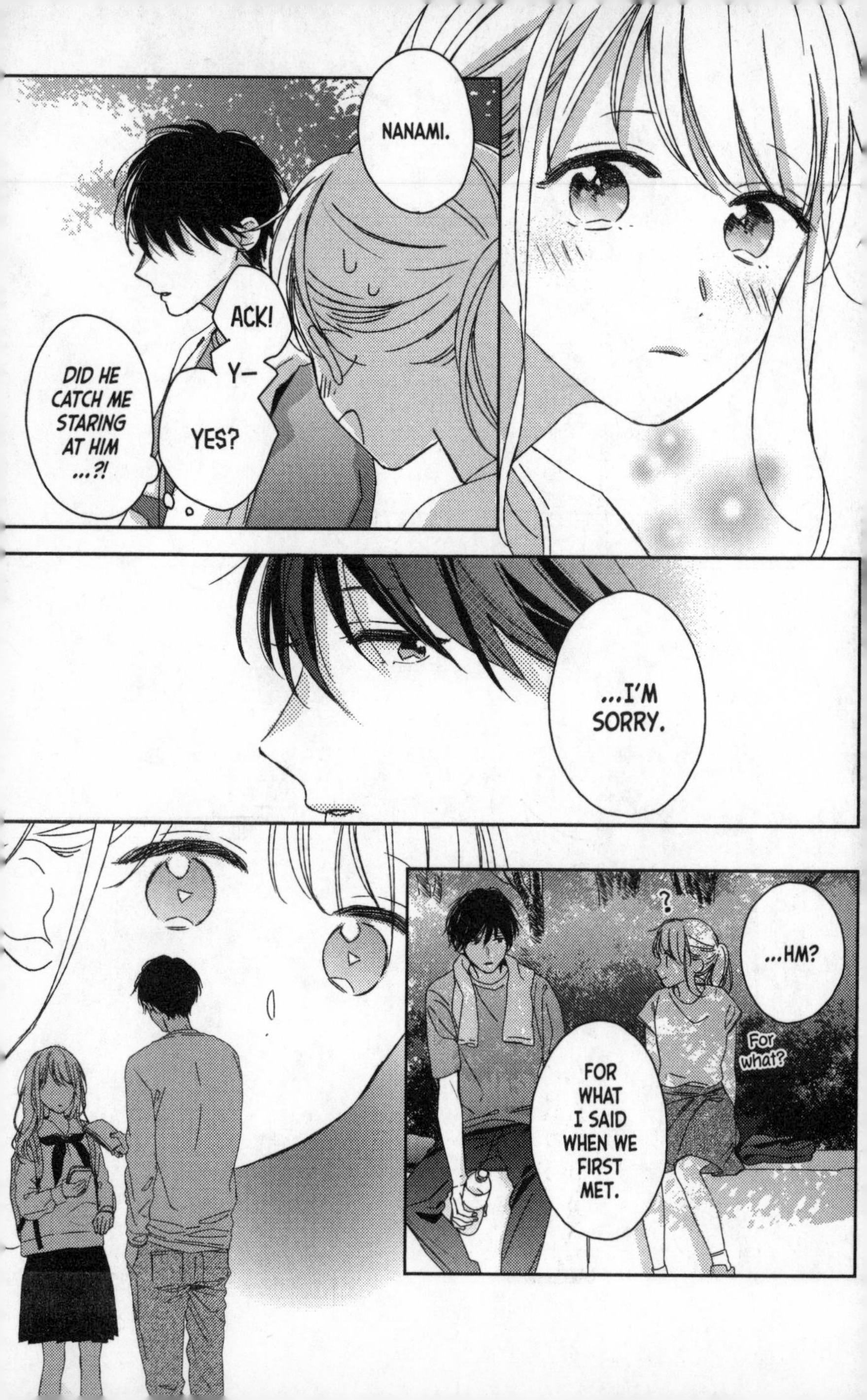
NANAMI.
ACK!
Y—
YES?
DID HE CATCH ME STARING AT HIM ...?!
...I'M SORRY.
?
...HM?
For what?
FOR WHAT I SAID WHEN WE FIRST MET.

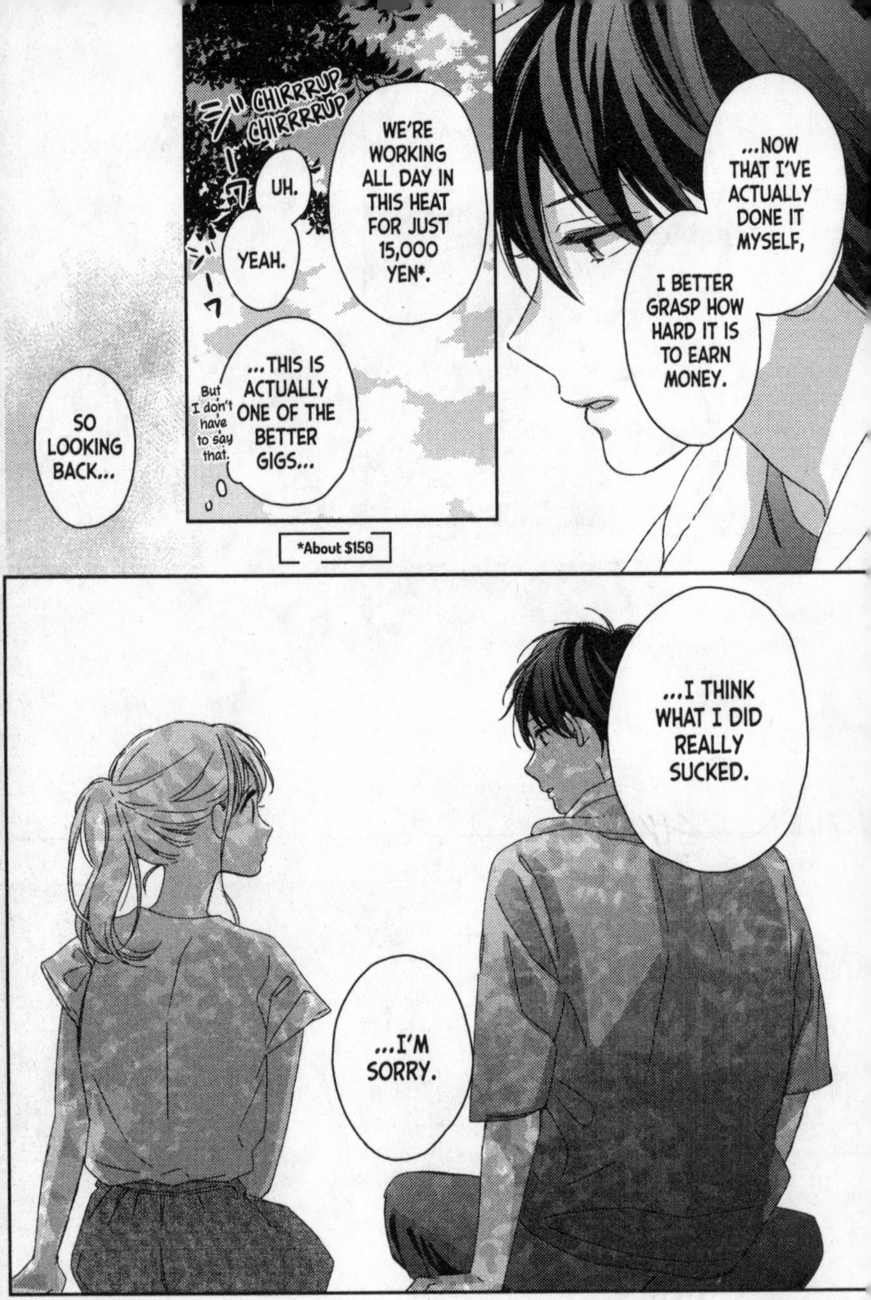
CHIRRRUP CHIRRRRUP
WE'RE WORKING ALL DAY IN THIS HEAT FOR JUST 15,000 YEN*.
UH.
YEAH.
...THIS IS ACTUALLY ONE OF THE BETTER GIGS...
But I don't have to say that.
...NOW THAT I'VE ACTUALLY DONE IT MYSELF,
I BETTER GRASP HOW HARD IT IS TO EARN MONEY.
SO LOOKING BACK...
*About $150
...I THINK WHAT I DID REALLY SUCKED.
...I'M SORRY.

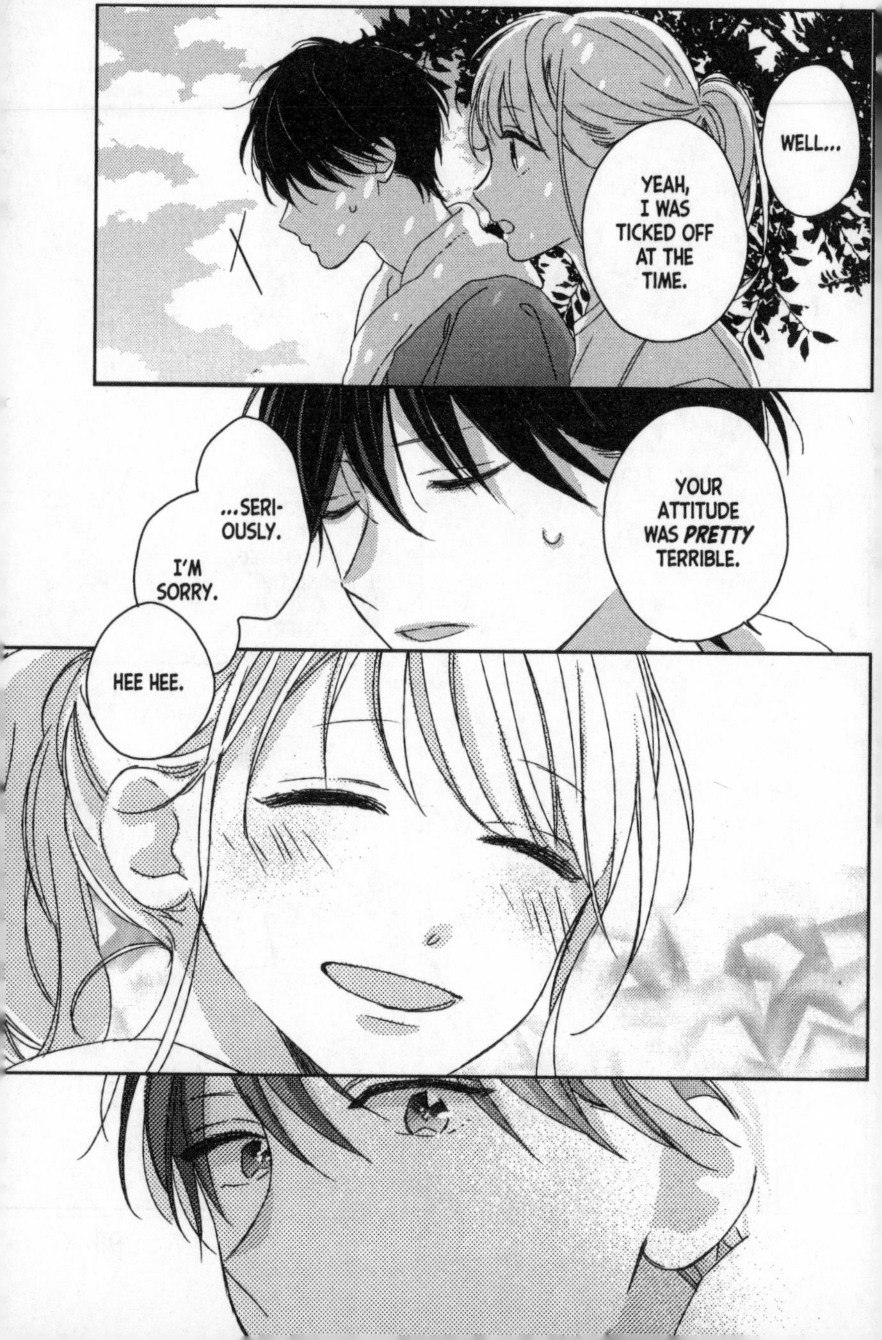
WELL...
YEAH, I WAS TICKED OFF AT THE TIME.
YOUR ATTITUDE WAS PRETTY TERRIBLE.
...SERIOUSLY. I'M SORRY.
HEE HEE.

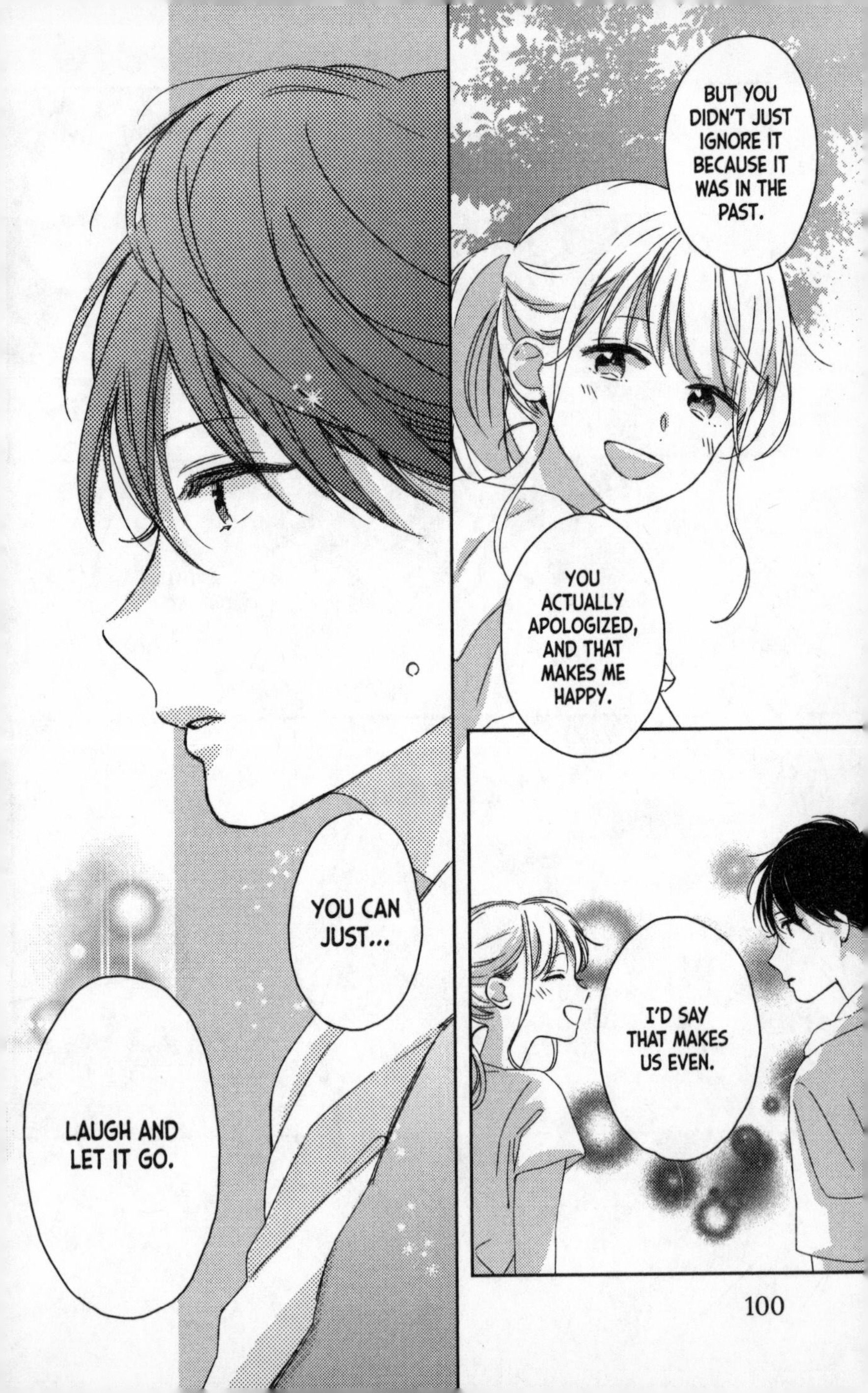
BUT YOU DIDN'T JUST IGNORE IT BECAUSE IT WAS IN THE PAST.
YOU ACTUALLY APOLOGIZED, AND THAT MAKES ME HAPPY.
I'D SAY THAT MAKES US EVEN.
YOU CAN JUST...
LAUGH AND LET IT GO.

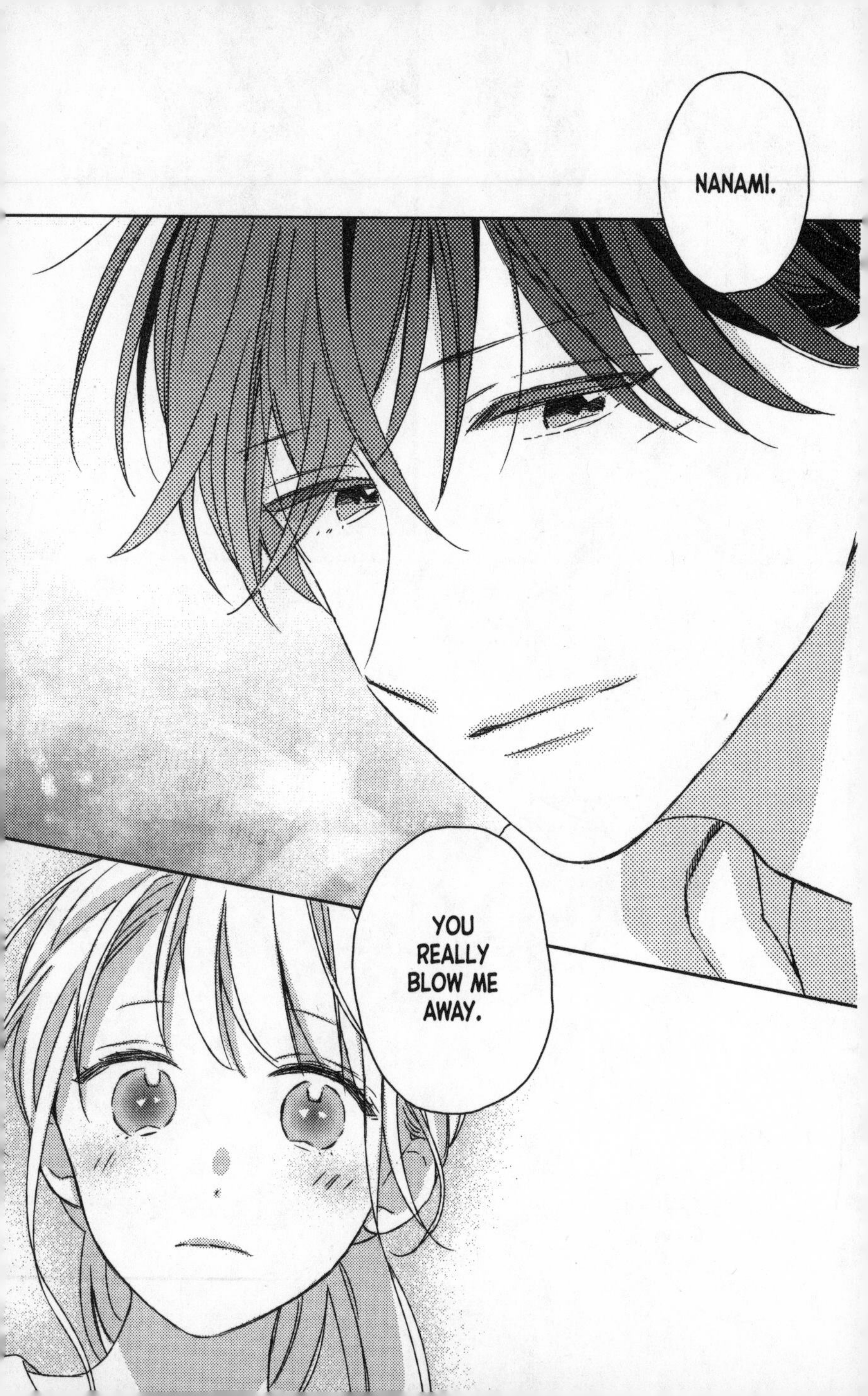
NANAMI.
YOU REALLY BLOW ME AWAY.

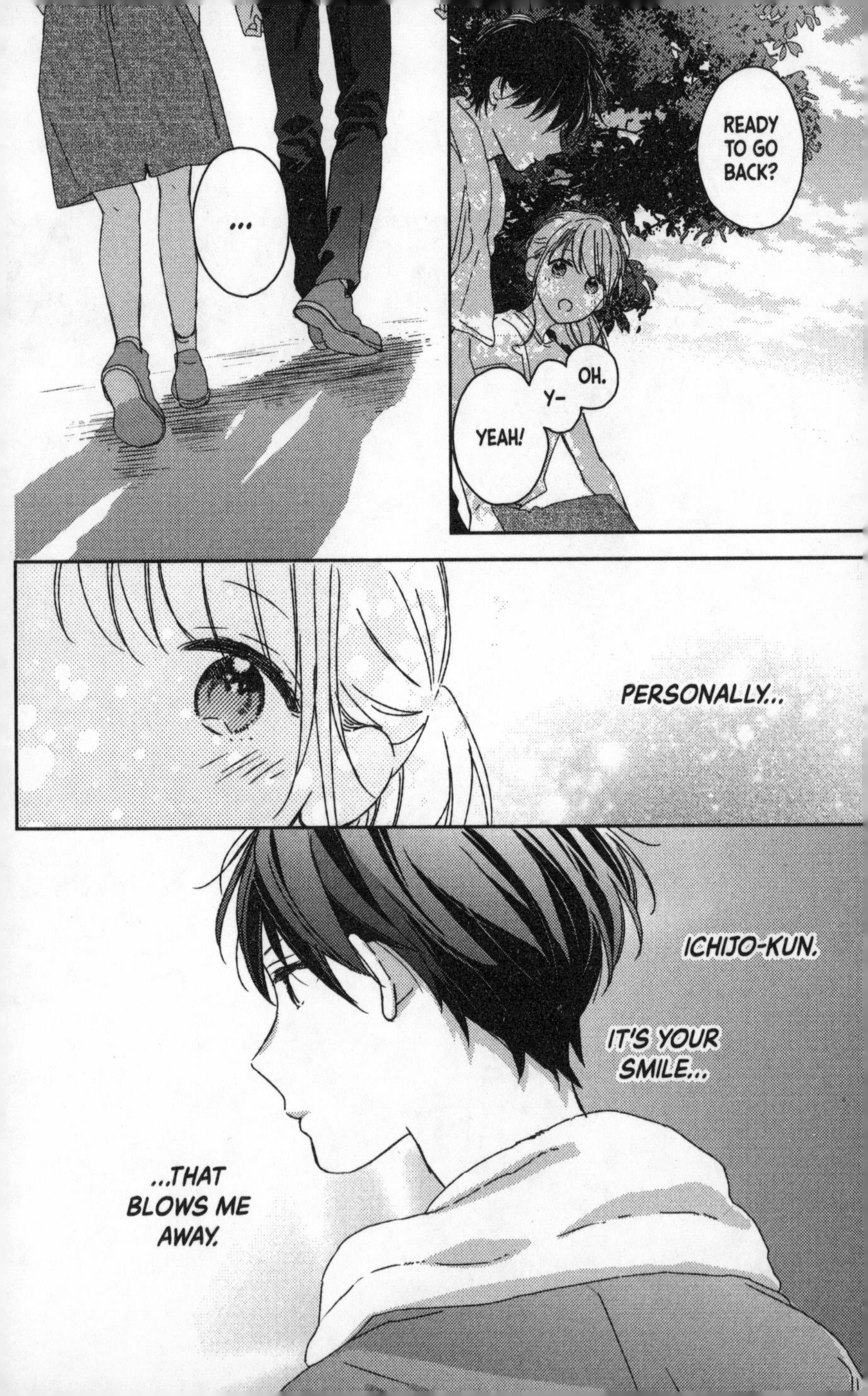
READY TO GO BACK?
OH. Y- YEAH!
...
PERSONALLY...
ICHIJO-KUN.
IT'S YOUR SMILE...
...THAT BLOWS ME AWAY.

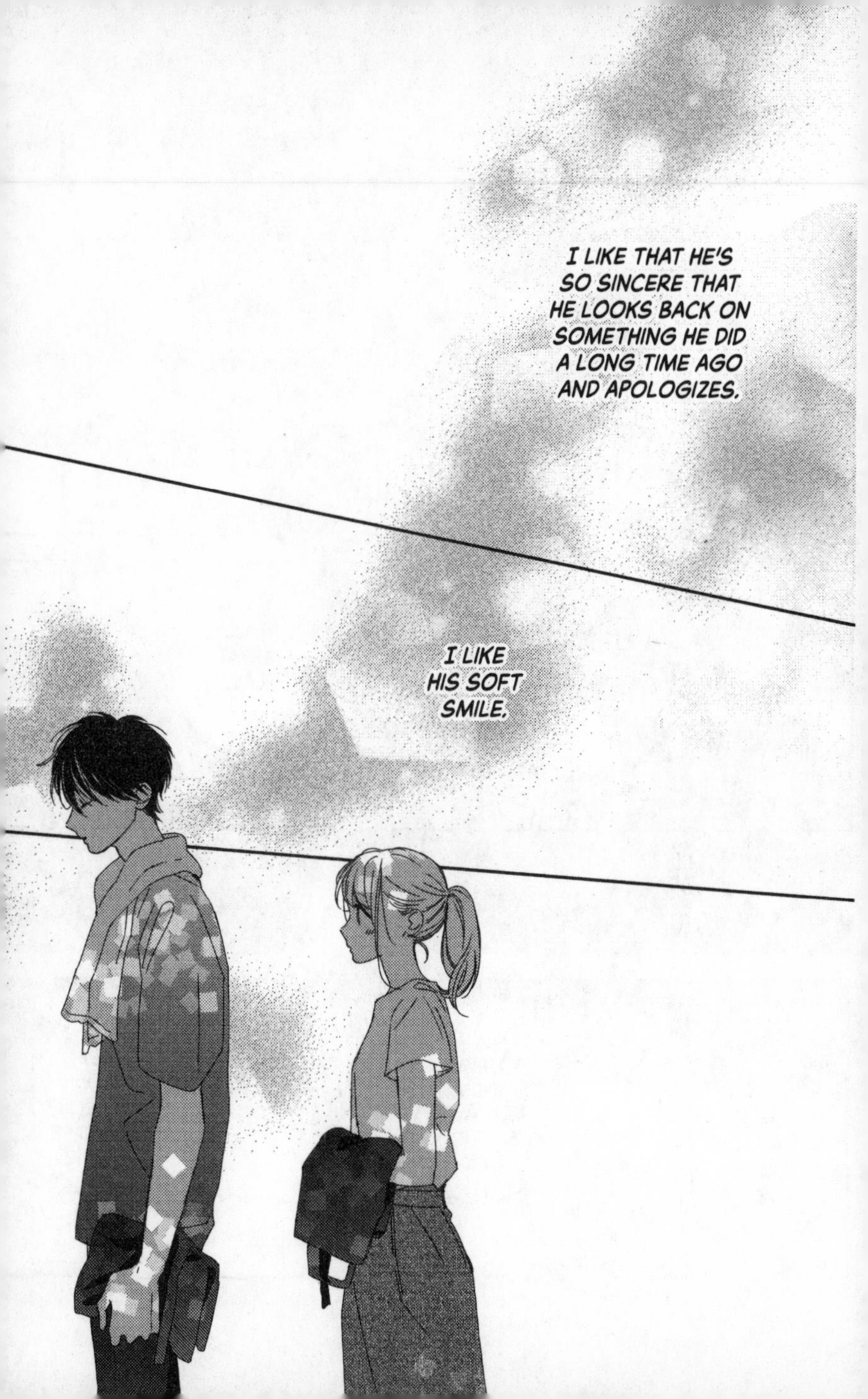
I LIKE THAT HE'S SO SINCERE THAT HE LOOKS BACK ON SOMETHING HE DID A LONG TIME AGO AND APOLOGIZES.
I LIKE HIS SOFT SMILE.

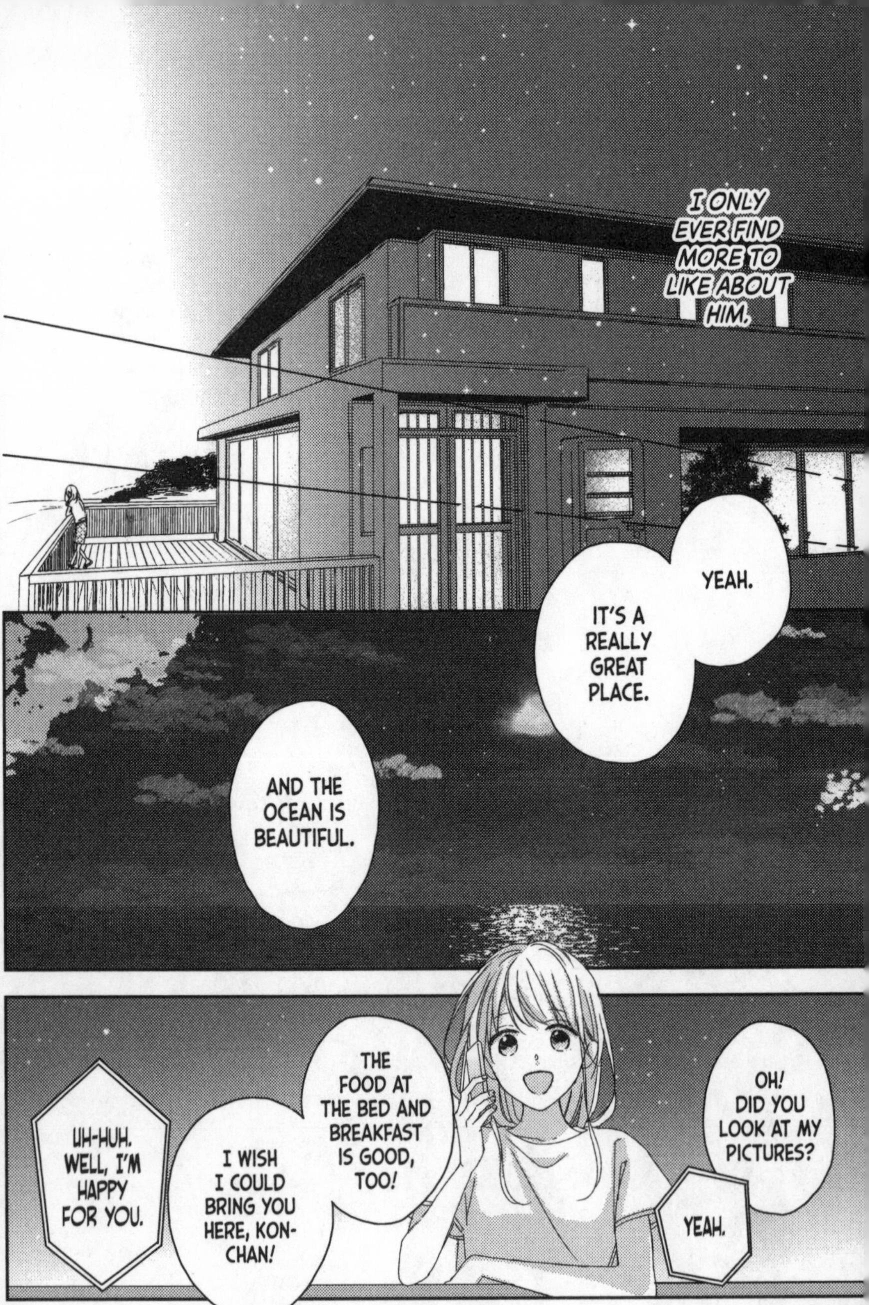
I ONLY EVER FIND MORE TO LIKE ABOUT HIM.
YEAH.
IT'S A REALLY GREAT PLACE.
AND THE OCEAN IS BEAUTIFUL.
OH! DID YOU LOOK AT MY PICTURES?
YEAH.
THE FOOD AT THE BED AND BREAKFAST IS GOOD, TOO!
I WISH I COULD BRING YOU HERE, KON-CHAN!
UH-HUH. WELL, I'M HAPPY FOR YOU.

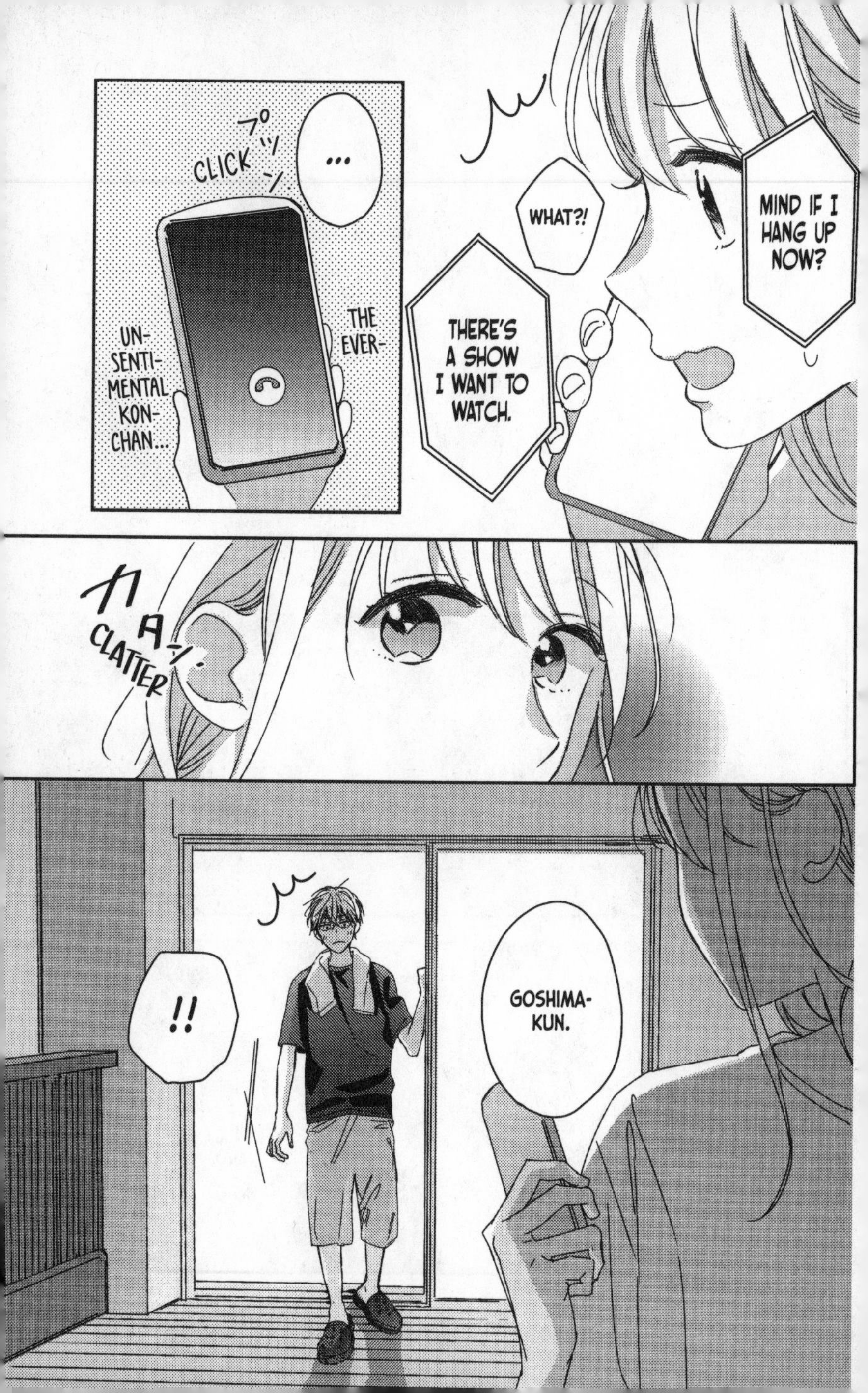
MIND IF I HANG UP NOW?
WHAT?!
THERE'S A SHOW I WANT TO WATCH.
...
CLICK
THE EVER-
UN-SENTI-MENTAL KON-CHAN...
CLATTER
GOSHIMA-KUN.
!!

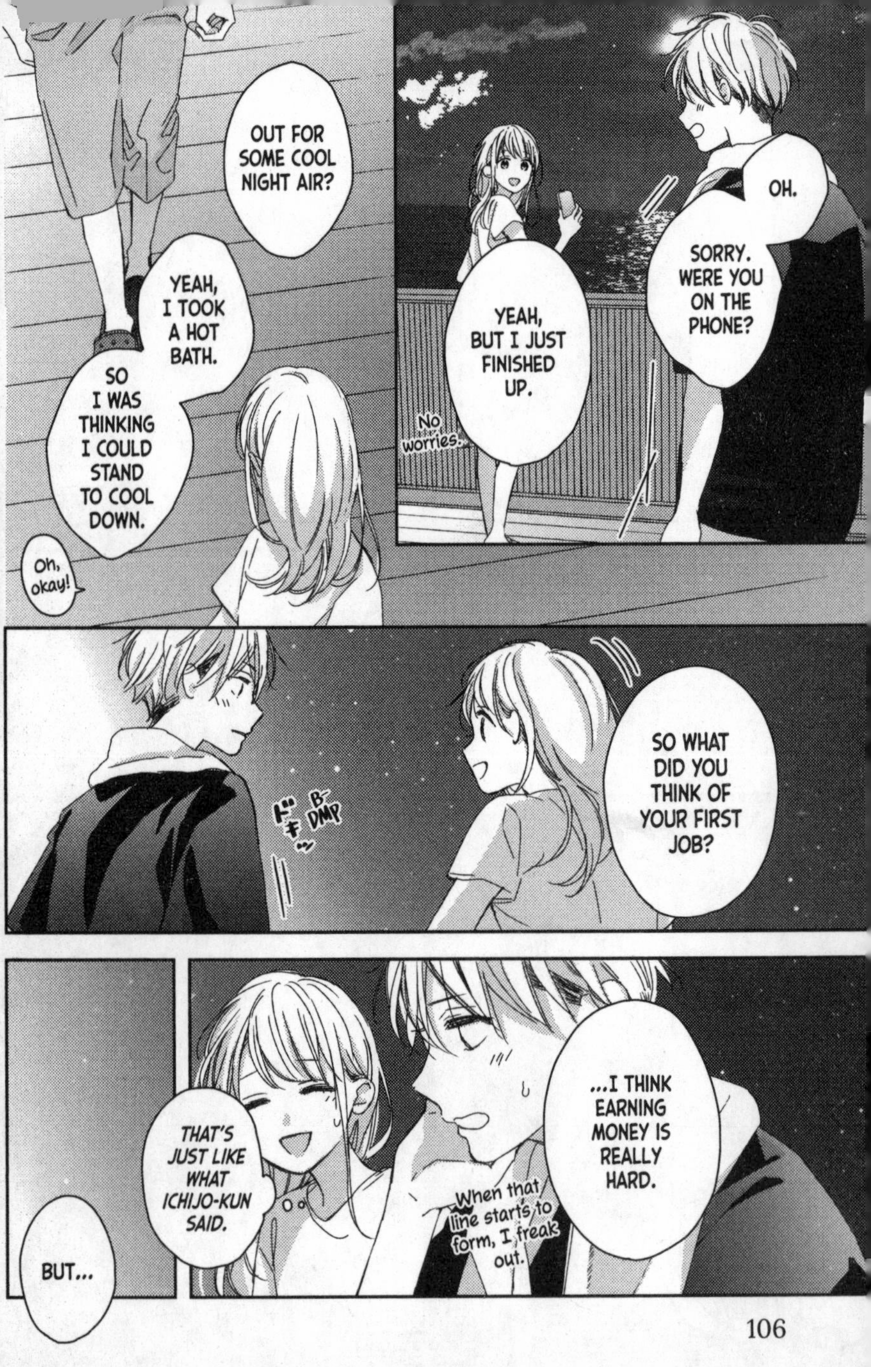
OH.
SORRY. WERE YOU ON THE PHONE?
YEAH, BUT I JUST FINISHED UP.
No worries.
OUT FOR SOME COOL NIGHT AIR?
YEAH, I TOOK A HOT BATH.
SO I WAS THINKING I COULD STAND TO COOL DOWN.
Oh, okay!
SO WHAT DID YOU THINK OF YOUR FIRST JOB?
B-DMP
...I THINK EARNING MONEY IS REALLY HARD.
When that line starts to form, I freak out.
THAT'S JUST LIKE WHAT ICHIJO-KUN SAID.
BUT...

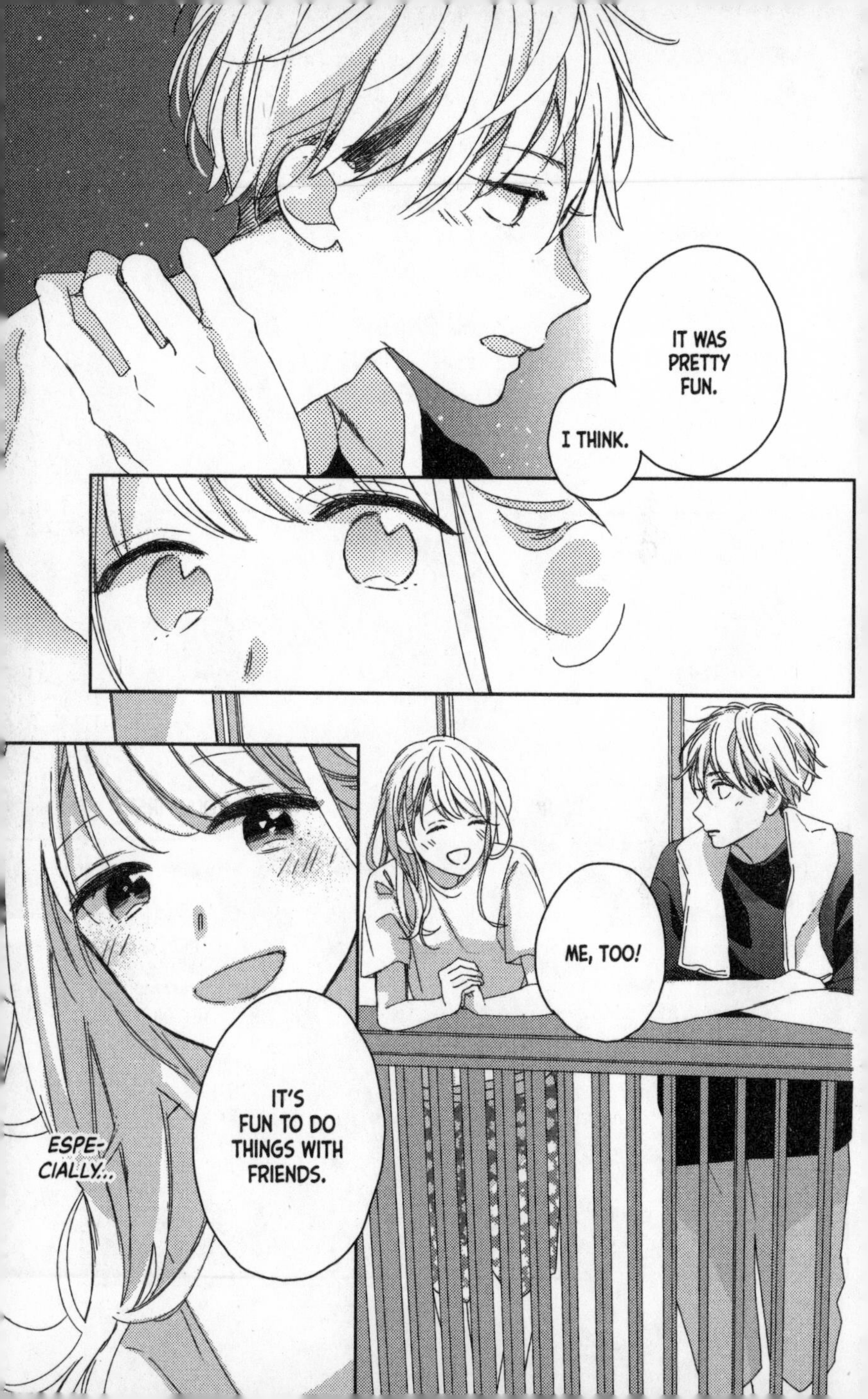
IT WAS PRETTY FUN.
I THINK.
ME, TOO!
IT'S FUN TO DO THINGS WITH FRIENDS.
ESPE-CIALLY...

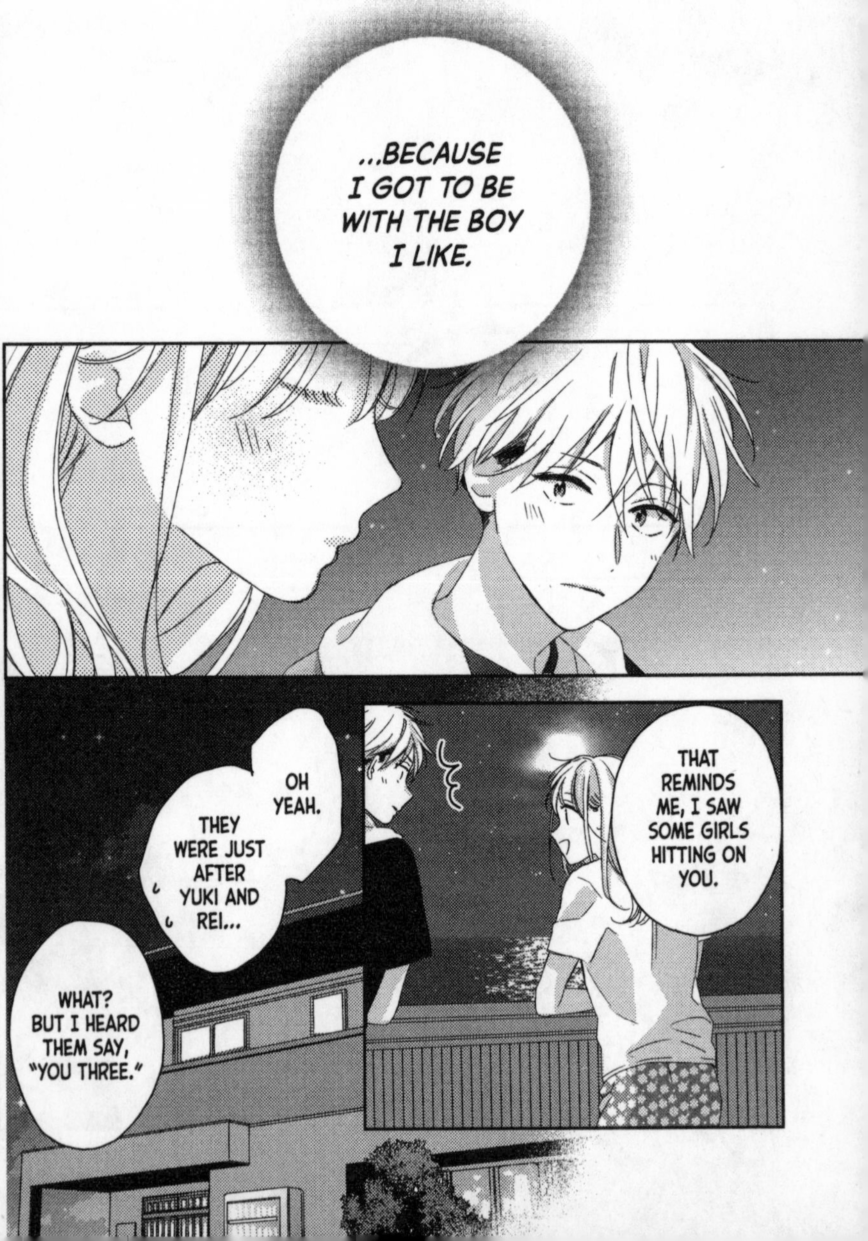
...BECAUSE I GOT TO BE WITH THE BOY I LIKE.
THAT REMINDS ME, I SAW SOME GIRLS HITTING ON YOU.
OH YEAH.
THEY WERE JUST AFTER YUKI AND REI...
WHAT? BUT I HEARD THEM SAY, "YOU THREE."

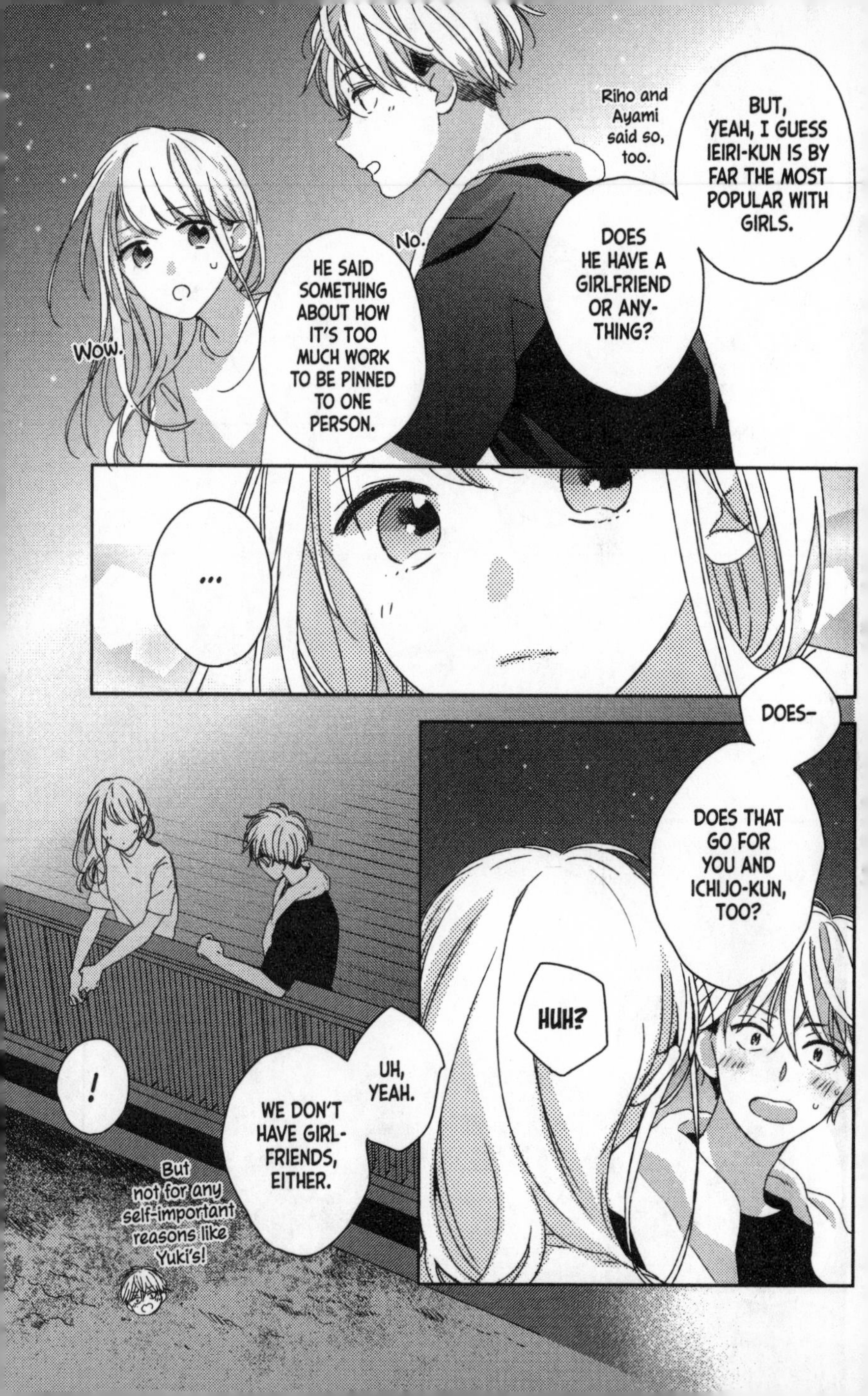
BUT, YEAH, I GUESS IEIRI-KUN IS BY FAR THE MOST POPULAR WITH GIRLS.
Riho and Ayami said so, too.
DOES HE HAVE A GIRLFRIEND OR ANY-THING?
No.
HE SAID SOMETHING ABOUT HOW IT'S TOO MUCH WORK TO BE PINNED TO ONE PERSON.
Wow.
...
DOES–
DOES THAT GO FOR YOU AND ICHIJO-KUN, TOO?
HUH?
UH, YEAH.
WE DON'T HAVE GIRL-FRIENDS, EITHER.
!
But not for any self-important reasons like Yuki's!

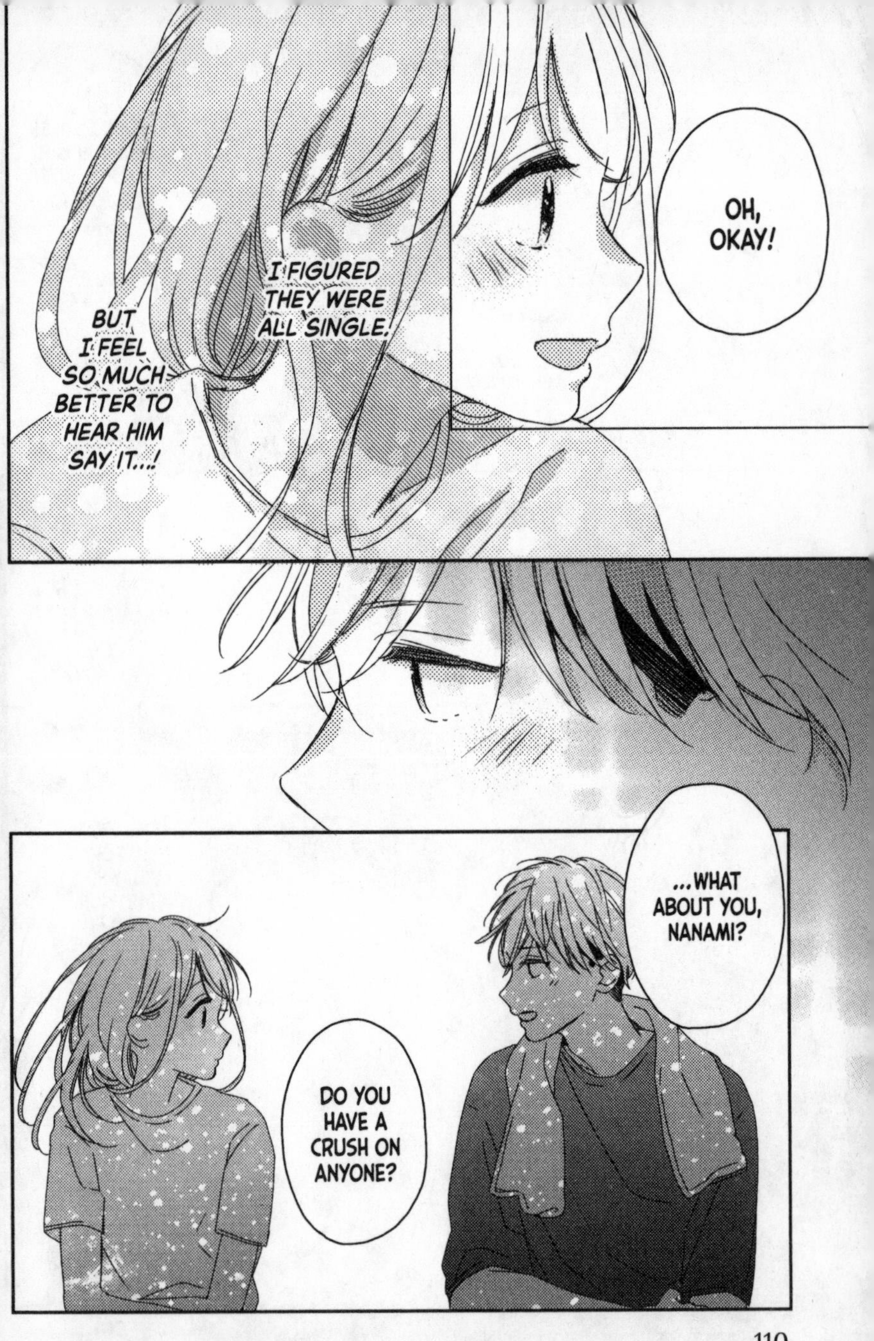
OH, OKAY!
I FIGURED THEY WERE ALL SINGLE.
BUT I FEEL SO MUCH BETTER TO HEAR HIM SAY IT...!
...WHAT ABOUT YOU, NANAMI?
DO YOU HAVE A CRUSH ON ANYONE?

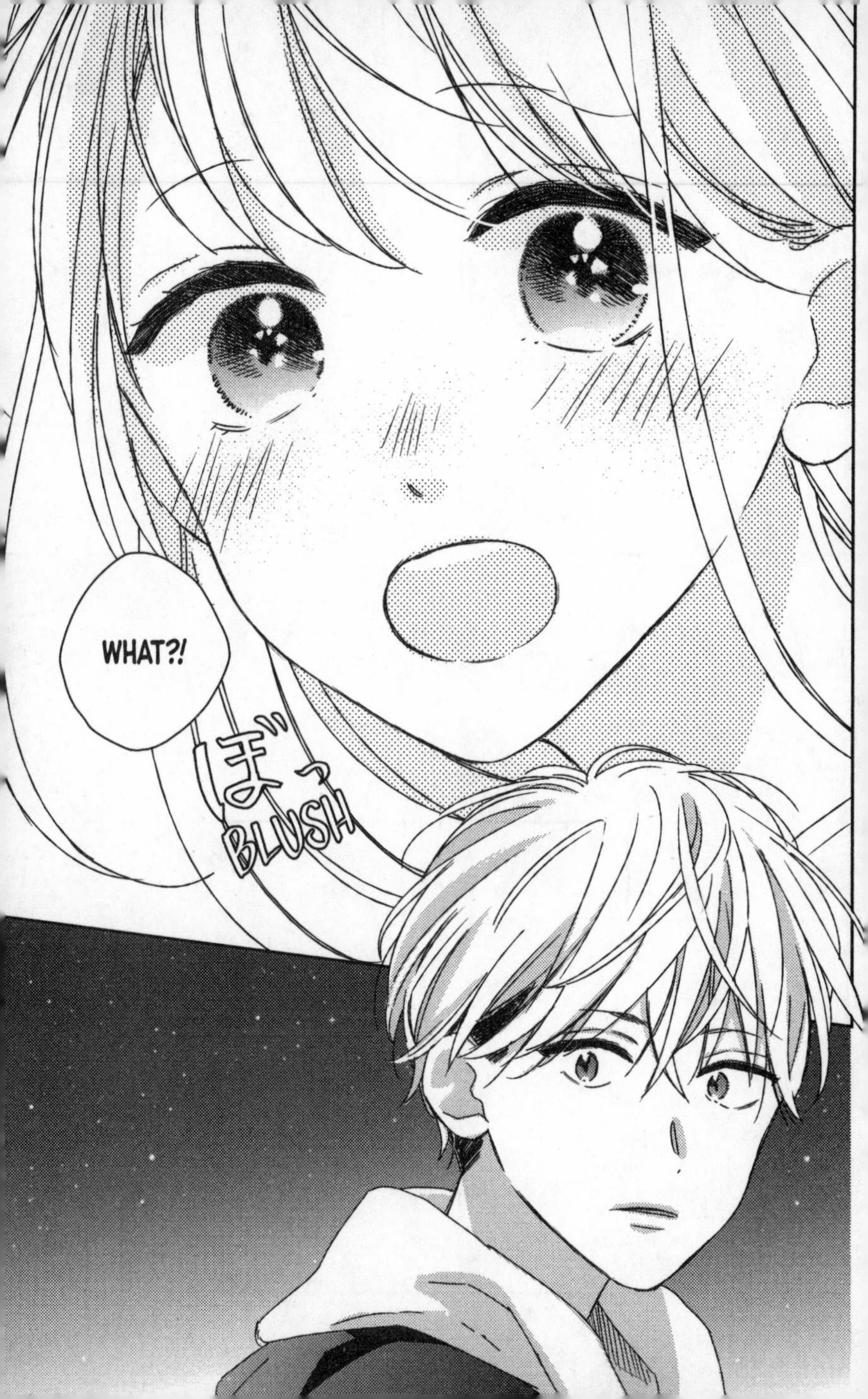
WHAT?!
ぼっ
BLUSH

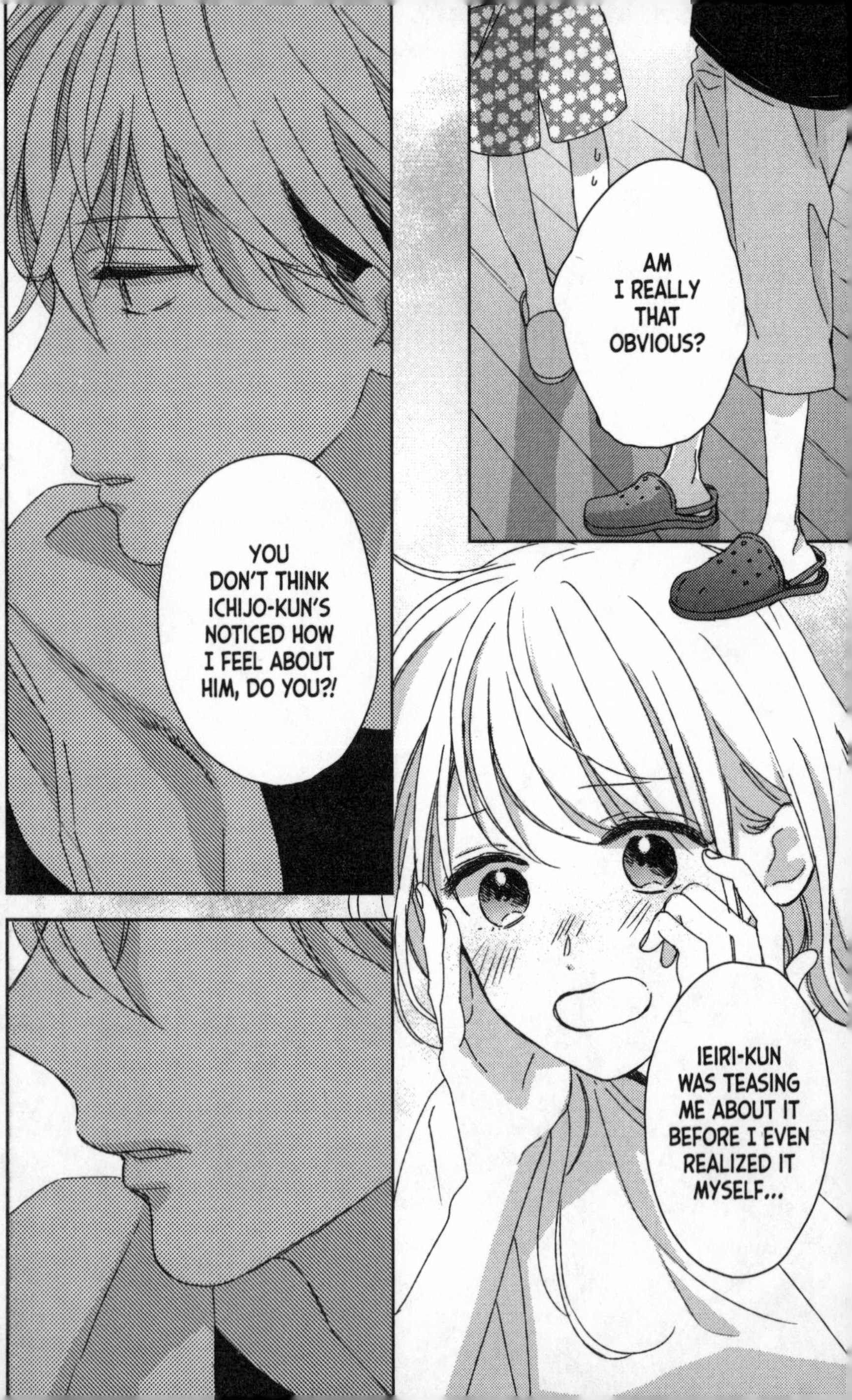
AM I REALLY THAT OBVIOUS?
YOU DON'T THINK ICHIJO-KUN'S NOTICED HOW I FEEL ABOUT HIM, DO YOU?!
IEIRI-KUN WAS TEASING ME ABOUT IT BEFORE I EVEN REALIZED IT MYSELF...

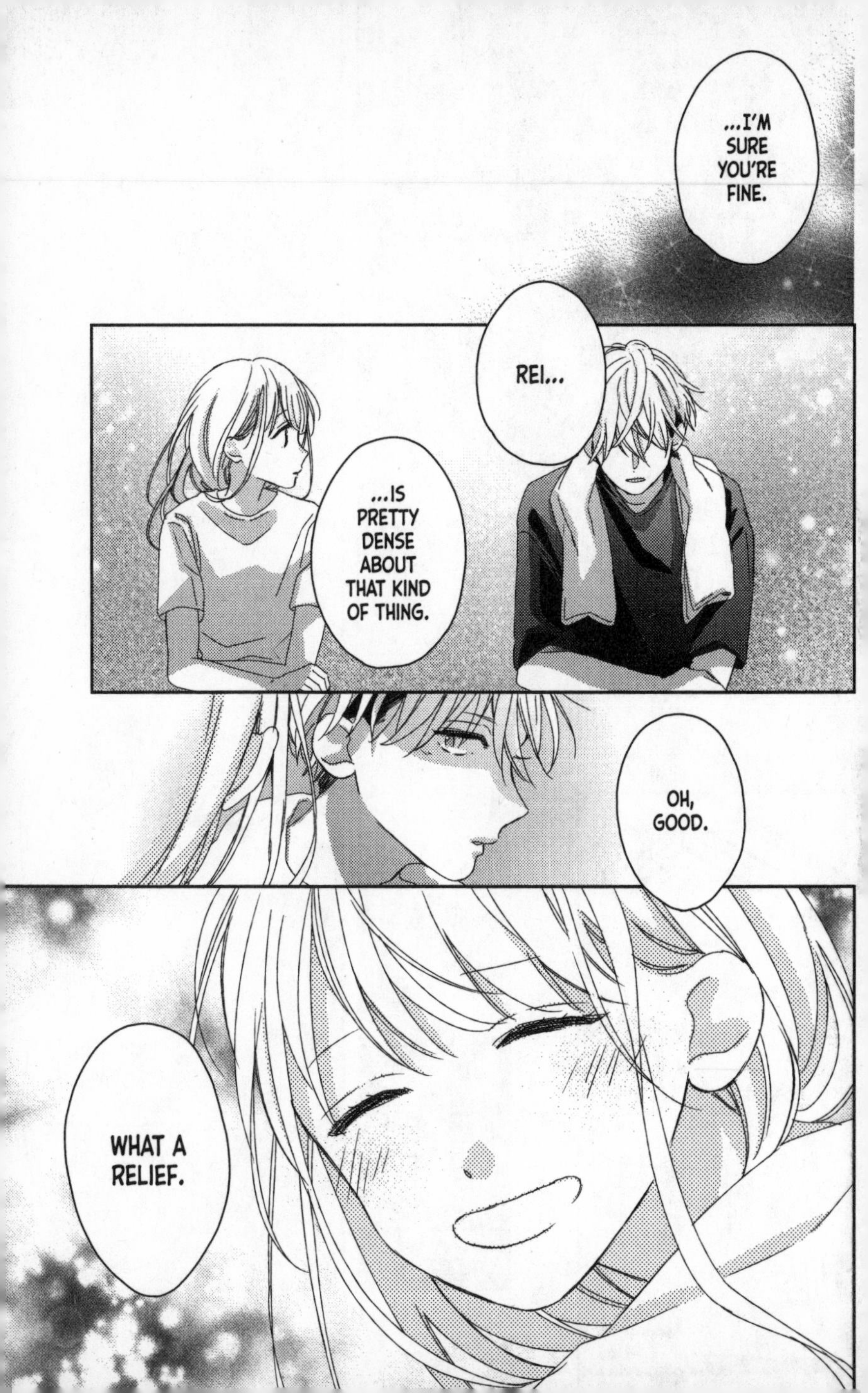
...I'M SURE YOU'RE FINE.
REI...
...IS PRETTY DENSE ABOUT THAT KIND OF THING.
OH, GOOD.
WHAT A RELIEF.

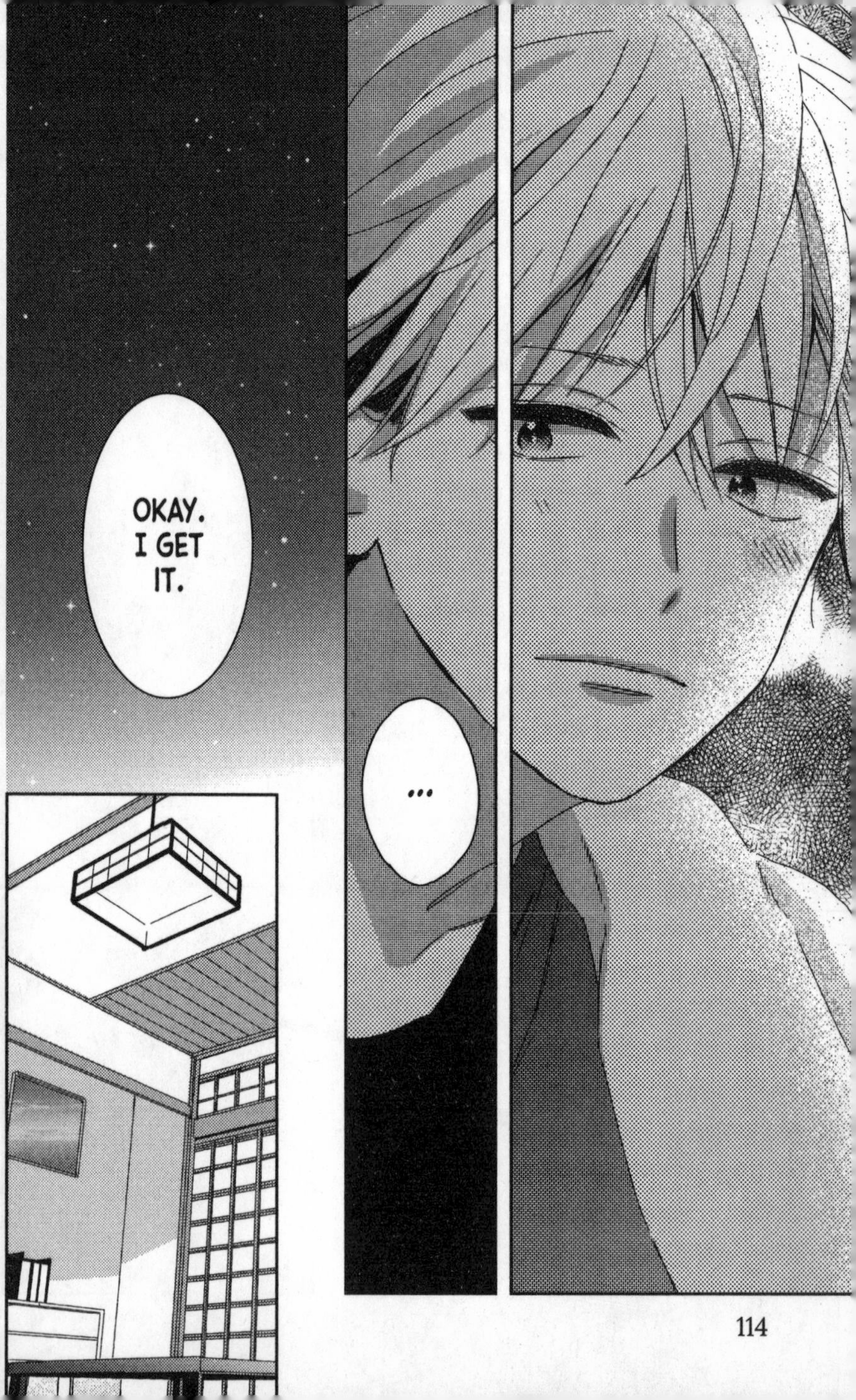
...
OKAY. I GET IT.

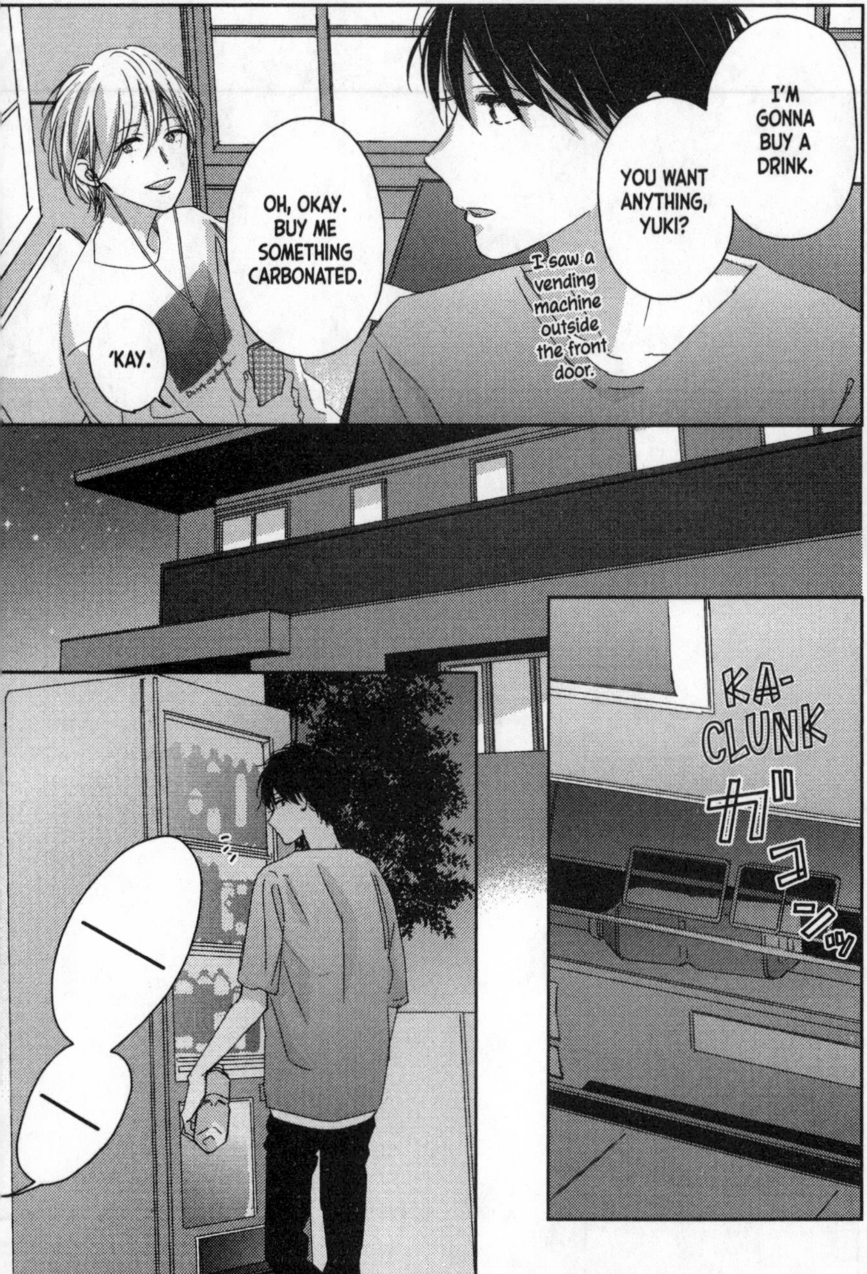
I'M GONNA BUY A DRINK.
YOU WANT ANYTHING, YUKI?
I saw a vending machine outside the front door.
OH, OKAY. BUY ME SOMETHING CARBONATED.
'KAY.
KA-CLUNK
ガコンッ
——

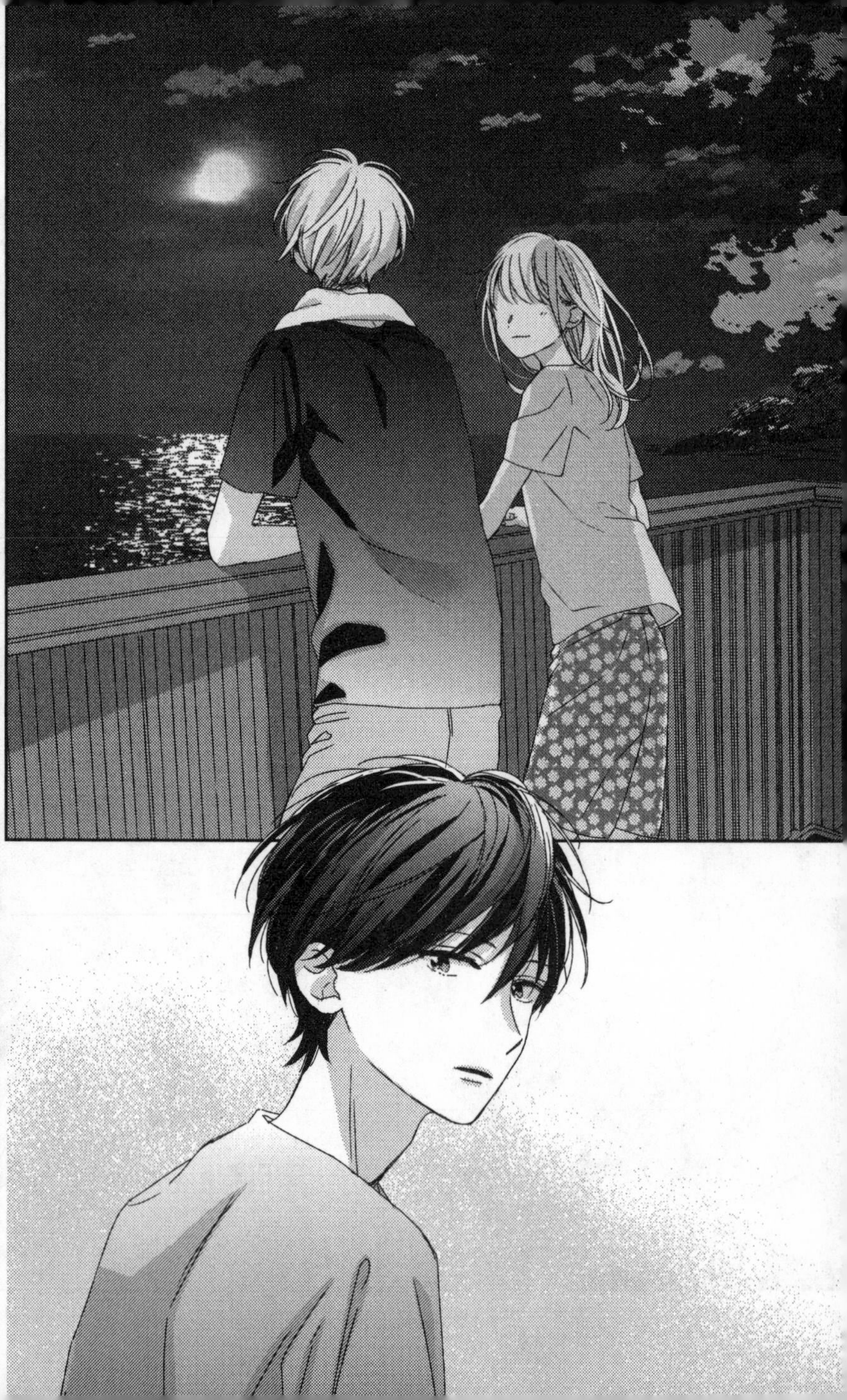

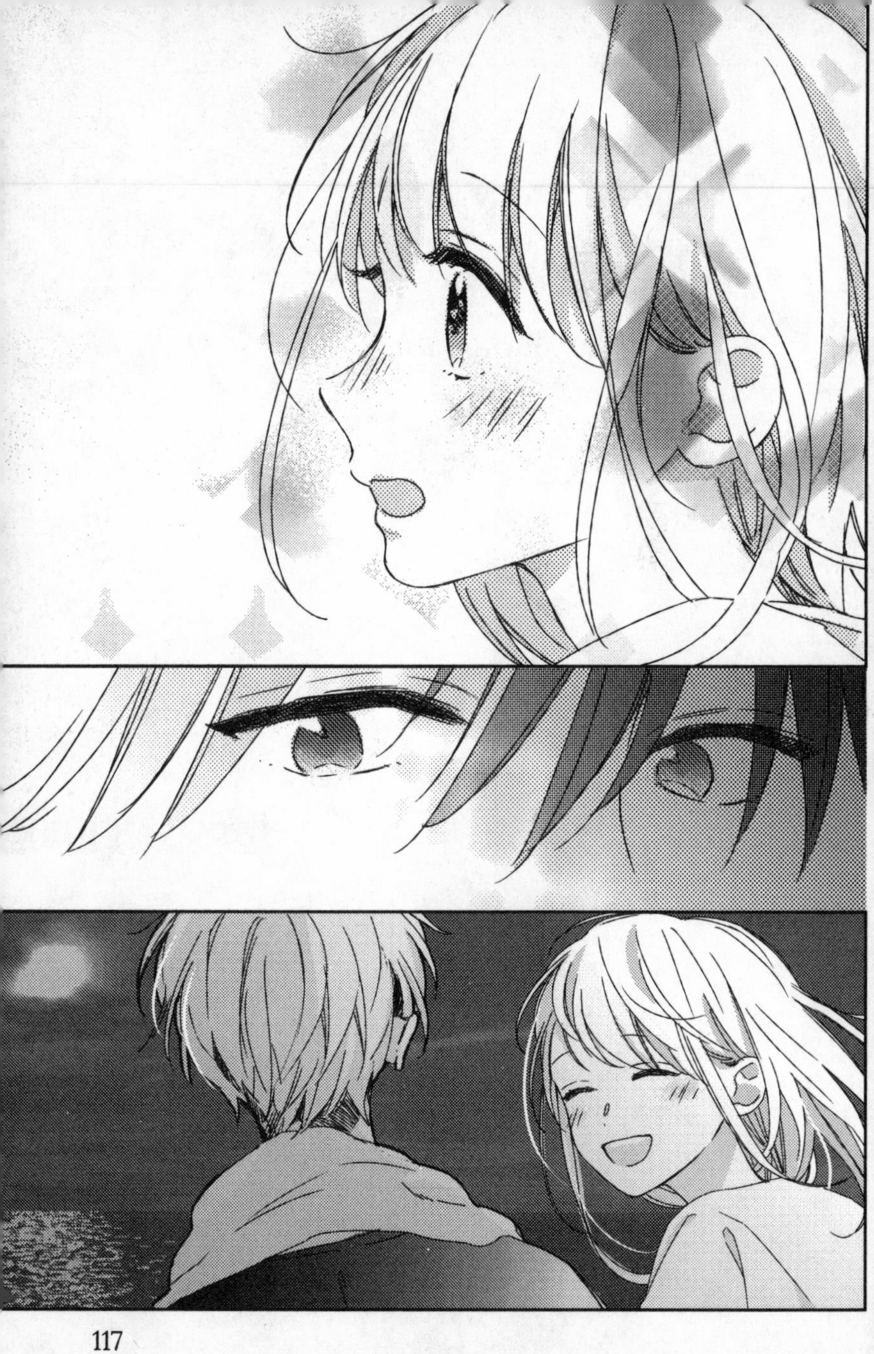

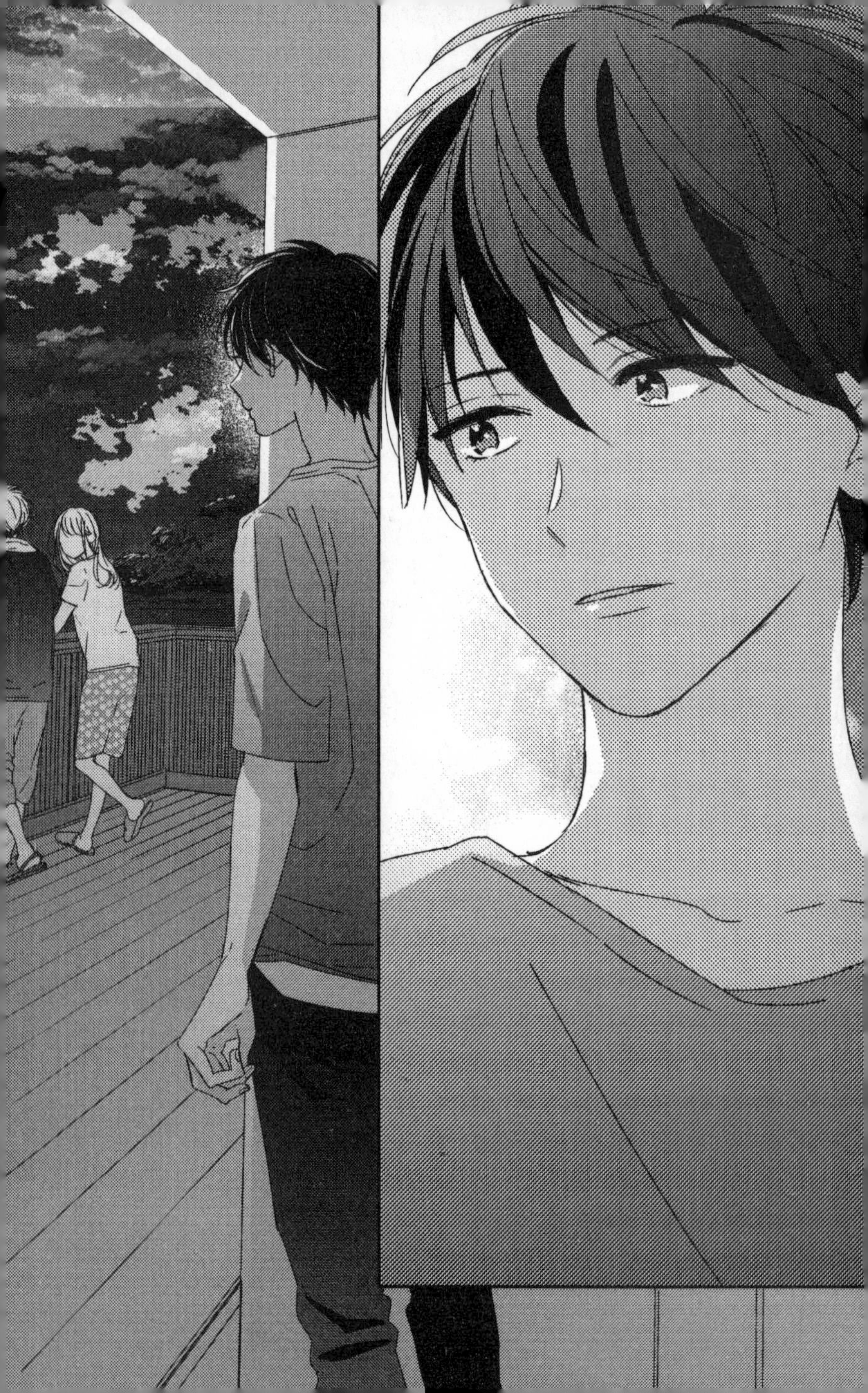

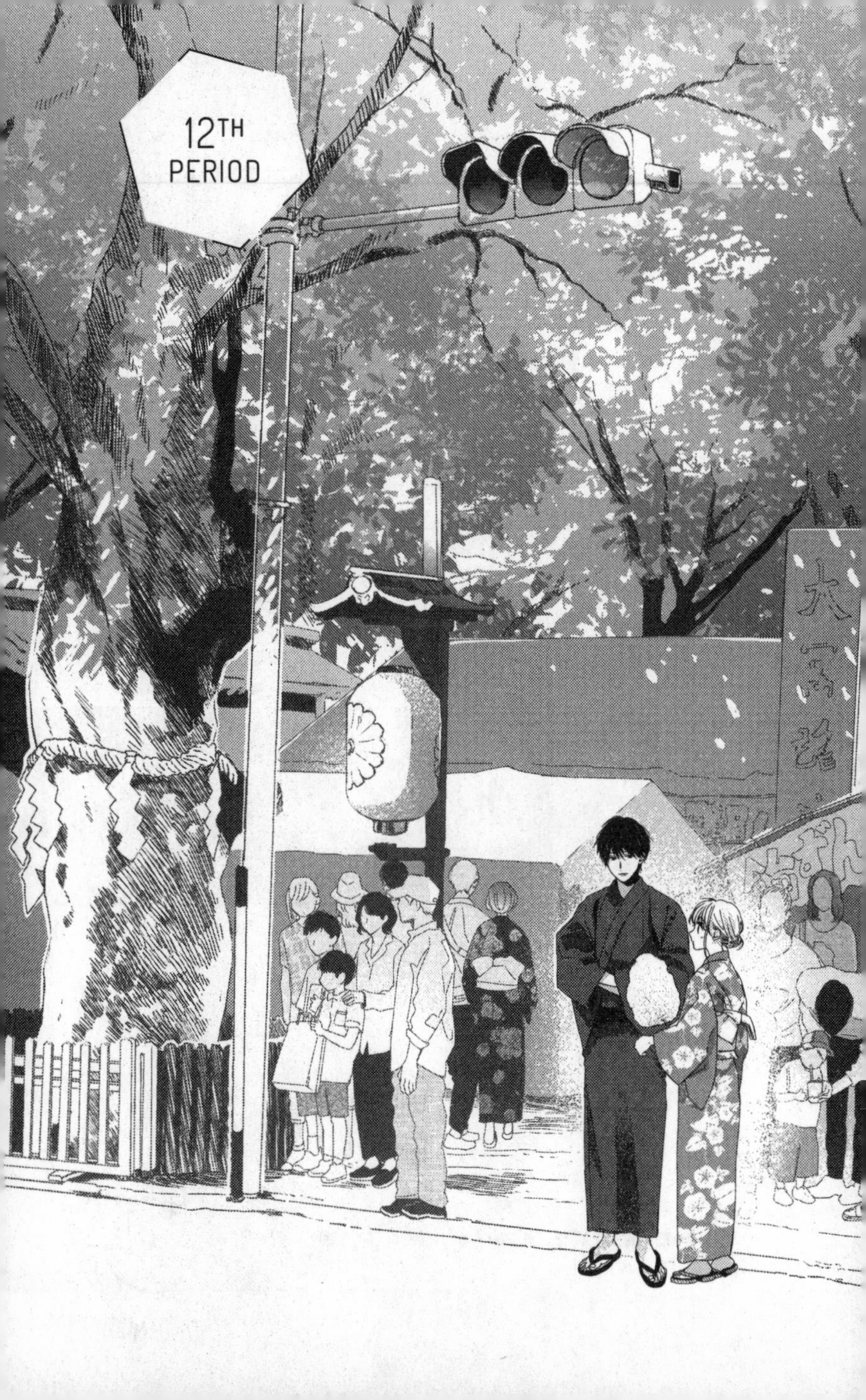
12TH
PERIOD

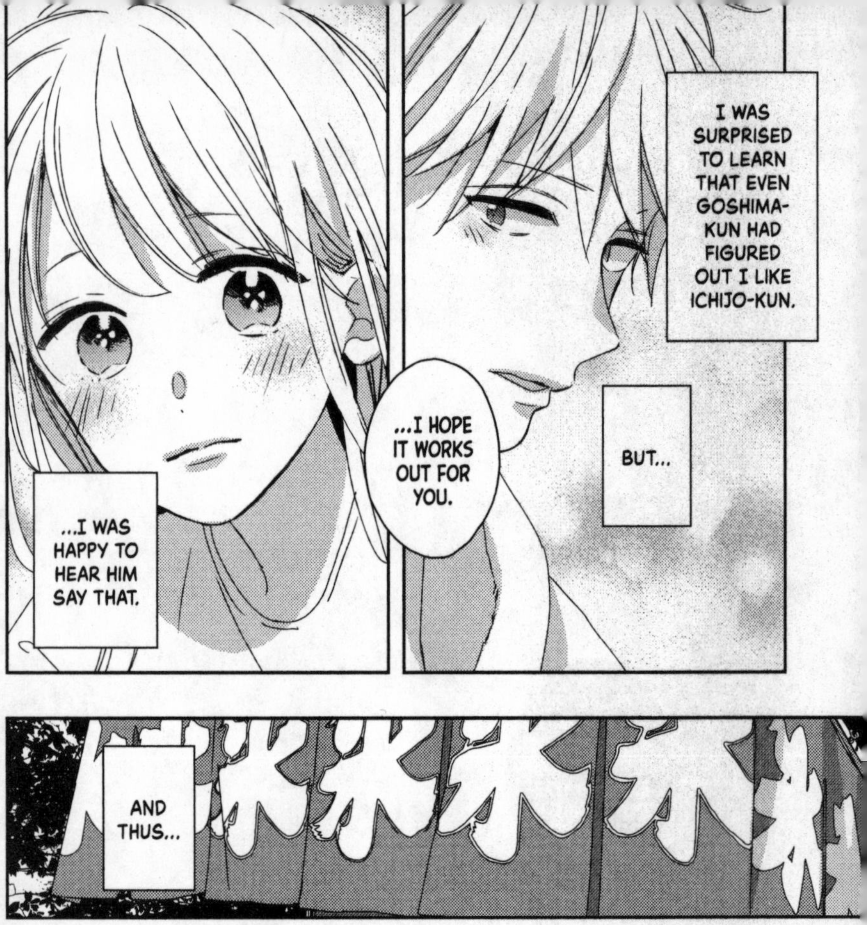
I WAS SURPRISED TO LEARN THAT EVEN GOSHIMA-KUN HAD FIGURED OUT I LIKE ICHIJO-KUN.
BUT...
...I HOPE IT WORKS OUT FOR YOU.
...I WAS HAPPY TO HEAR HIM SAY THAT.
AND THUS...

Special Thanks

AKI NISHIHIRO-CHAN
FRIENDS, FAMILY

MY EDITOR
KODAMA-SAN
EVERYONE AT THE DESSERT EDITORIAL DEPARTMENT

ARCO INC.
EVERYONE WHO WAS INVOLVED IN THE CREATION AND SELLING OF THIS WORK

I HOPE WE MEET AGAIN
IN VOLUME 4.

野切耀子

YOKO NOGIRI

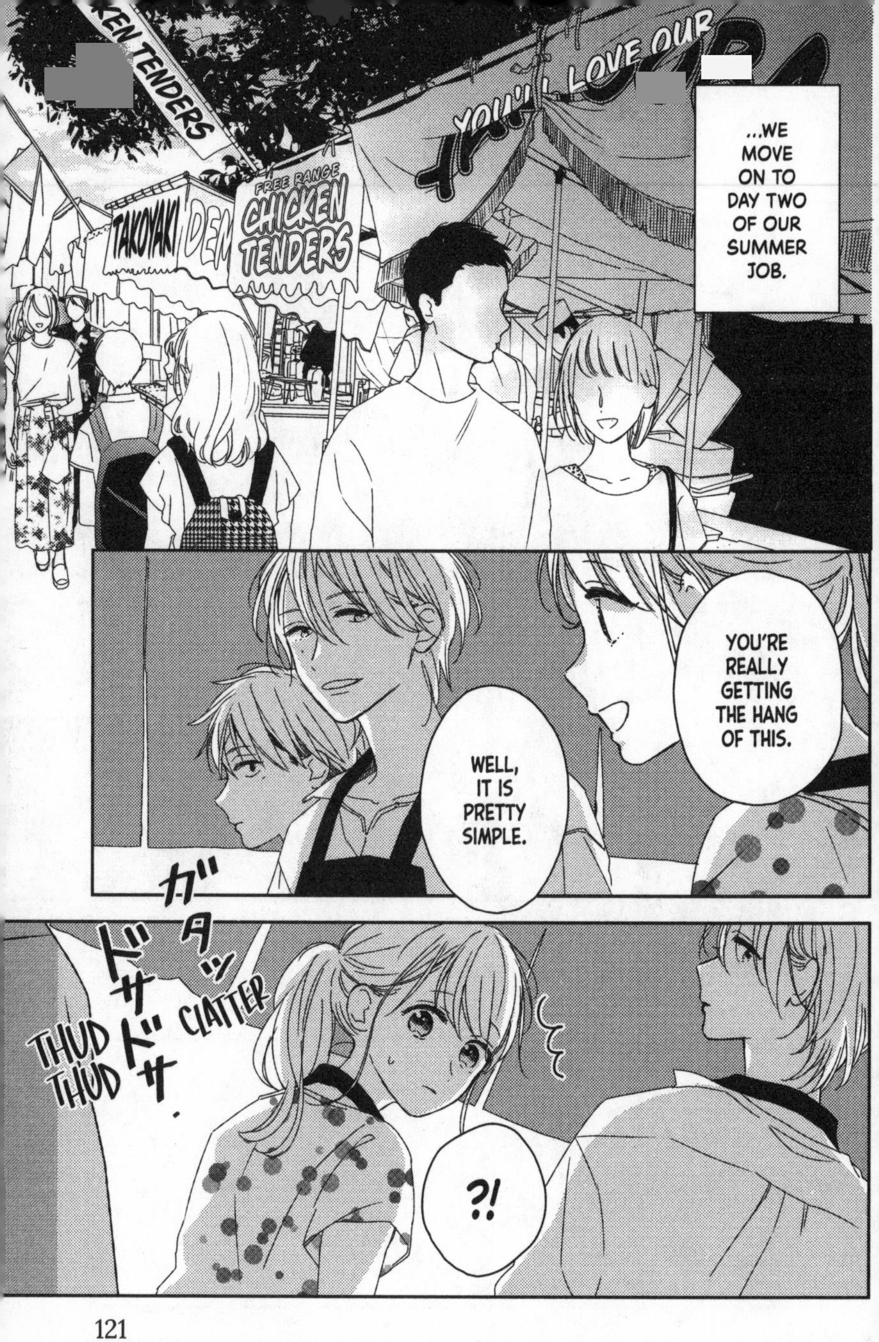
KEN TENDERS
YOU'LL LOVE OUR
FREE RANGE CHICKEN TENDERS
TAKOYAKI
...WE MOVE ON TO DAY TWO OF OUR SUMMER JOB.
YOU'RE REALLY GETTING THE HANG OF THIS.
WELL, IT IS PRETTY SIMPLE.
ガタッ
CLATTER
ドサドサ
THUD THUD
?!

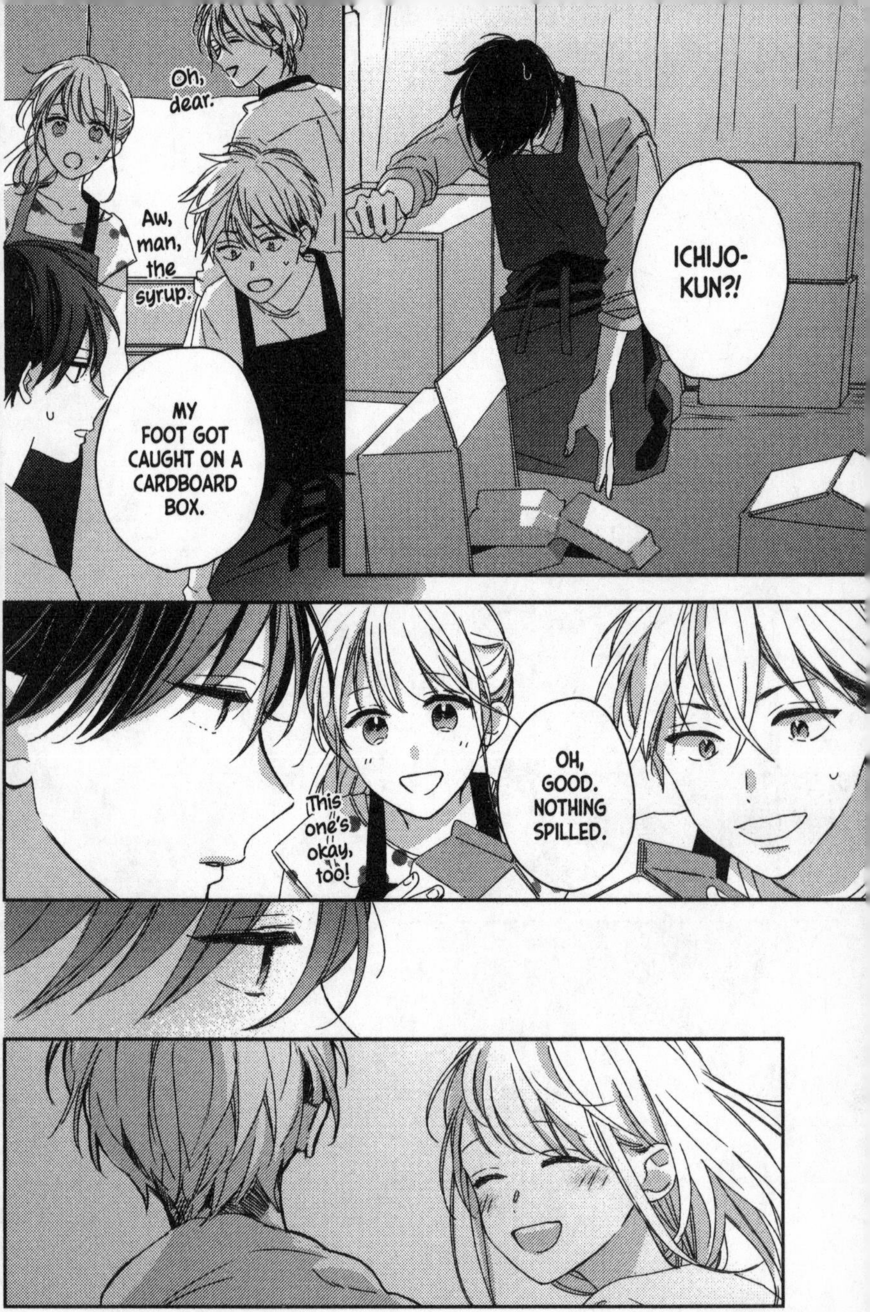
ICHIJO-KUN?!
Oh, dear.
Aw, man, the syrup.
MY FOOT GOT CAUGHT ON A CARDBOARD BOX.
OH, GOOD. NOTHING SPILLED.
This one's okay, too!

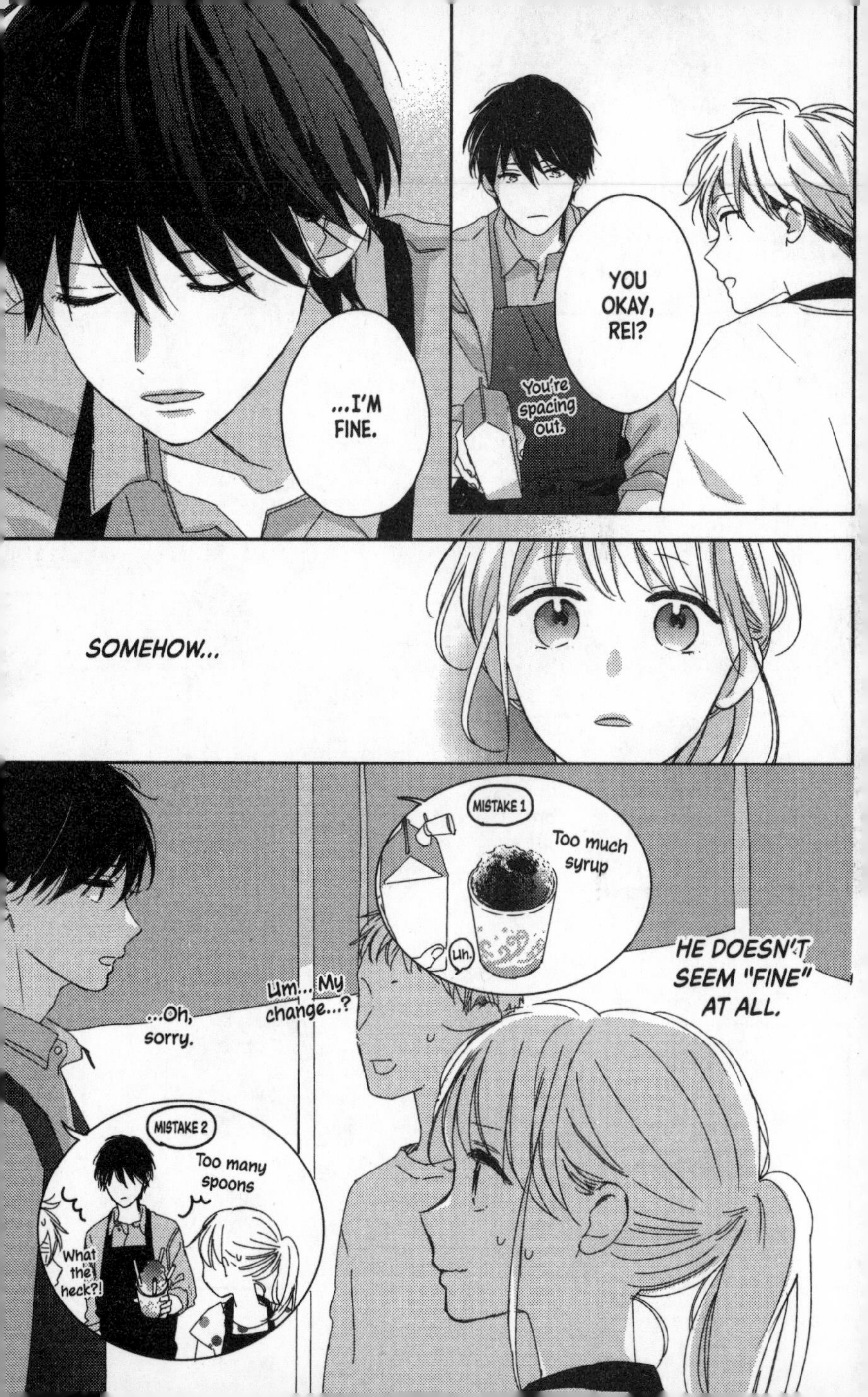
YOU OKAY, REI?
You're spacing out.
...I'M FINE.
SOMEHOW...
HE DOESN'T SEEM "FINE" AT ALL.
MISTAKE 1
Too much syrup
Uh.
Um... My change...?
...Oh, sorry.
MISTAKE 2
Too many spoons
What the heck?!

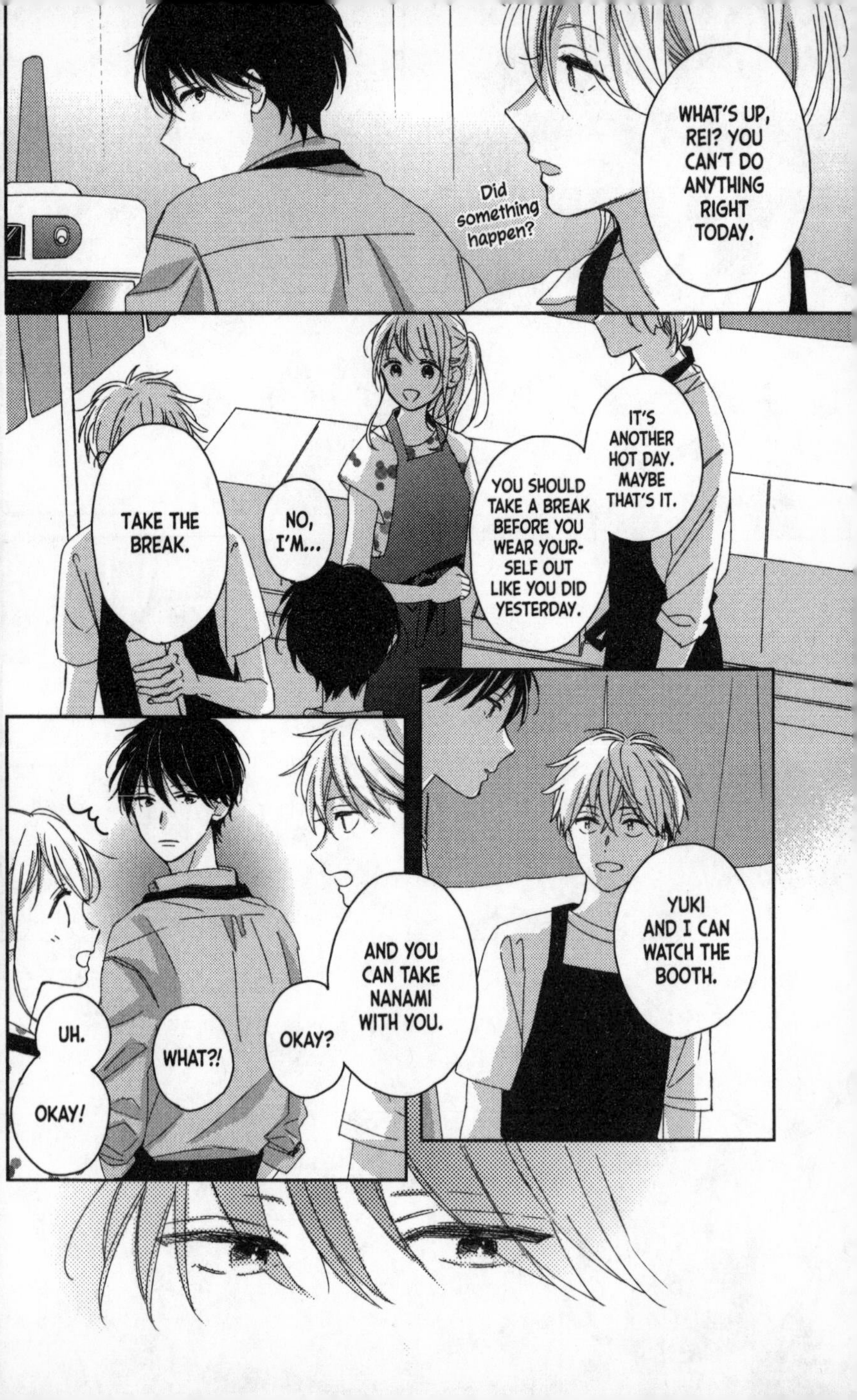
WHAT'S UP, REI? YOU CAN'T DO ANYTHING RIGHT TODAY.
Did something happen?
IT'S ANOTHER HOT DAY. MAYBE THAT'S IT.
YOU SHOULD TAKE A BREAK BEFORE YOU WEAR YOUR-SELF OUT LIKE YOU DID YESTERDAY.
NO, I'M...
TAKE THE BREAK.
YUKI AND I CAN WATCH THE BOOTH.
AND YOU CAN TAKE NANAMI WITH YOU.
OKAY?
WHAT?!
UH.
OKAY!

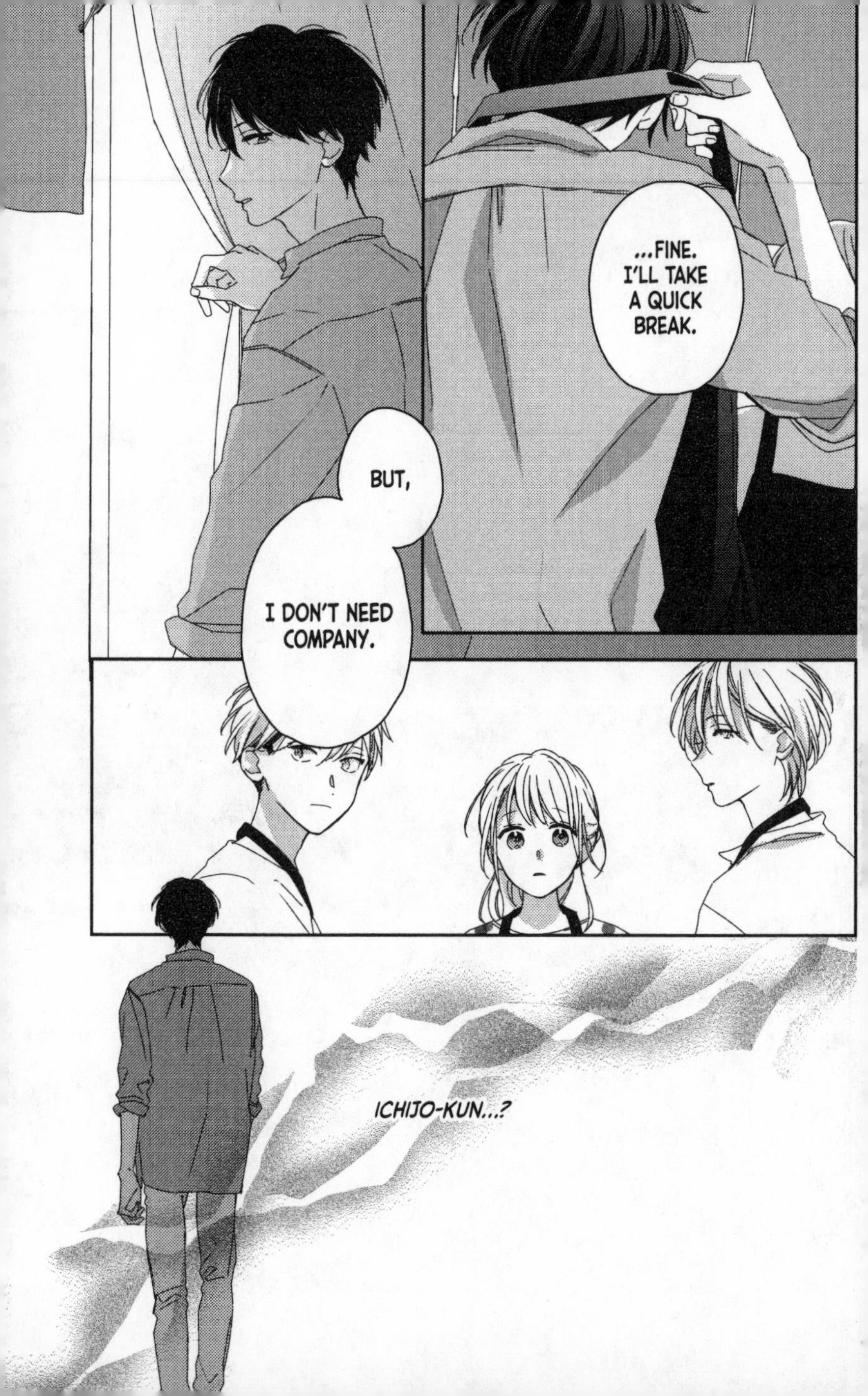
...FINE. I'LL TAKE A QUICK BREAK.
BUT,
I DON'T NEED COMPANY.
ICHIJO-KUN...?

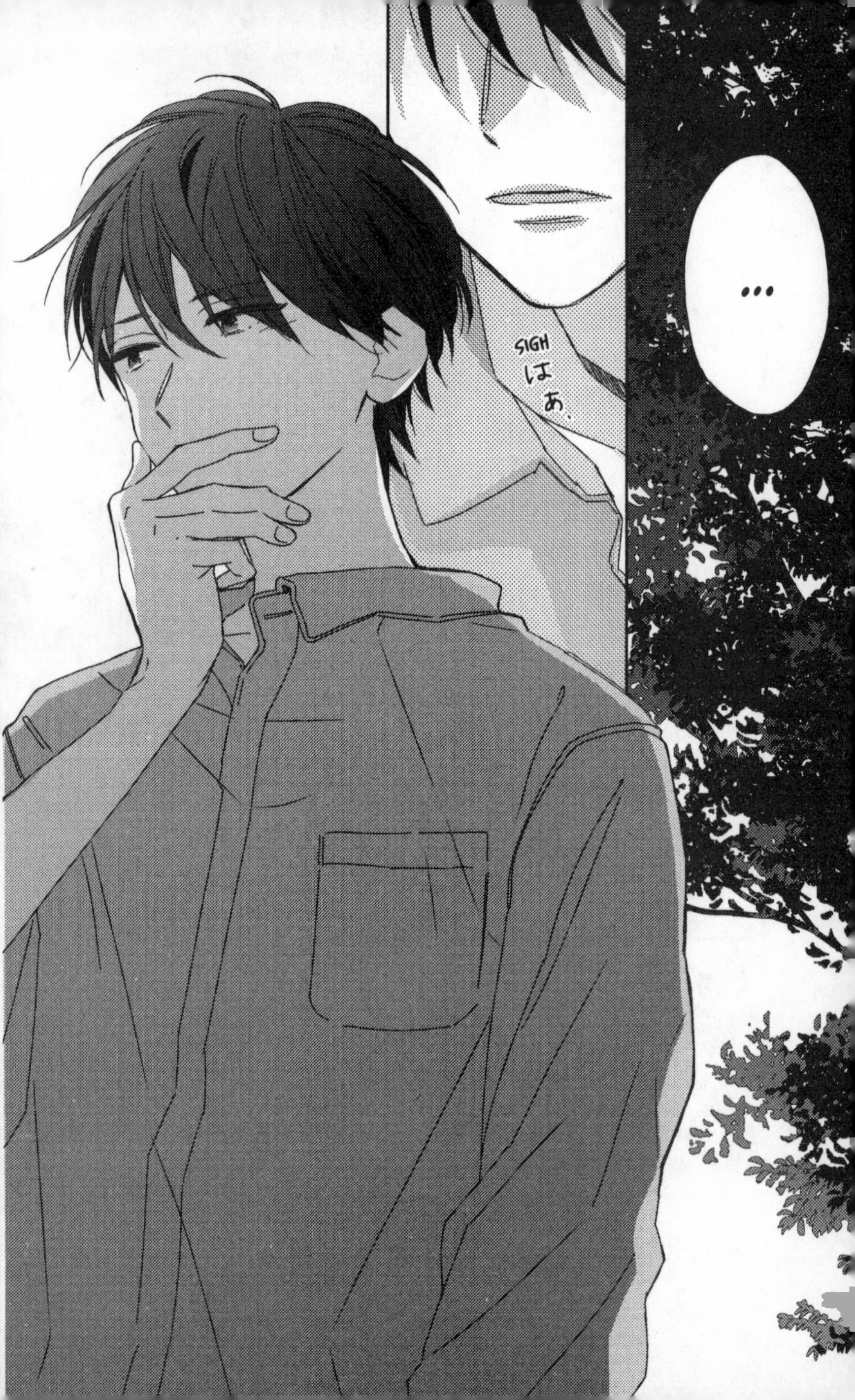
...
SIGH
はあ

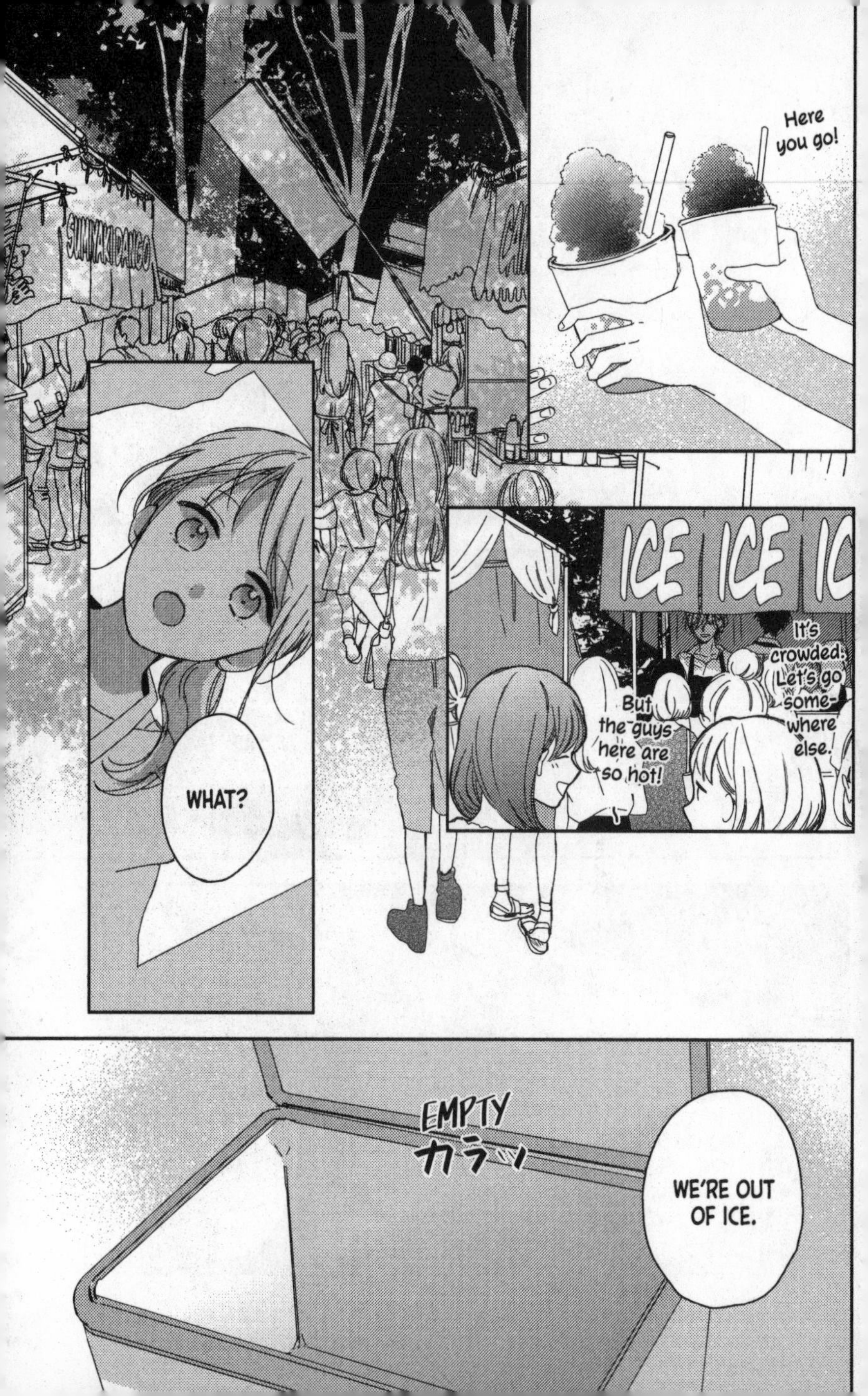
Here you go!
ICE ICE IC
It's crowded. Let's go some-where else.
But the guys here are so hot!
SUMIYAKI DANGO
WHAT?
EMPTY
カラッ
WE'RE OUT OF ICE.

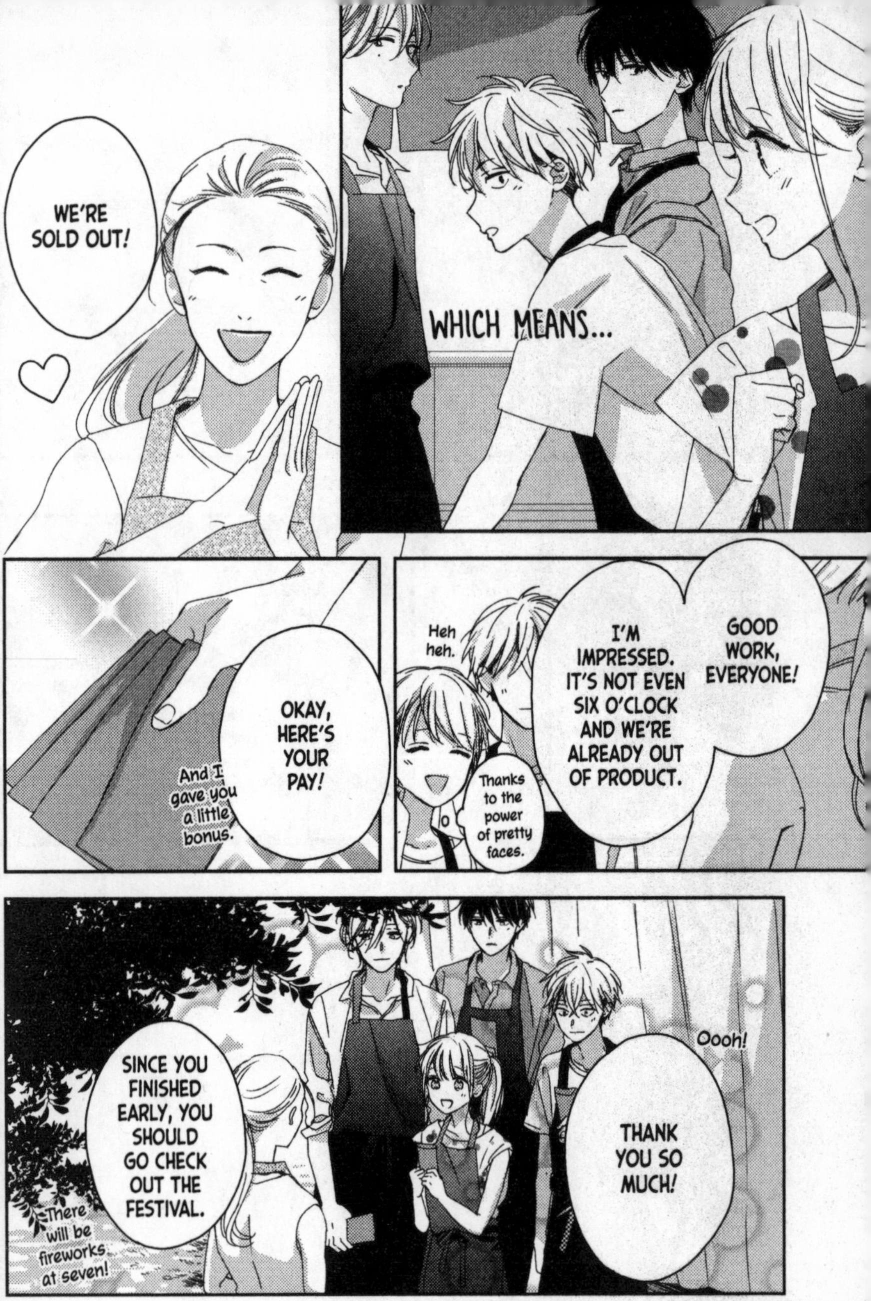
WHICH MEANS...
WE'RE SOLD OUT!
GOOD WORK, EVERYONE!
I'M IMPRESSED. IT'S NOT EVEN SIX O'CLOCK AND WE'RE ALREADY OUT OF PRODUCT.
Heh heh.
Thanks to the power of pretty faces.
OKAY, HERE'S YOUR PAY!
And I gave you a little bonus.
Oooh!
THANK YOU SO MUCH!
SINCE YOU FINISHED EARLY, YOU SHOULD GO CHECK OUT THE FESTIVAL.
There will be fireworks at seven!

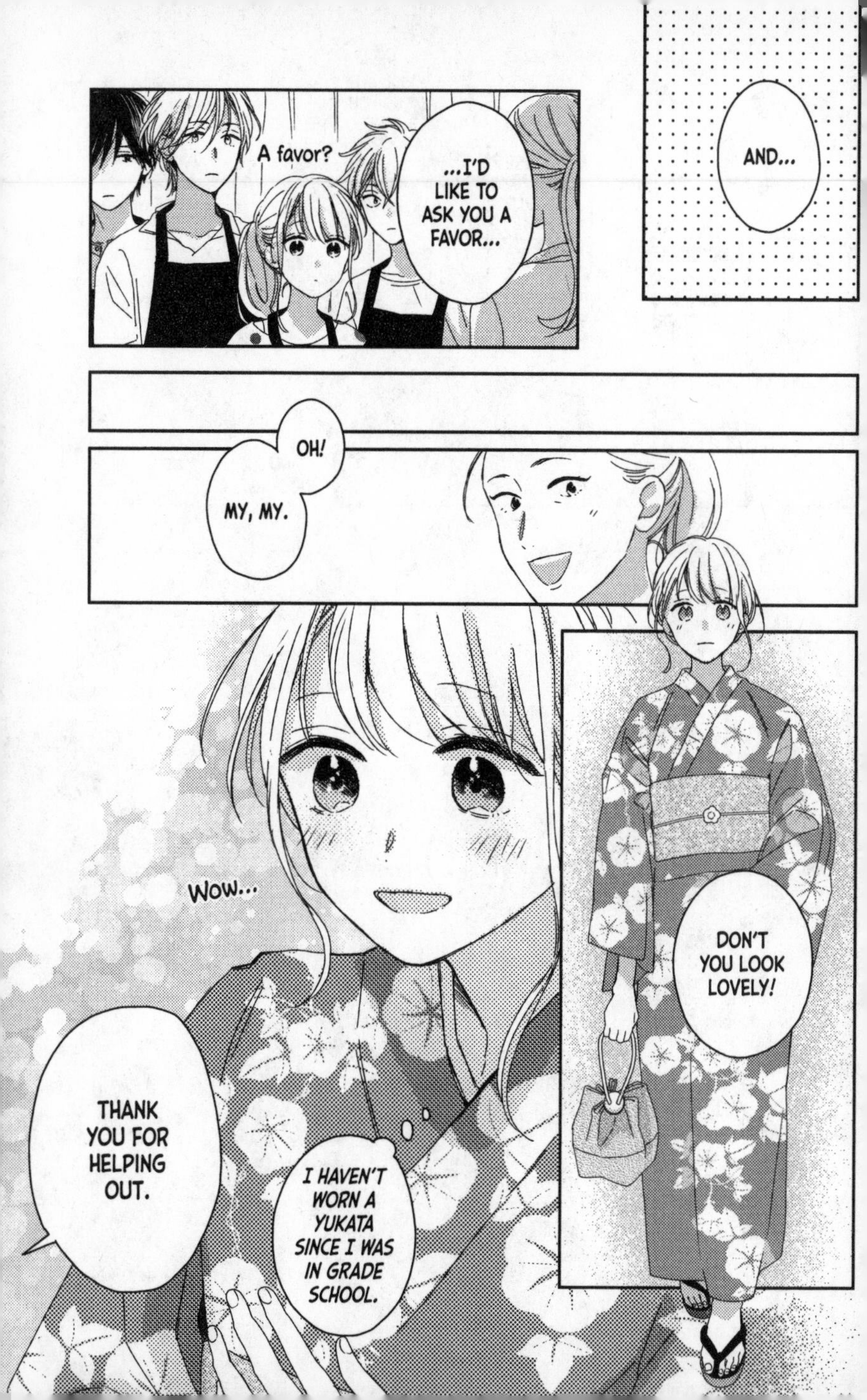
AND...
...I'D LIKE TO ASK YOU A FAVOR...
A favor?
OH!
MY, MY.
DON'T YOU LOOK LOVELY!
WOW...
I HAVEN'T WORN A YUKATA SINCE I WAS IN GRADE SCHOOL.
THANK YOU FOR HELPING OUT.

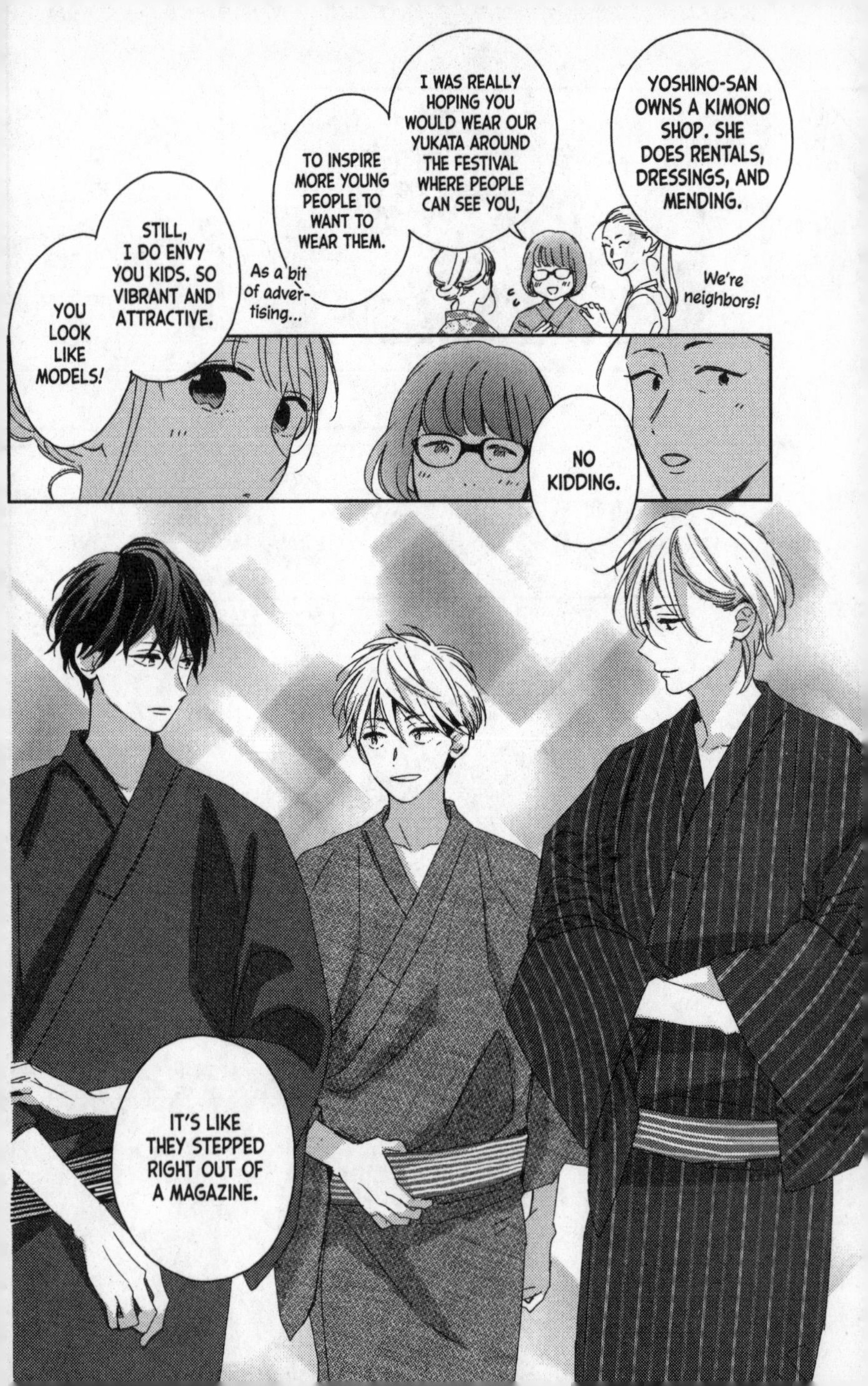
YOSHINO-SAN OWNS A KIMONO SHOP. SHE DOES RENTALS, DRESSINGS, AND MENDING.
We're neighbors!
I WAS REALLY HOPING YOU WOULD WEAR OUR YUKATA AROUND THE FESTIVAL WHERE PEOPLE CAN SEE YOU,
TO INSPIRE MORE YOUNG PEOPLE TO WANT TO WEAR THEM.
As a bit of advertising...
STILL, I DO ENVY YOU KIDS. SO VIBRANT AND ATTRACTIVE.
YOU LOOK LIKE MODELS!
NO KIDDING.
IT'S LIKE THEY STEPPED RIGHT OUT OF A MAGAZINE.

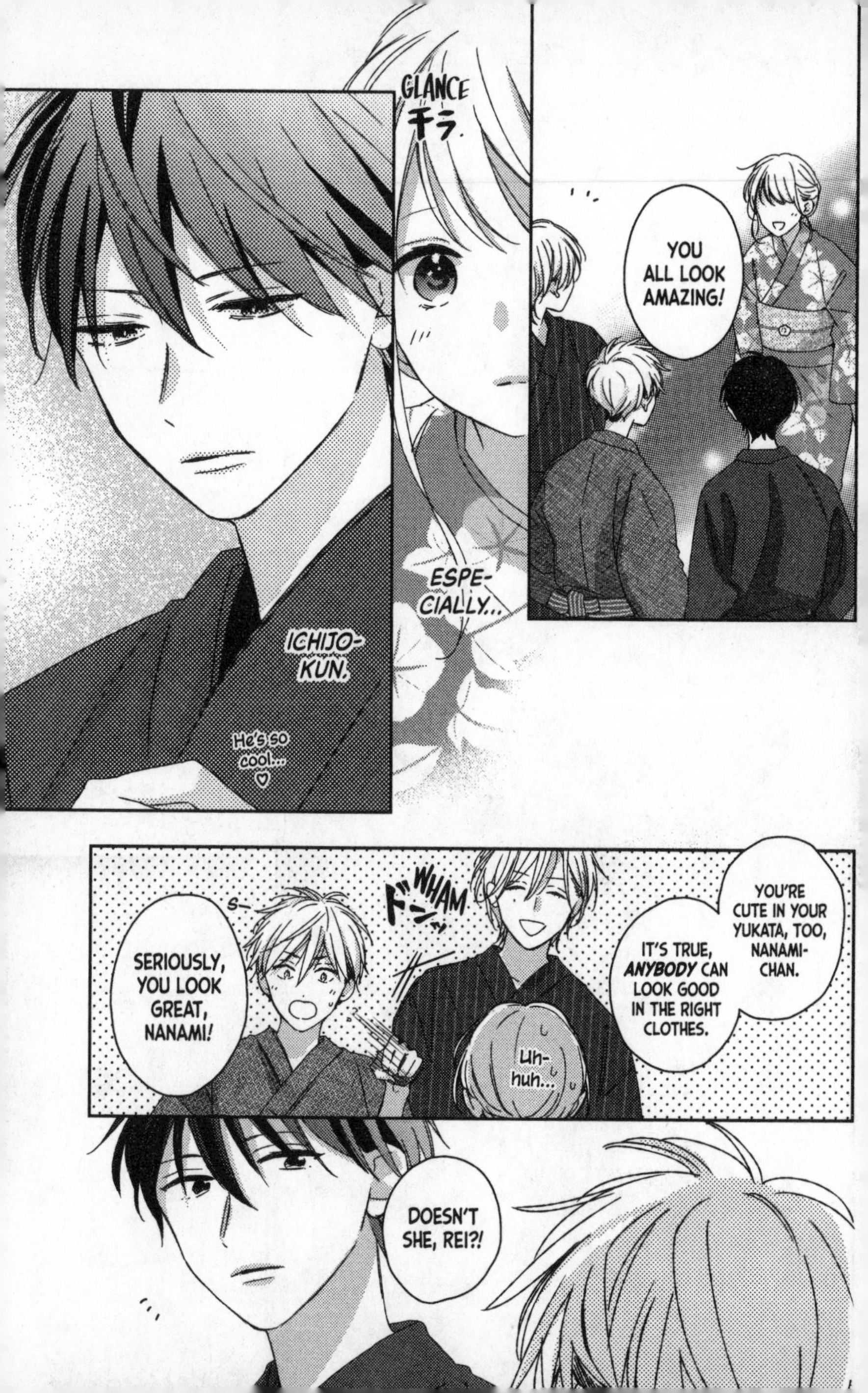
YOU ALL LOOK AMAZING!
GLANCE
チラ
ESPE-CIALLY...
ICHIJO-KUN.
He's so cool... ♡
YOU'RE CUTE IN YOUR YUKATA, TOO, NANAMI-CHAN.
IT'S TRUE, ***ANYBODY*** CAN LOOK GOOD IN THE RIGHT CLOTHES.
WHAM
ドン
Uh-huh...
S-
SERIOUSLY, YOU LOOK GREAT, NANAMI!
DOESN'T SHE, REI?!

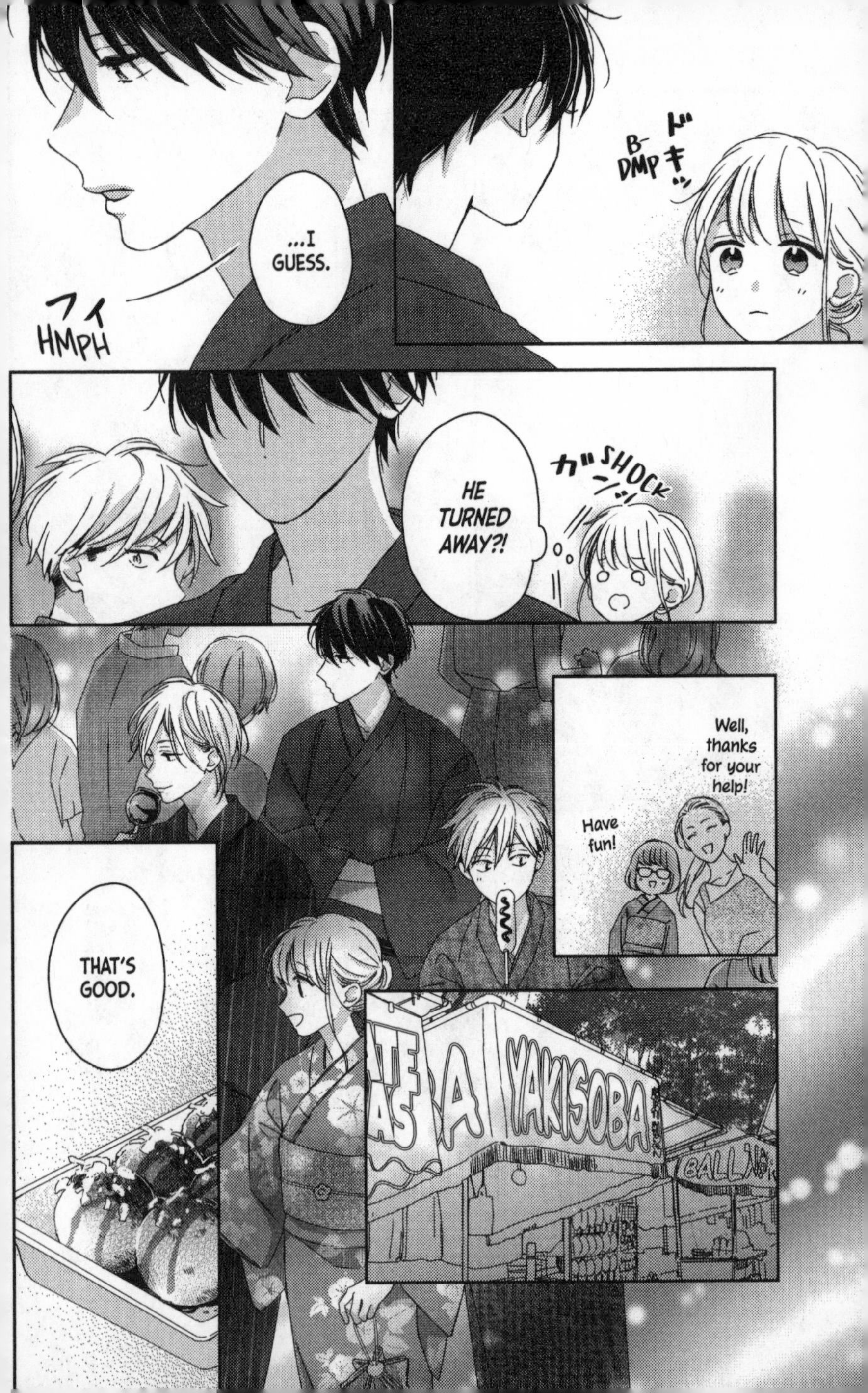
B-DMP
ドキッ
...I GUESS.
フイ
HMPH
HE TURNED AWAY?!
ガーン
SHOCK
Well, thanks for your help!
Have fun!
YAKISOBA
BALL
THAT'S GOOD.

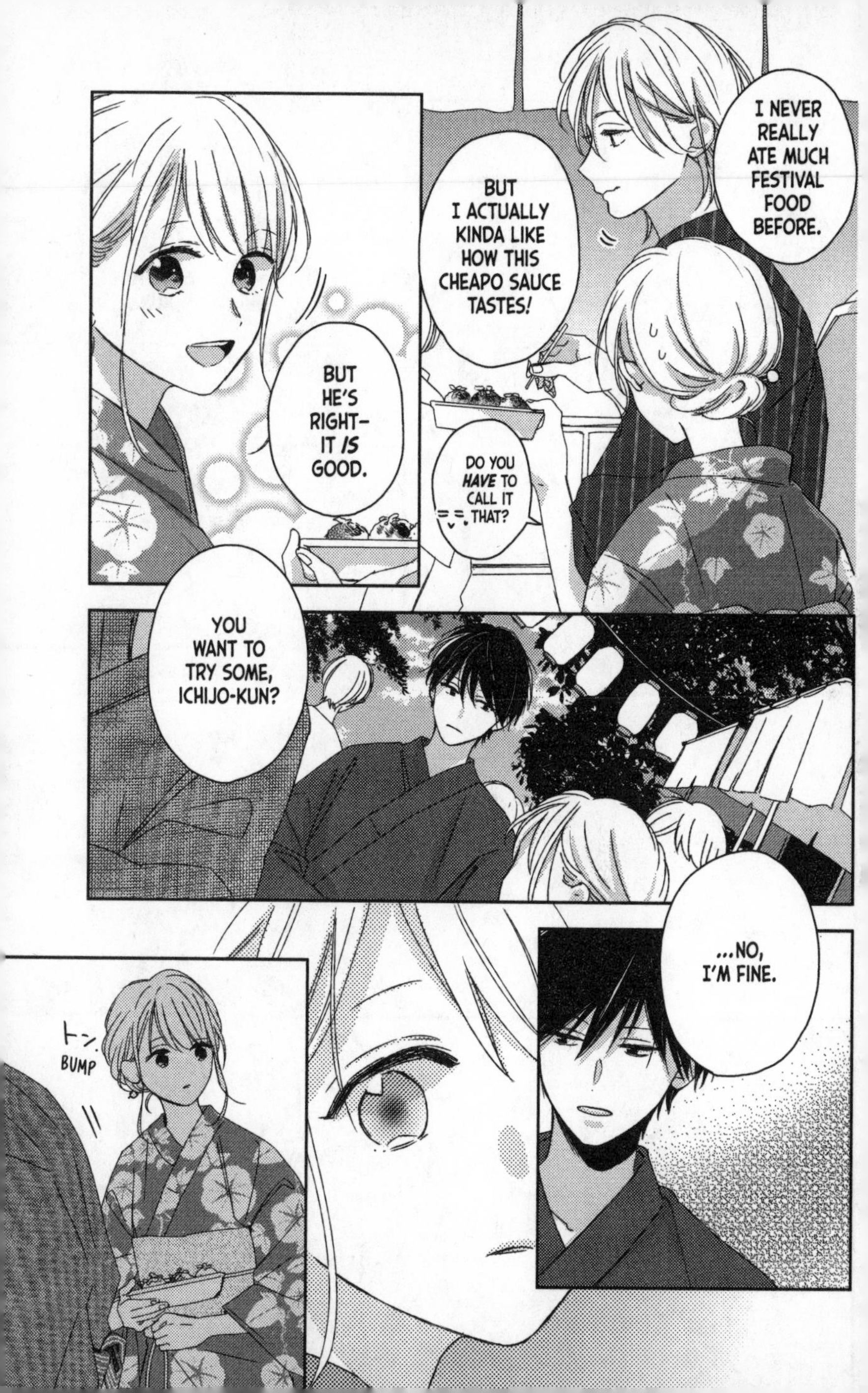
I NEVER REALLY ATE MUCH FESTIVAL FOOD BEFORE.
BUT I ACTUALLY KINDA LIKE HOW THIS CHEAPO SAUCE TASTES!
DO YOU *HAVE* TO CALL IT THAT?
BUT HE'S RIGHT— IT *IS* GOOD.
YOU WANT TO TRY SOME, ICHIJO-KUN?
...NO, I'M FINE.
トン
BUMP

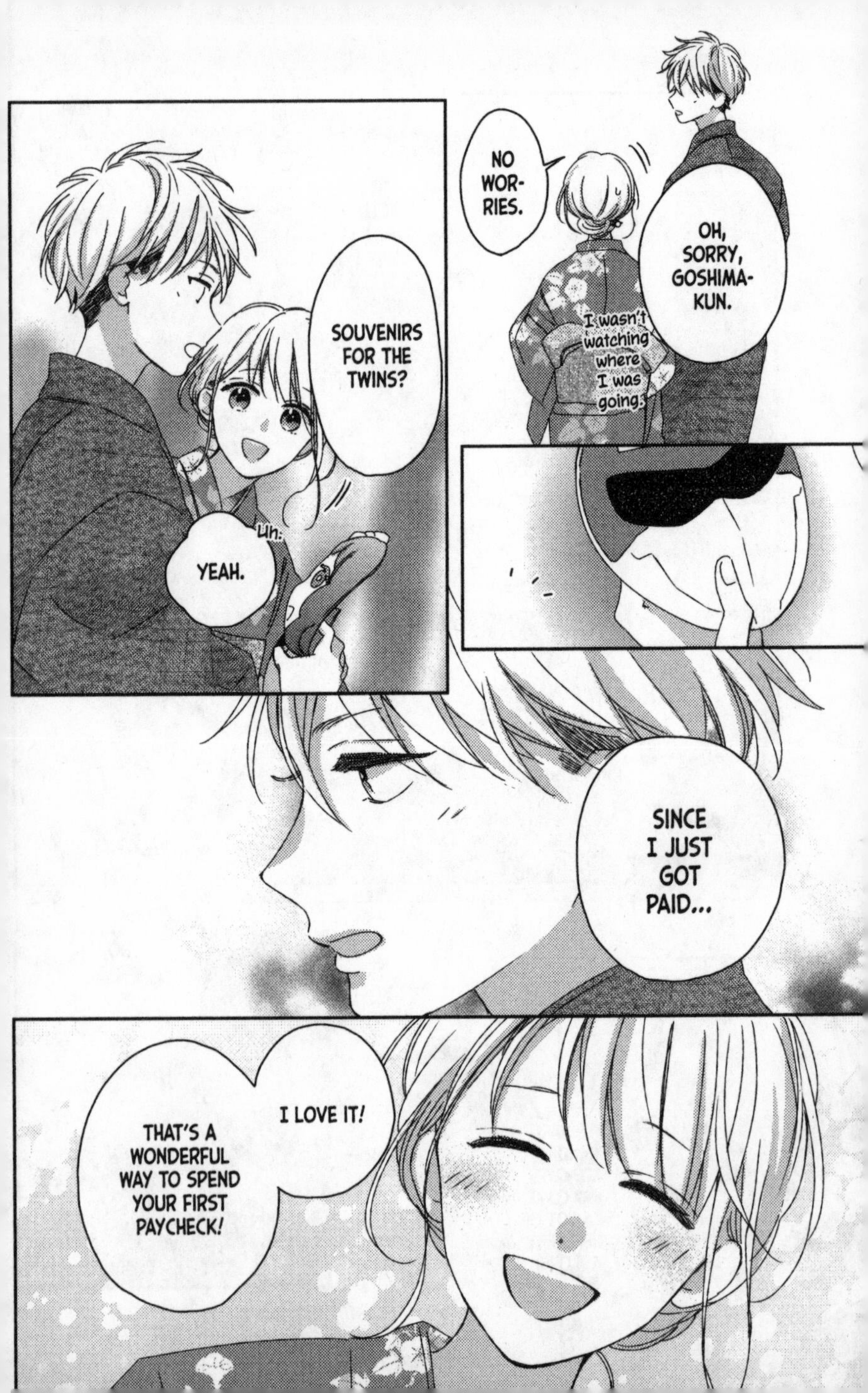
OH, SORRY, GOSHIMA-KUN.
I wasn't watching where I was going.
NO WOR-RIES.
SOUVENIRS FOR THE TWINS?
Uh.
YEAH.
SINCE I JUST GOT PAID...
I LOVE IT!
THAT'S A WONDERFUL WAY TO SPEND YOUR FIRST PAYCHECK!

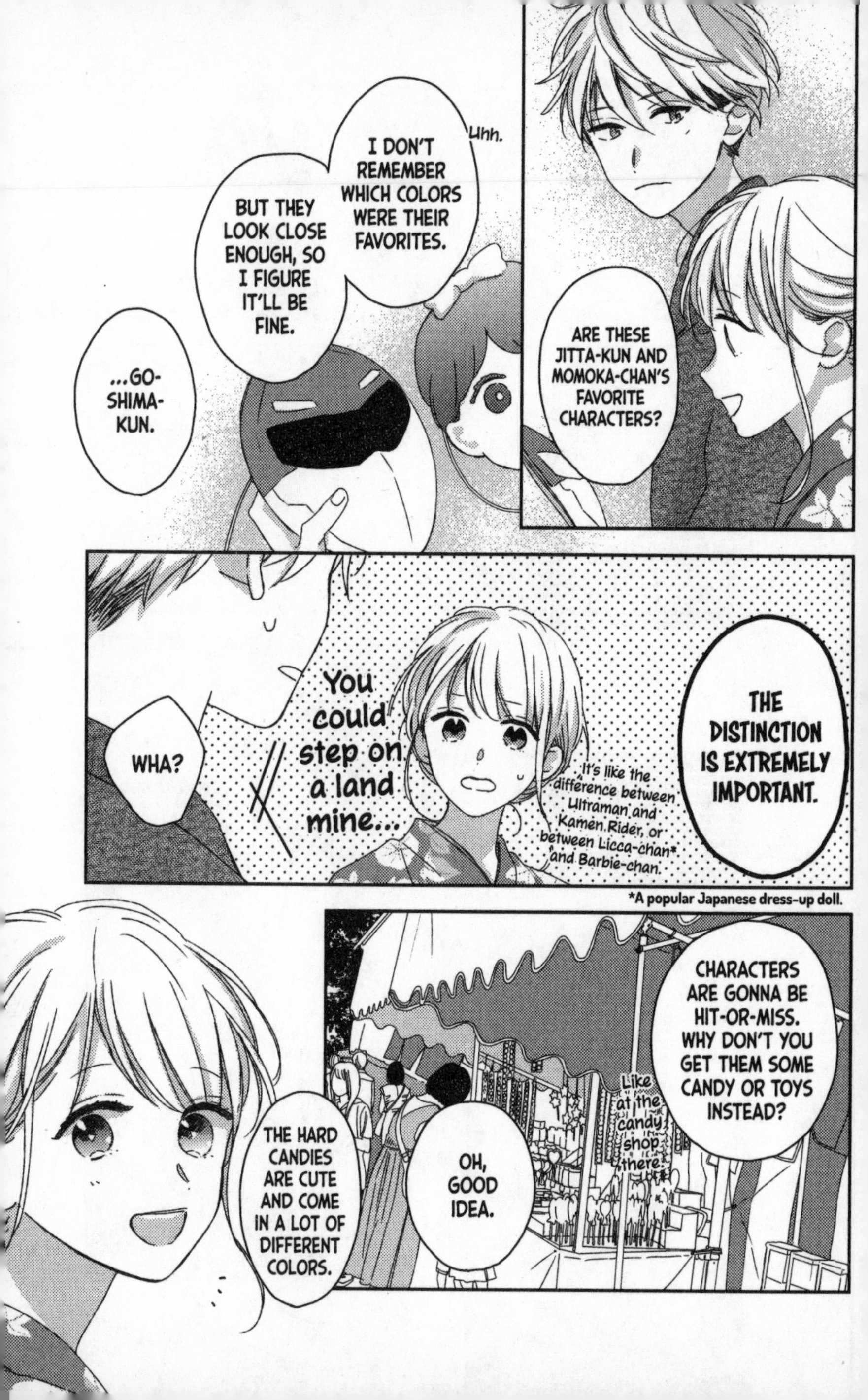
ARE THESE JITTA-KUN AND MOMOKA-CHAN'S FAVORITE CHARACTERS?
Uhh.
I DON'T REMEMBER WHICH COLORS WERE THEIR FAVORITES.
BUT THEY LOOK CLOSE ENOUGH, SO I FIGURE IT'LL BE FINE.
...GO-SHIMA-KUN.
THE DISTINCTION IS EXTREMELY IMPORTANT.
It's like the difference between Ultraman and Kamen Rider, or between Licca-chan* and Barbie-chan.
You could step on a land mine...
WHA?
*A popular Japanese dress-up doll.
CHARACTERS ARE GONNA BE HIT-OR-MISS. WHY DON'T YOU GET THEM SOME CANDY OR TOYS INSTEAD?
Like at the candy shop there.
OH, GOOD IDEA.
THE HARD CANDIES ARE CUTE AND COME IN A LOT OF DIFFERENT COLORS.

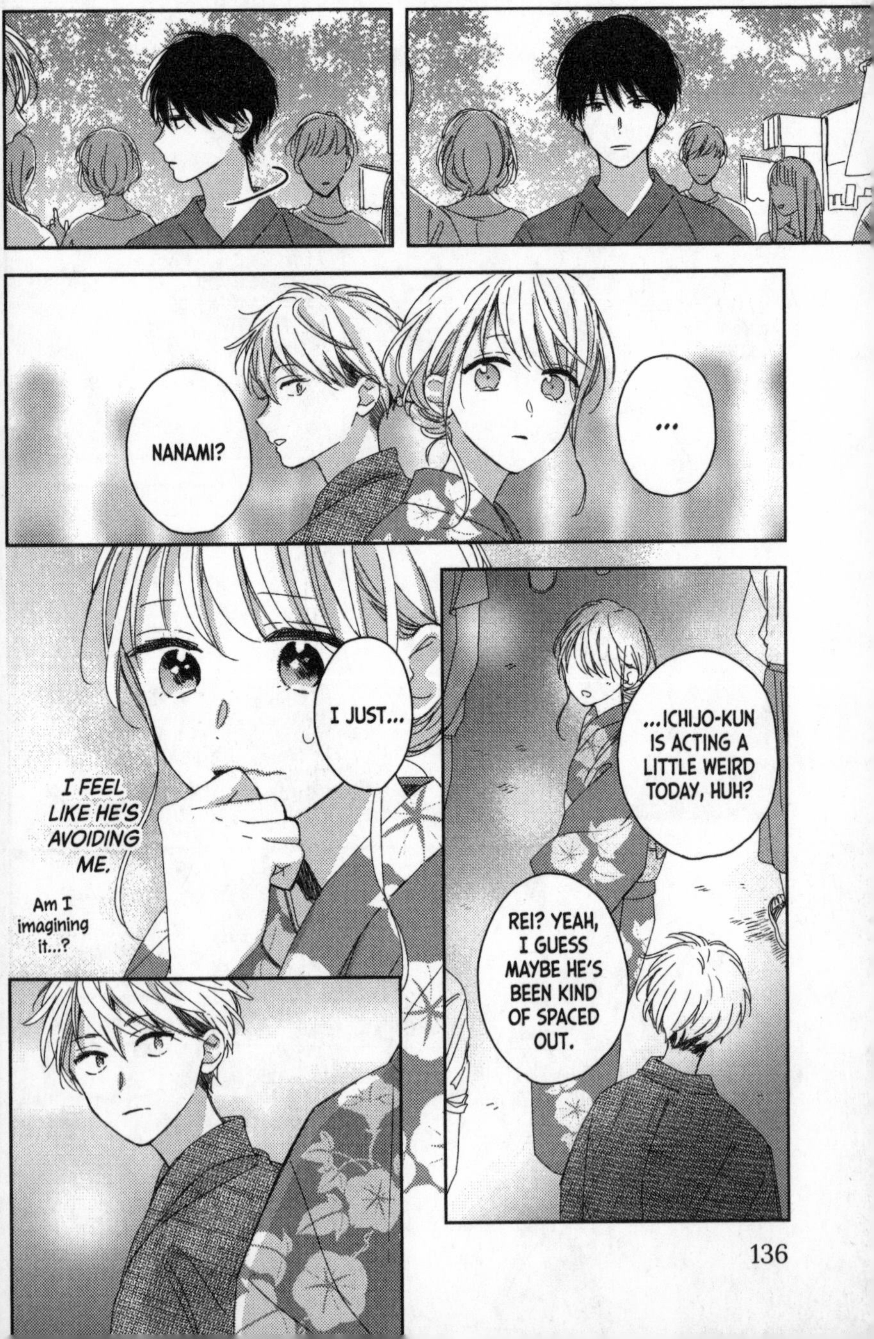
...
NANAMI?
...ICHIJO-KUN IS ACTING A LITTLE WEIRD TODAY, HUH?
REI? YEAH, I GUESS MAYBE HE'S BEEN KIND OF SPACED OUT.
I JUST...
I FEEL LIKE HE'S AVOIDING ME.
Am I imagining it...?

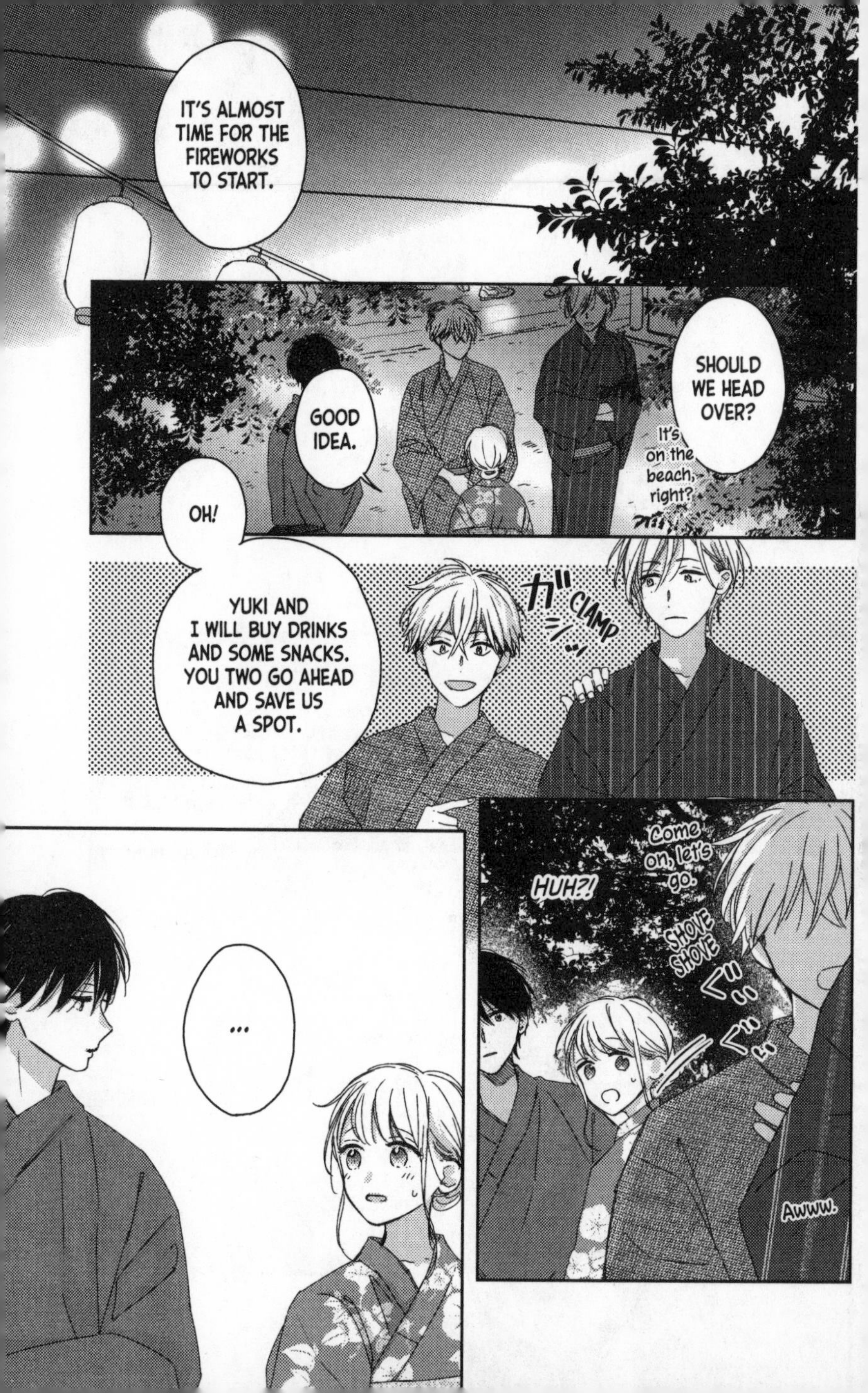
IT'S ALMOST TIME FOR THE FIREWORKS TO START.
SHOULD WE HEAD OVER?
It's on the beach, right?
GOOD IDEA.
OH!
YUKI AND I WILL BUY DRINKS AND SOME SNACKS. YOU TWO GO AHEAD AND SAVE US A SPOT.
CLAMP
Come on, let's go.
HUH?!
SHOVE SHOVE
AWWW.
...

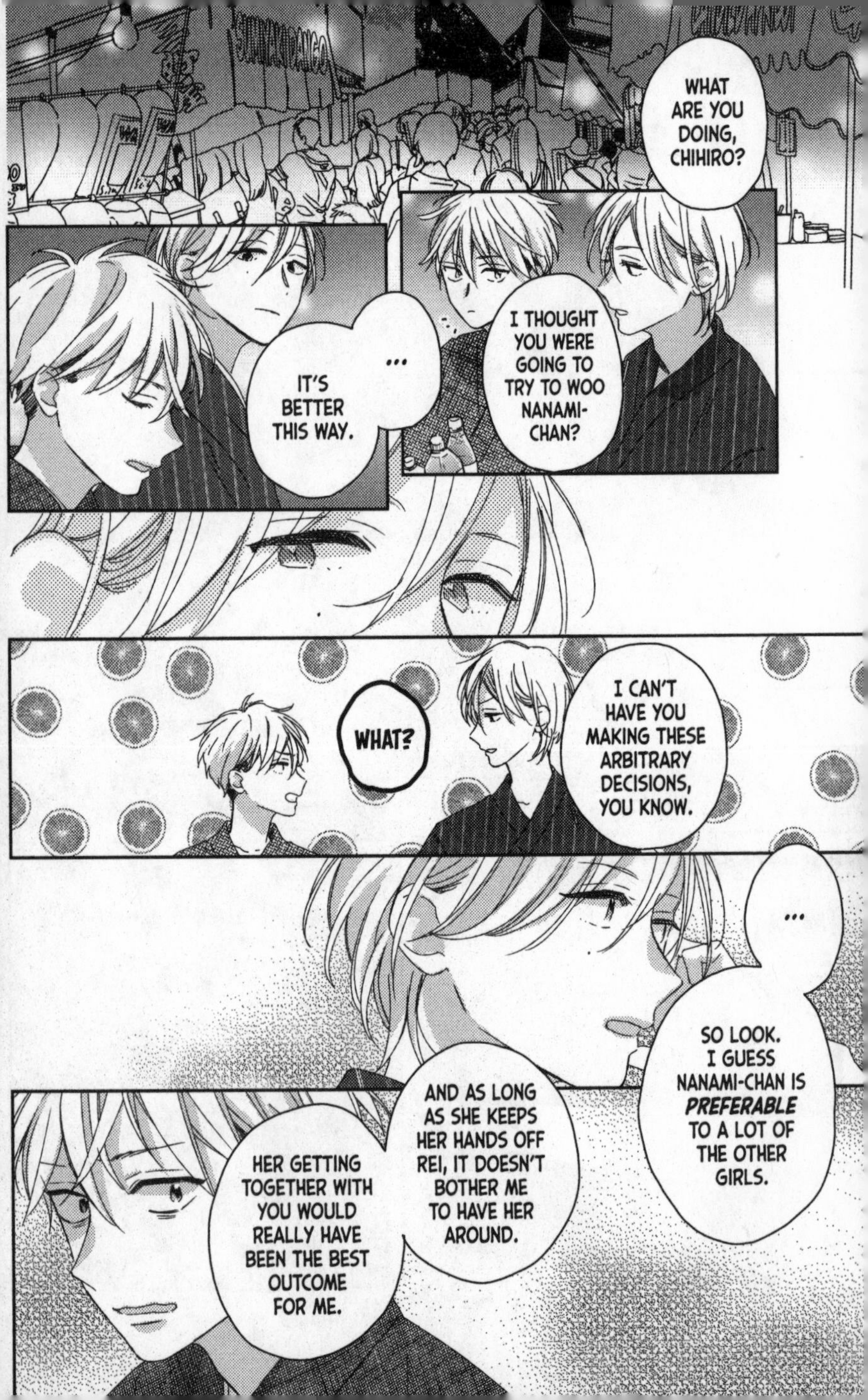
WHAT ARE YOU DOING, CHIHIRO?
I THOUGHT YOU WERE GOING TO TRY TO WOO NANAMI-CHAN?
...
IT'S BETTER THIS WAY.
I CAN'T HAVE YOU MAKING THESE ARBITRARY DECISIONS, YOU KNOW.
WHAT?
...
SO LOOK. I GUESS NANAMI-CHAN IS *PREFERABLE* TO A LOT OF THE OTHER GIRLS.
AND AS LONG AS SHE KEEPS HER HANDS OFF REI, IT DOESN'T BOTHER ME TO HAVE HER AROUND.
HER GETTING TOGETHER WITH YOU WOULD REALLY HAVE BEEN THE BEST OUTCOME FOR ME.

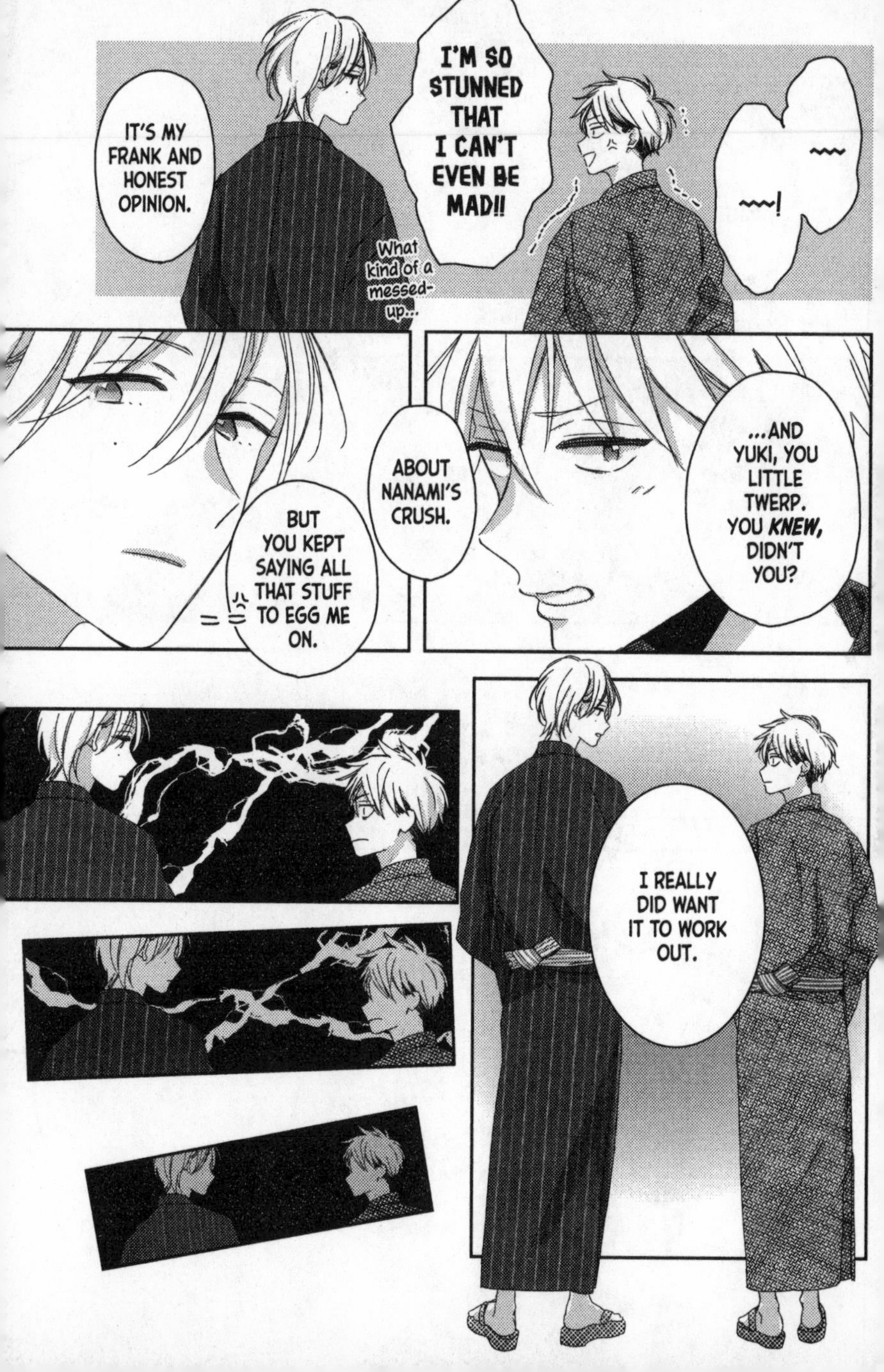
~~~
~~~!
I'M SO STUNNED THAT I CAN'T EVEN BE MAD!!
What kind of a messed-up...
IT'S MY FRANK AND HONEST OPINION.
...AND YUKI, YOU LITTLE TWERP. YOU *KNEW*, DIDN'T YOU?
ABOUT NANAMI'S CRUSH.
BUT YOU KEPT SAYING ALL THAT STUFF TO EGG ME ON.
I REALLY DID WANT IT TO WORK OUT.

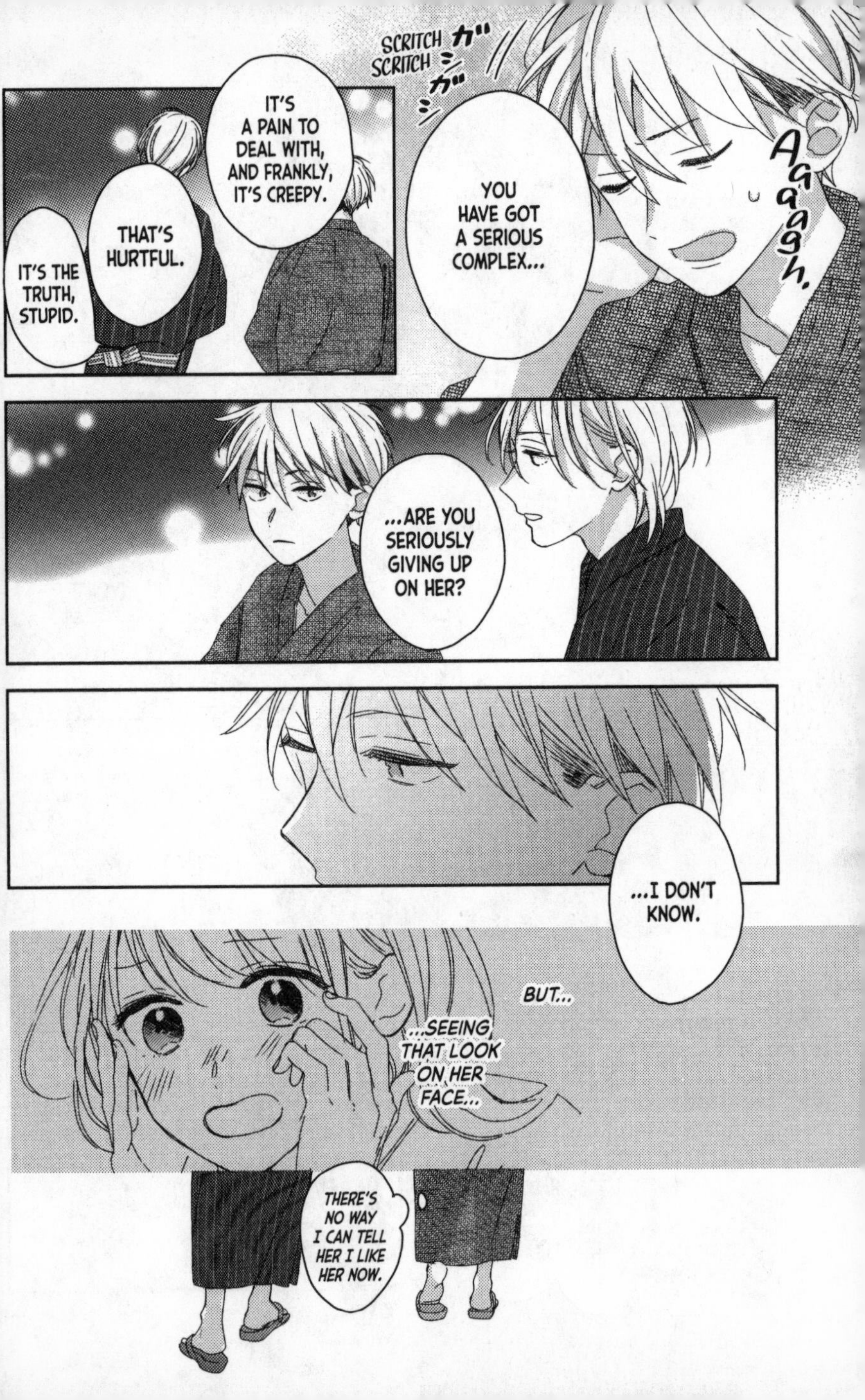
SCRITCH SCRITCH
ガシガシ
Aaaagh.
YOU HAVE GOT A SERIOUS COMPLEX...
IT'S A PAIN TO DEAL WITH, AND FRANKLY, IT'S CREEPY.
THAT'S HURTFUL.
IT'S THE TRUTH, STUPID.
...ARE YOU SERIOUSLY GIVING UP ON HER?
...I DON'T KNOW.
BUT...
...SEEING THAT LOOK ON HER FACE...
THERE'S NO WAY I CAN TELL HER I LIKE HER NOW.

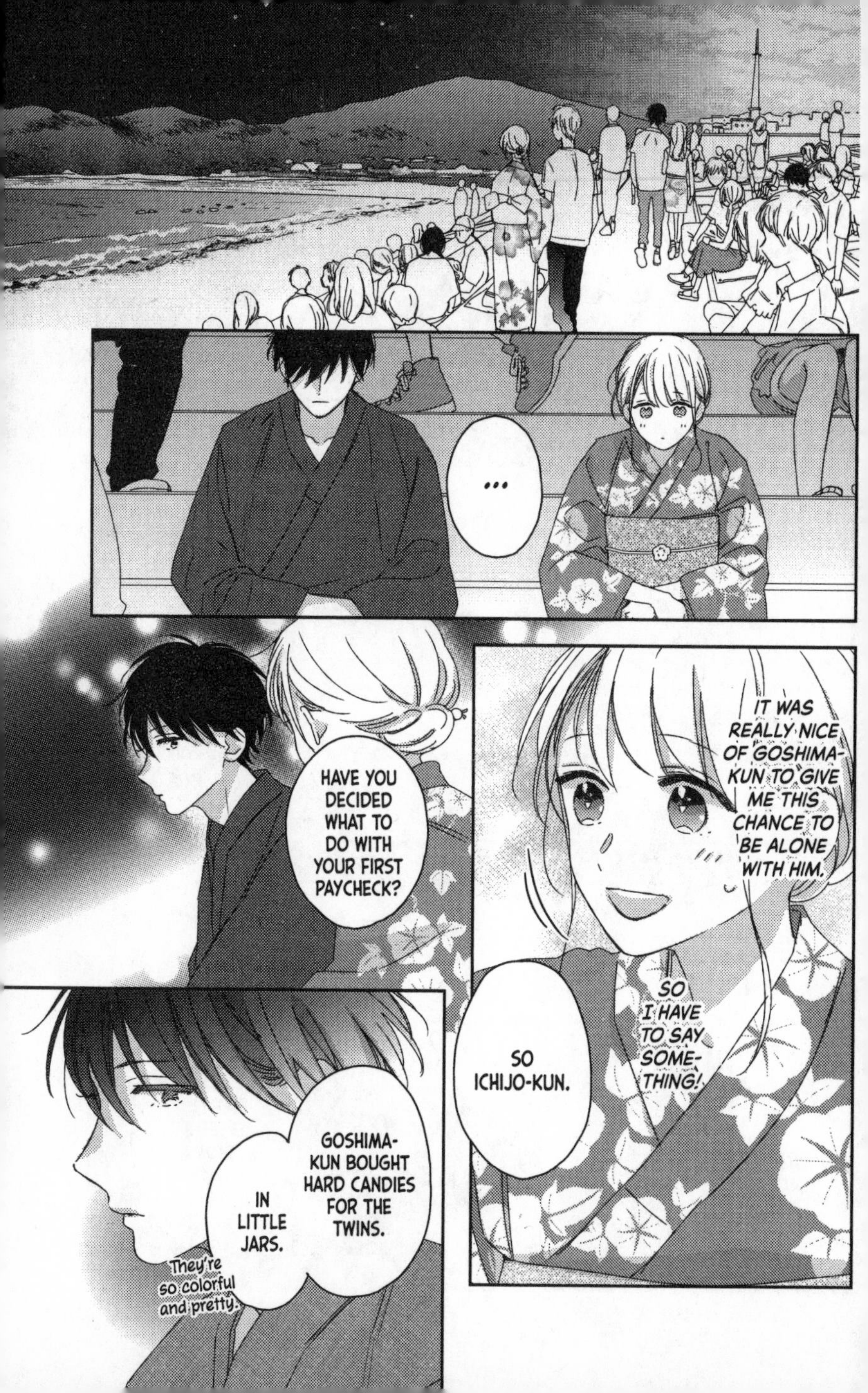
...
IT WAS REALLY NICE OF GOSHIMA-KUN TO GIVE ME THIS CHANCE TO BE ALONE WITH HIM.
SO I HAVE TO SAY SOME-THING!
SO ICHIJO-KUN.
HAVE YOU DECIDED WHAT TO DO WITH YOUR FIRST PAYCHECK?
GOSHIMA-KUN BOUGHT HARD CANDIES FOR THE TWINS.
IN LITTLE JARS.
They're so colorful and pretty.

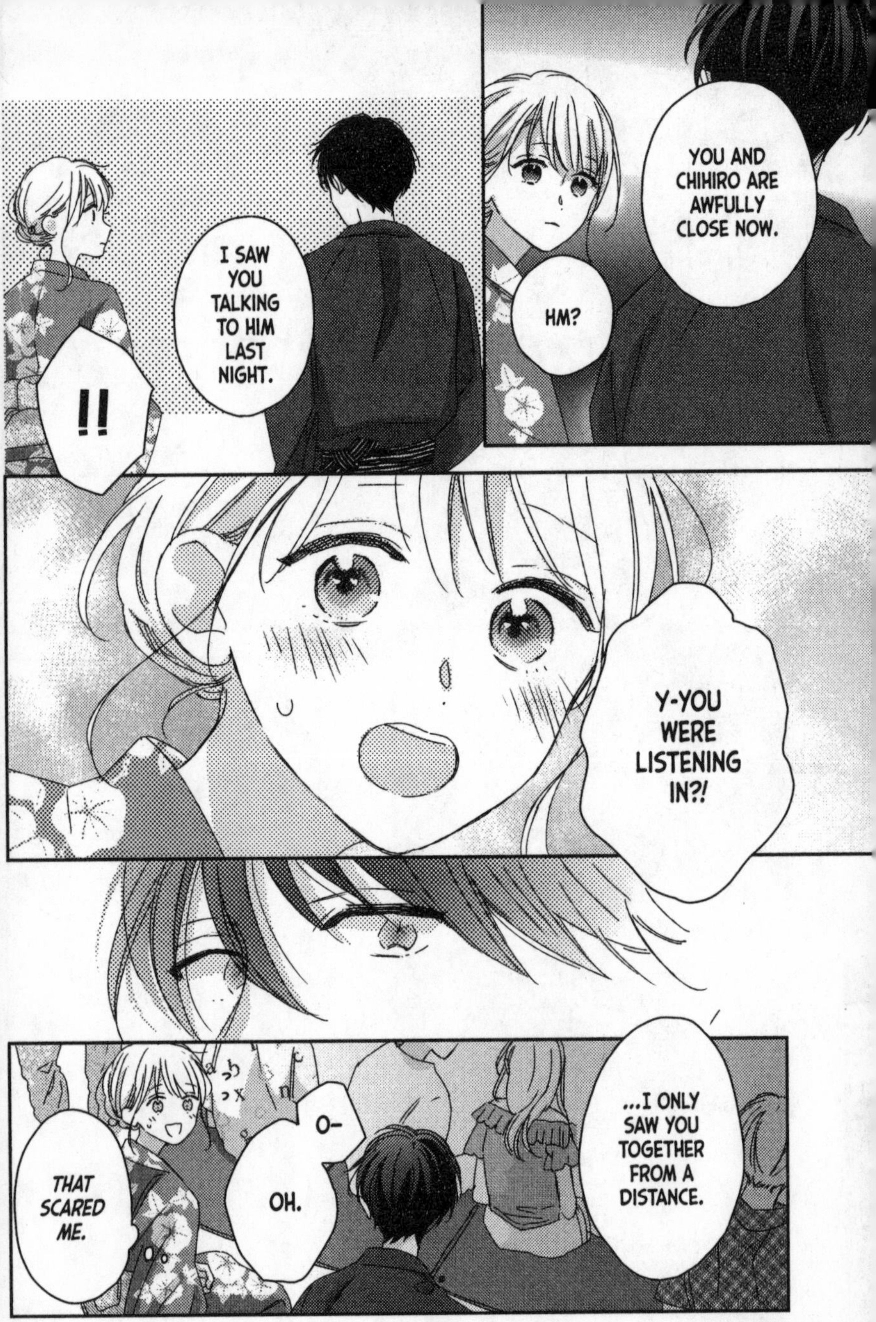
YOU AND CHIHIRO ARE AWFULLY CLOSE NOW.
HM?
I SAW YOU TALKING TO HIM LAST NIGHT.
!!
Y-YOU WERE LISTENING IN?!
...I ONLY SAW YOU TOGETHER FROM A DISTANCE.
O-
OH.
THAT SCARED ME.

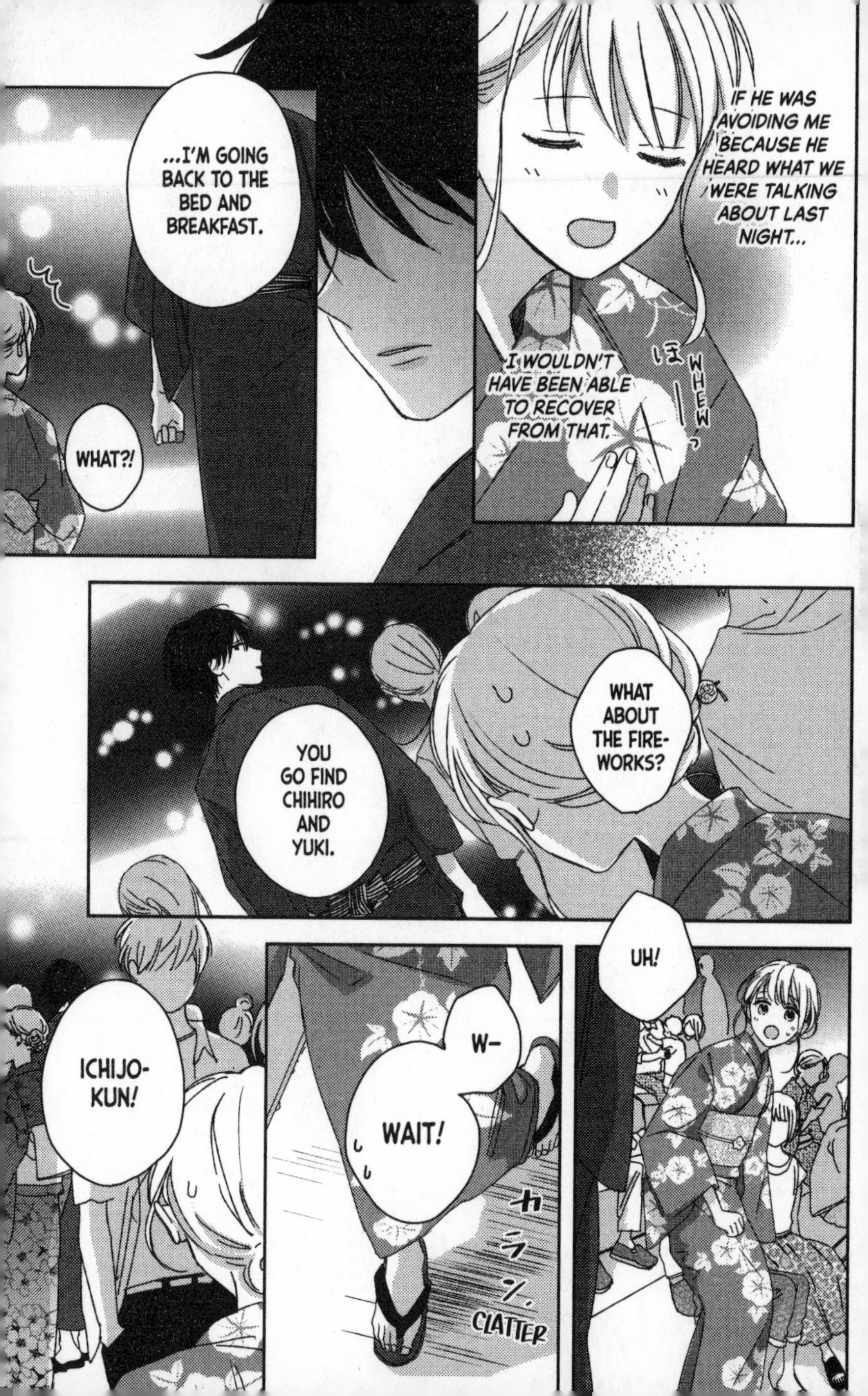
IF HE WAS AVOIDING ME BECAUSE HE HEARD WHAT WE WERE TALKING ABOUT LAST NIGHT...
I WOULDN'T HAVE BEEN ABLE TO RECOVER FROM THAT.
WHEW
...I'M GOING BACK TO THE BED AND BREAKFAST.
WHAT?!
WHAT ABOUT THE FIRE-WORKS?
YOU GO FIND CHIHIRO AND YUKI.
UH!
W-
WAIT!
CLATTER
ICHIJO-KUN!

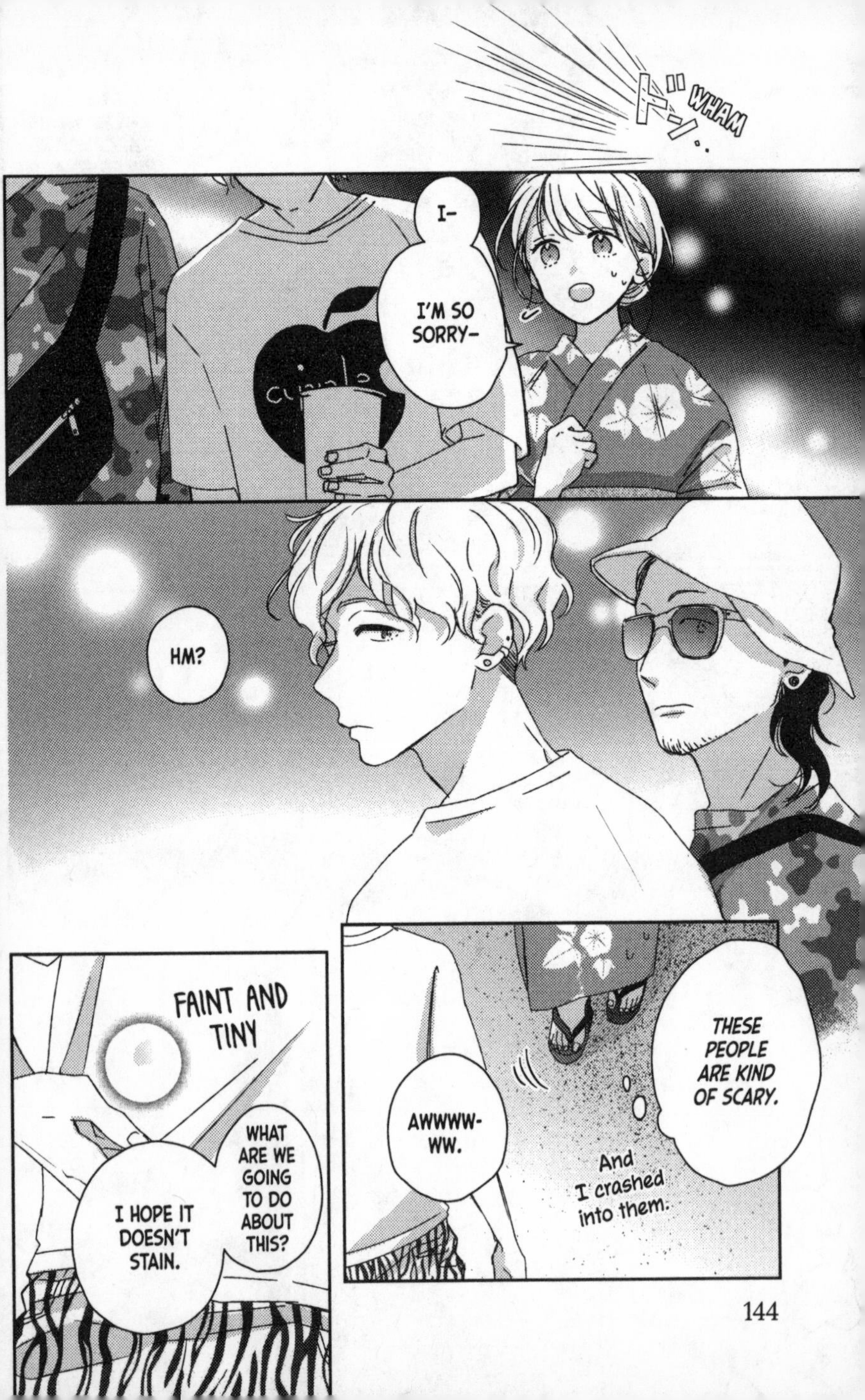
ドーン
WHAM
I–
I'M SO SORRY–
HM?
THESE PEOPLE ARE KIND OF SCARY.
AWWWW-WW.
And I crashed into them.
FAINT AND TINY
WHAT ARE WE GOING TO DO ABOUT THIS?
I HOPE IT DOESN'T STAIN.

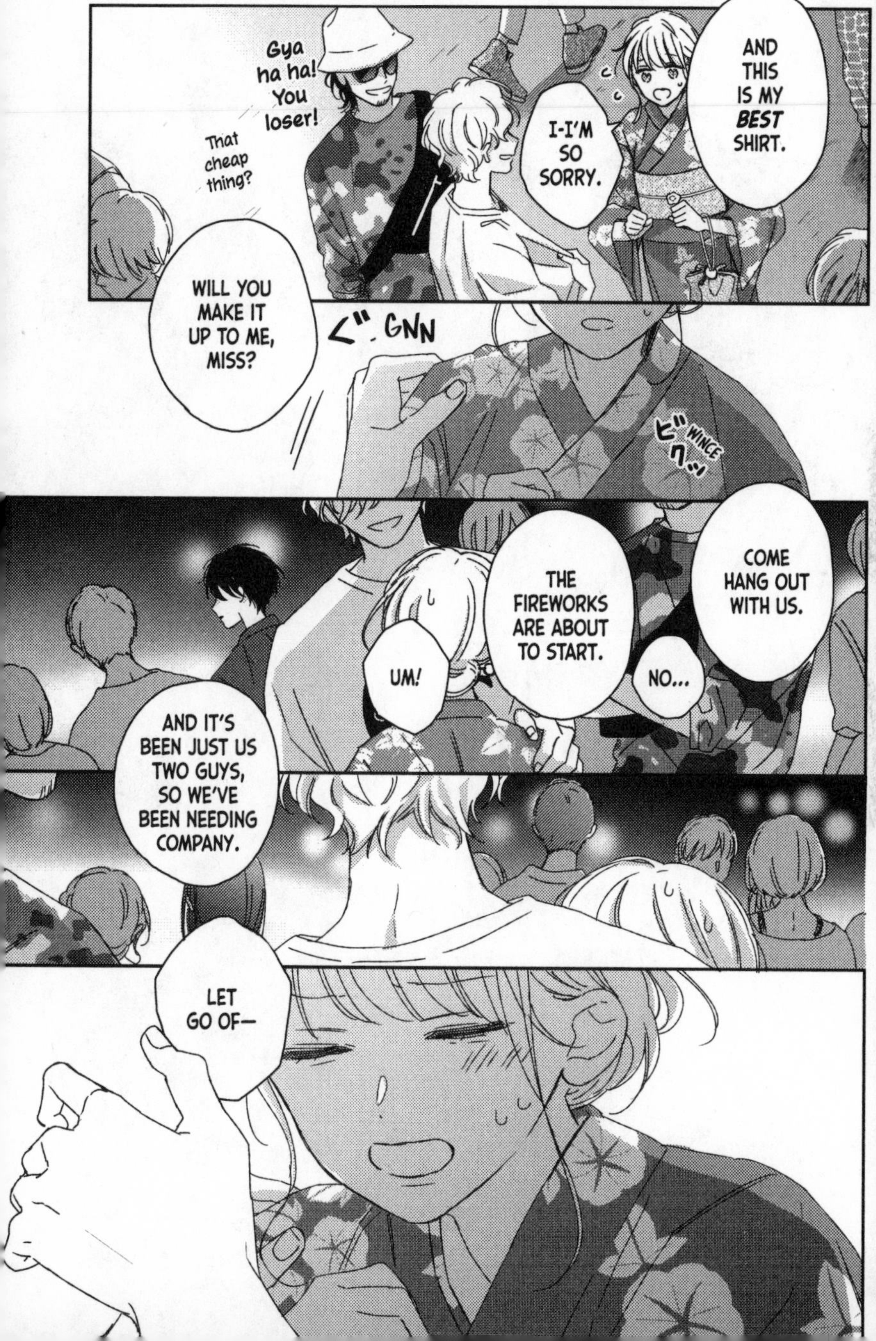
AND THIS IS MY *BEST* SHIRT.
I-I'M SO SORRY.
Gya ha ha! You loser!
That cheap thing?
WILL YOU MAKE IT UP TO ME, MISS?
GNN
WINCE
COME HANG OUT WITH US.
NO...
THE FIREWORKS ARE ABOUT TO START.
UM!
AND IT'S BEEN JUST US TWO GUYS, SO WE'VE BEEN NEEDING COMPANY.
LET GO OF—

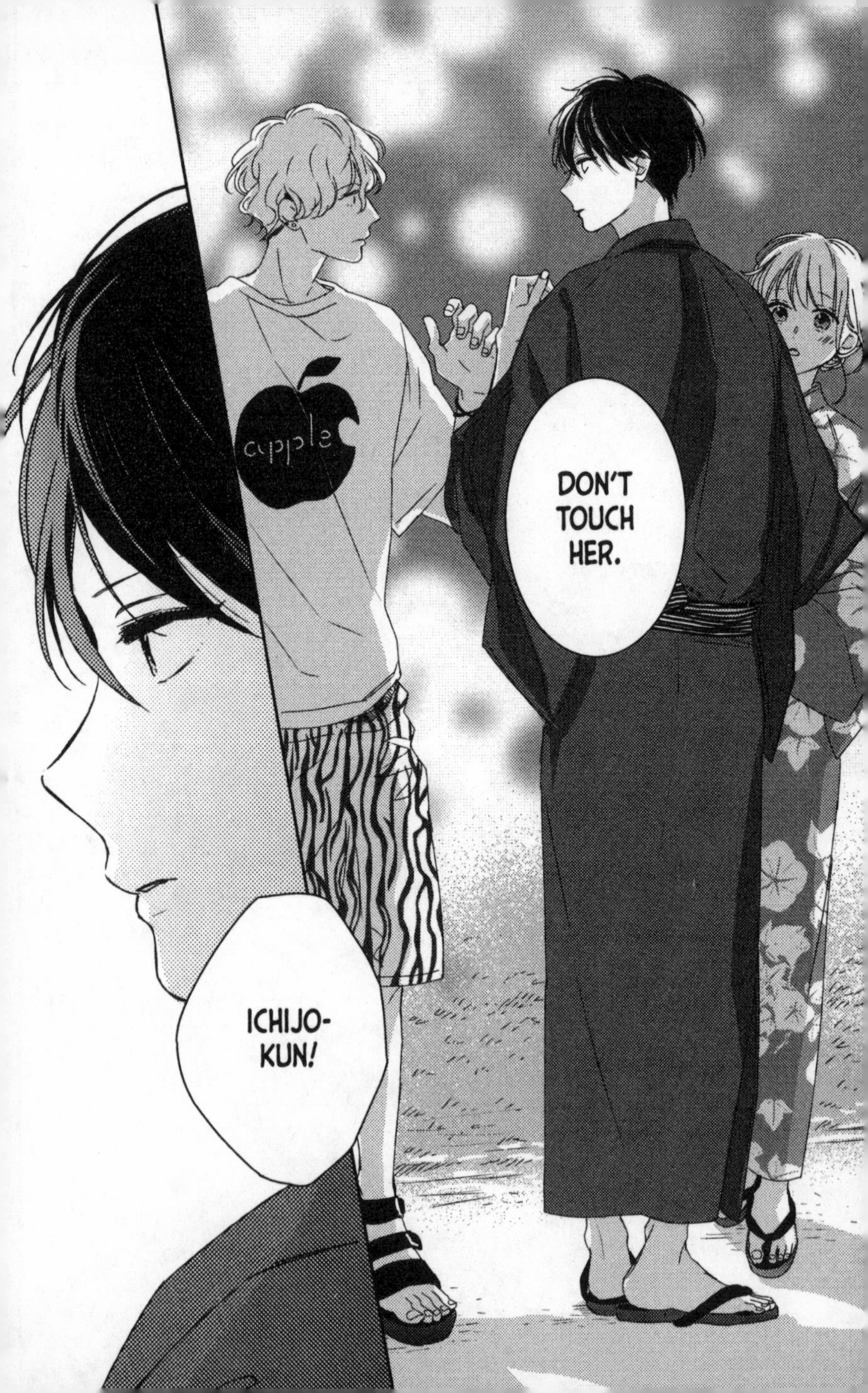
DON'T TOUCH HER.
ICHIJO-KUN!

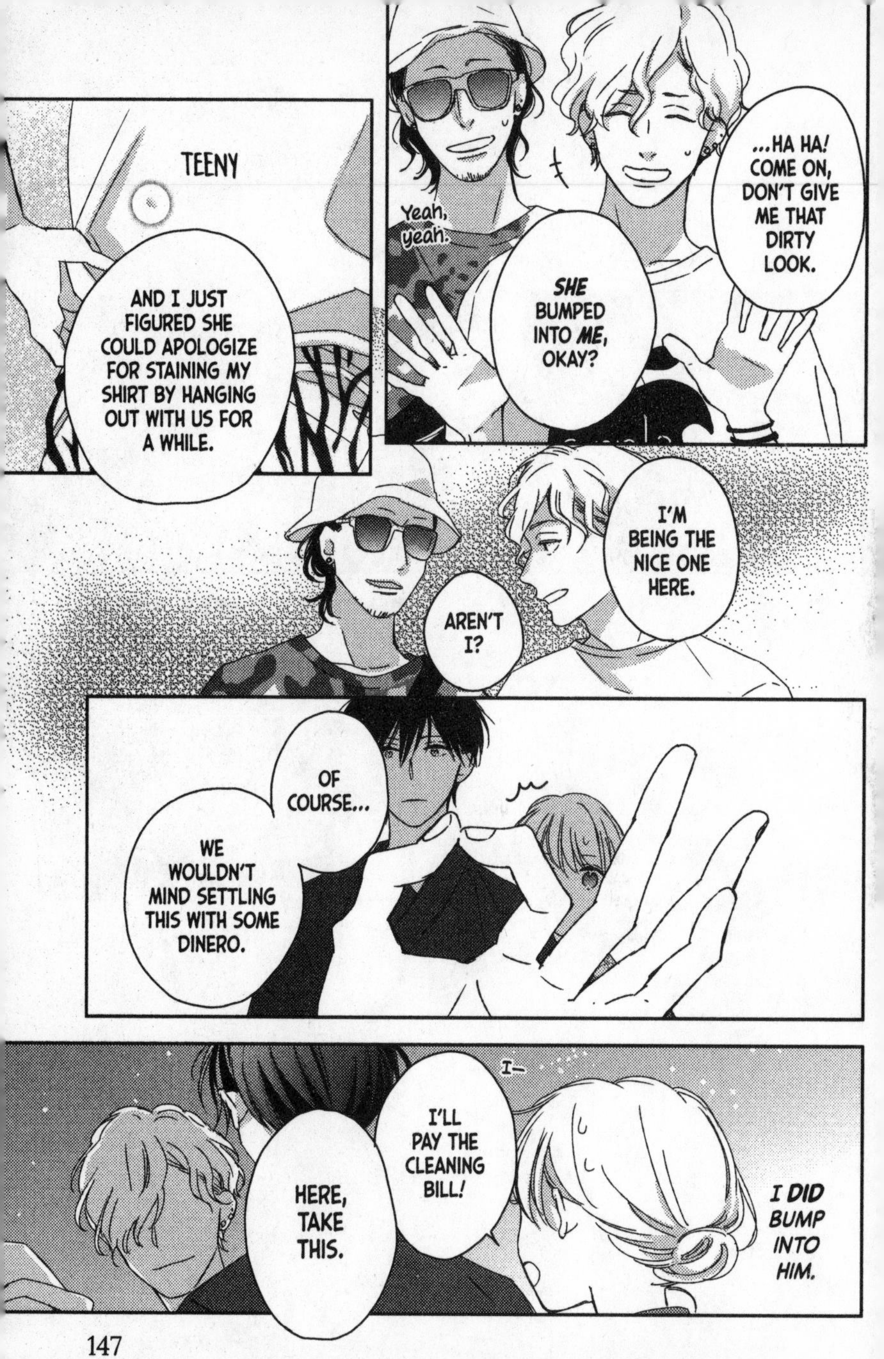
...HA HA! COME ON, DON'T GIVE ME THAT DIRTY LOOK.
Yeah, yeah.
SHE BUMPED INTO *ME*, OKAY?
TEENY
AND I JUST FIGURED SHE COULD APOLOGIZE FOR STAINING MY SHIRT BY HANGING OUT WITH US FOR A WHILE.
I'M BEING THE NICE ONE HERE.
AREN'T I?
OF COURSE...
WE WOULDN'T MIND SETTLING THIS WITH SOME DINERO.
I DID BUMP INTO HIM.
I—
I'LL PAY THE CLEANING BILL!
HERE, TAKE THIS.

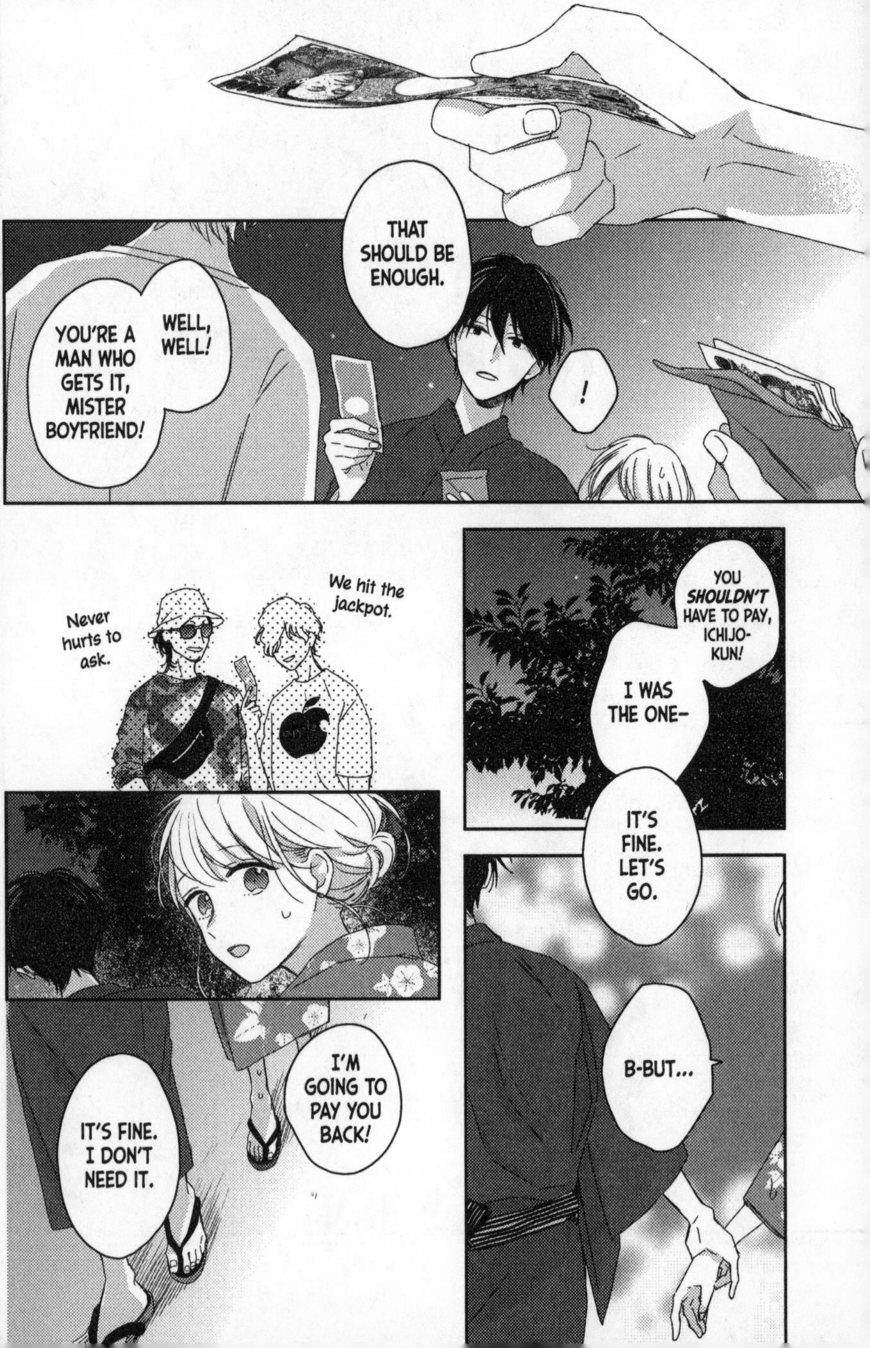
THAT SHOULD BE ENOUGH.
!
WELL, WELL!
YOU'RE A MAN WHO GETS IT, MISTER BOYFRIEND!
YOU *SHOULDN'T* HAVE TO PAY, ICHIJO-KUN!
I WAS THE ONE–
IT'S FINE. LET'S GO.
B-BUT...
We hit the jackpot.
Never hurts to ask.
I'M GOING TO PAY YOU BACK!
IT'S FINE. I DON'T NEED IT.

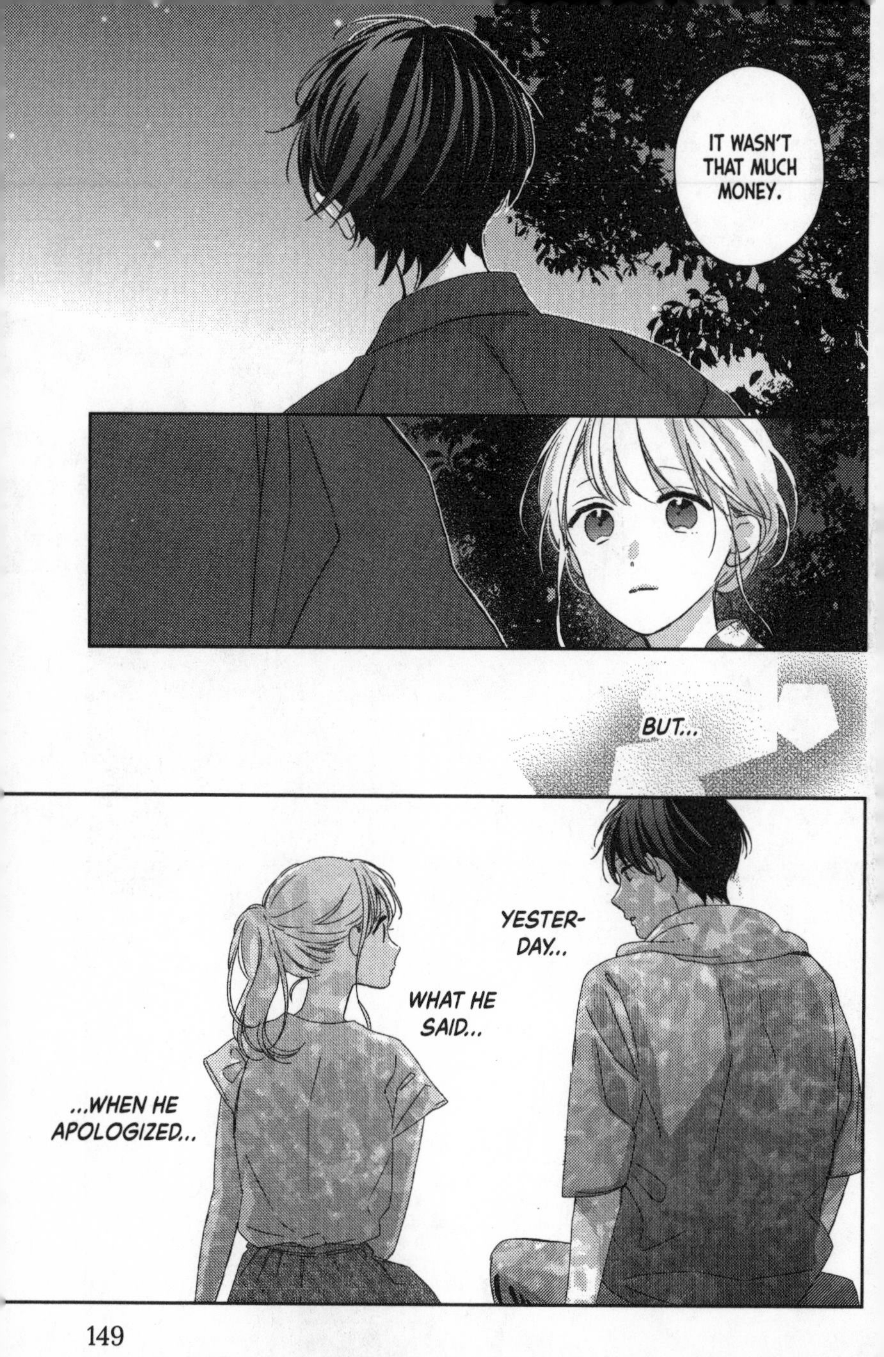
IT WASN'T THAT MUCH MONEY.
BUT...
YESTER-DAY...
WHAT HE SAID...
...WHEN HE APOLOGIZED...

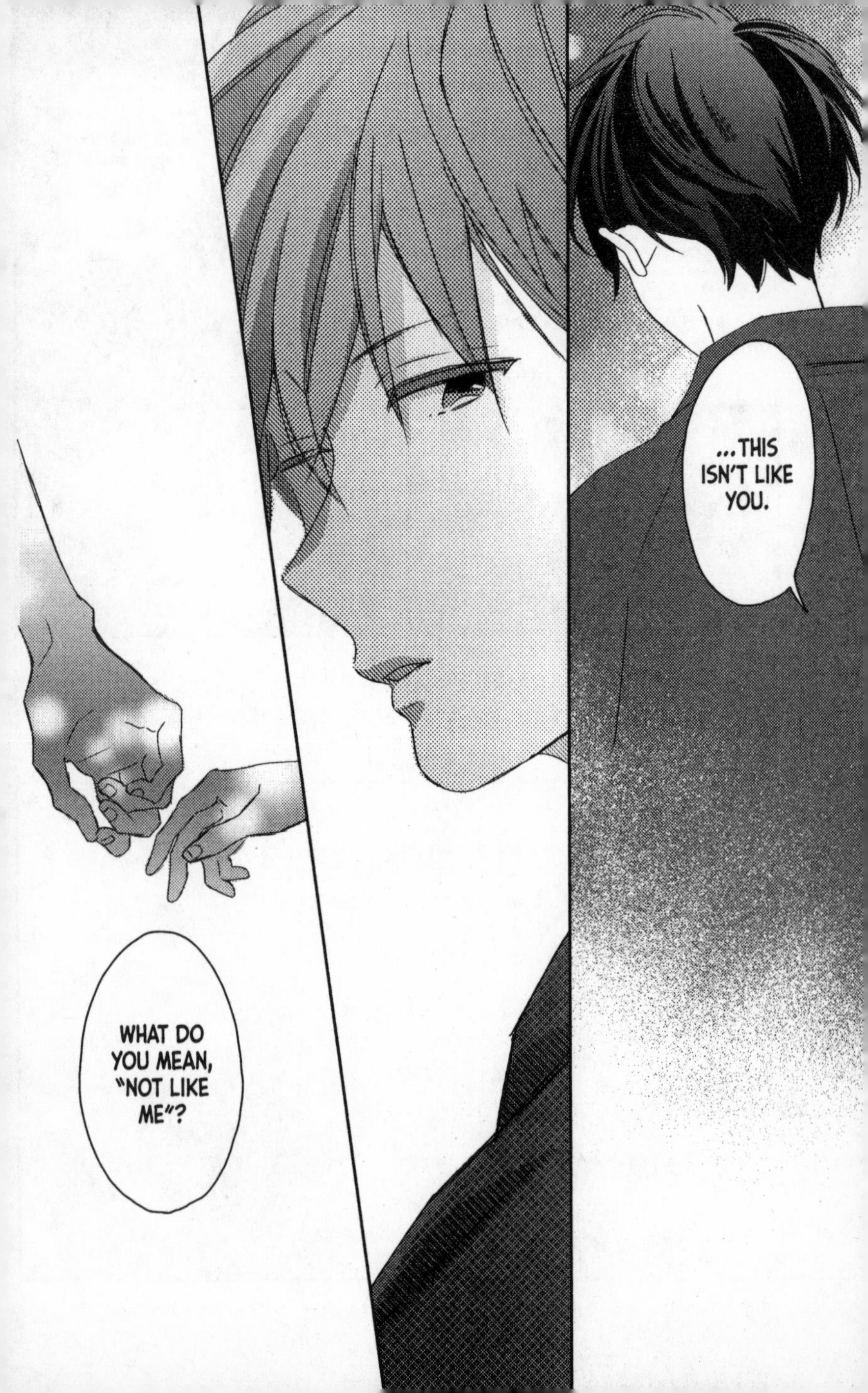
...THIS ISN'T LIKE YOU.
WHAT DO YOU MEAN, "NOT LIKE ME"?

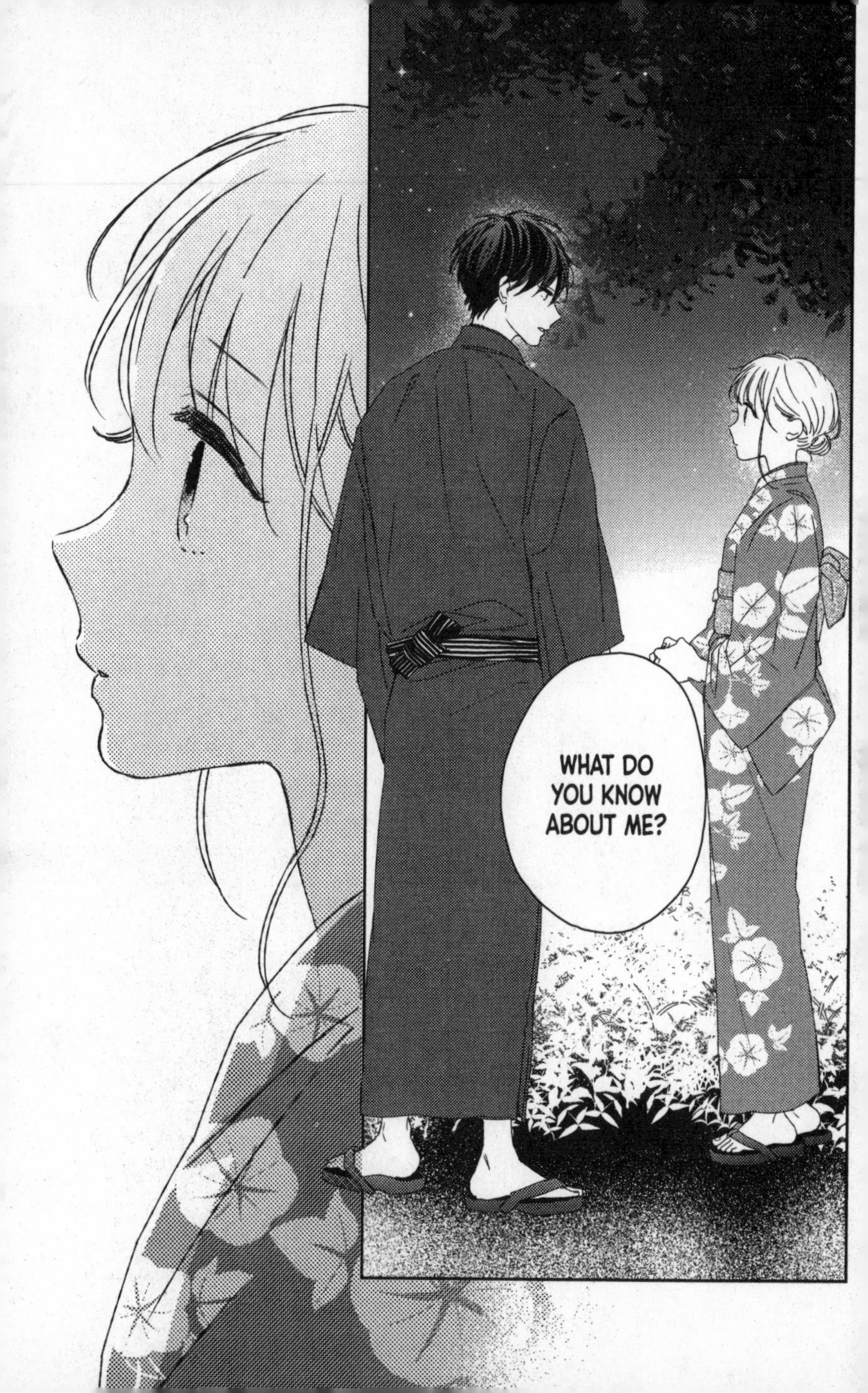
WHAT DO YOU KNOW ABOUT ME?

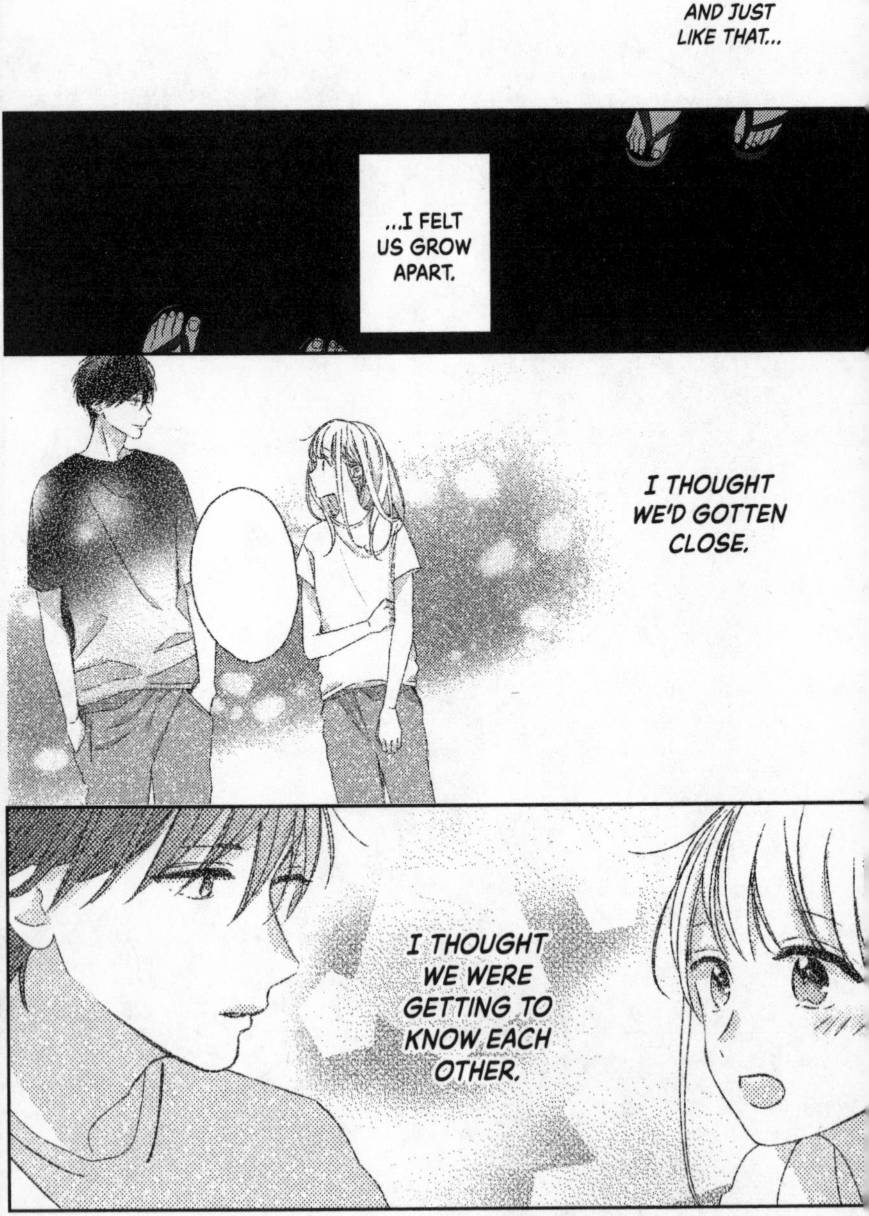
AND JUST LIKE THAT...
...I FELT US GROW APART.
I THOUGHT WE'D GOTTEN CLOSE.
I THOUGHT WE WERE GETTING TO KNOW EACH OTHER.

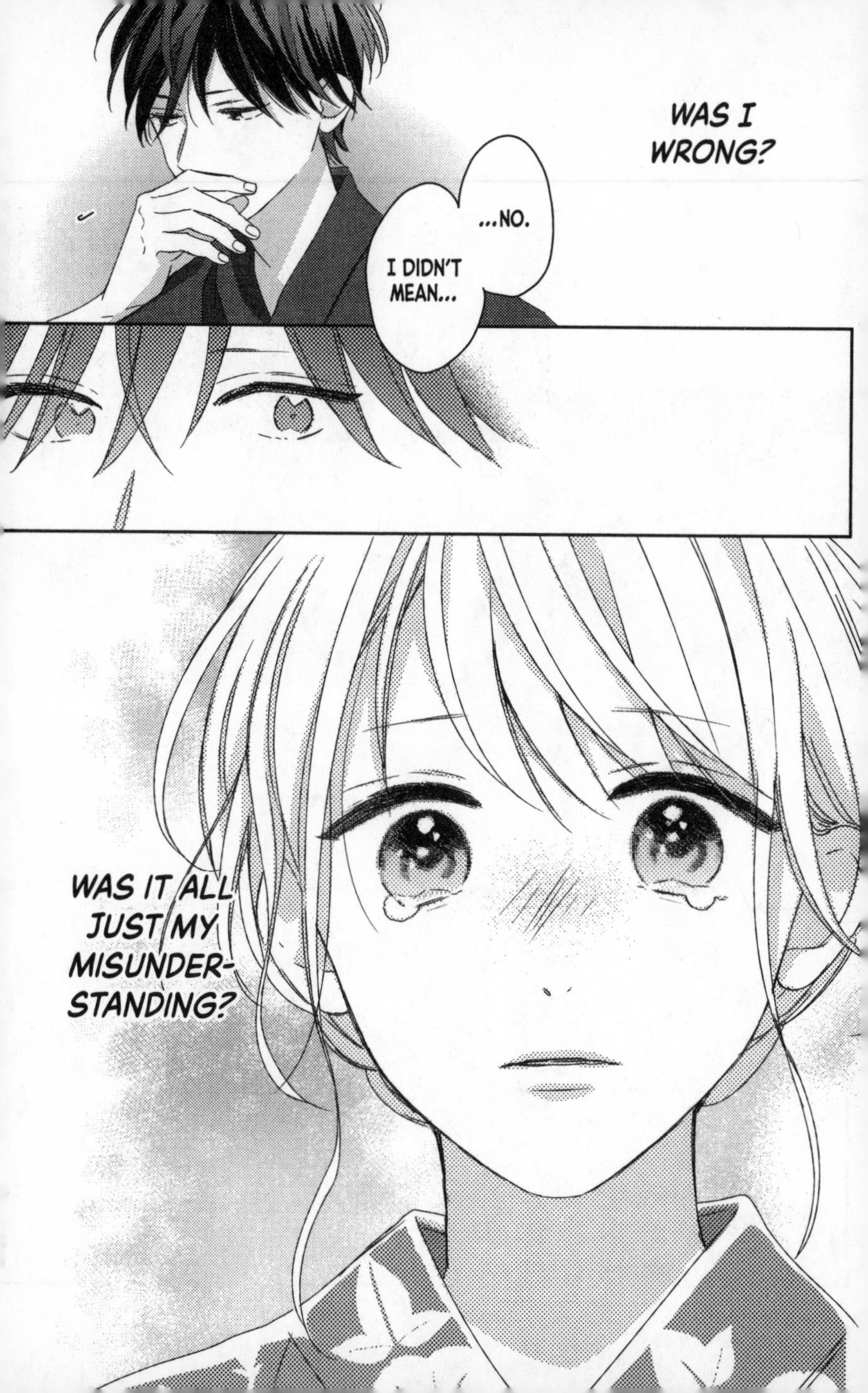
WAS I WRONG?
...NO.
I DIDN'T MEAN...
WAS IT ALL JUST MY MISUNDERSTANDING?

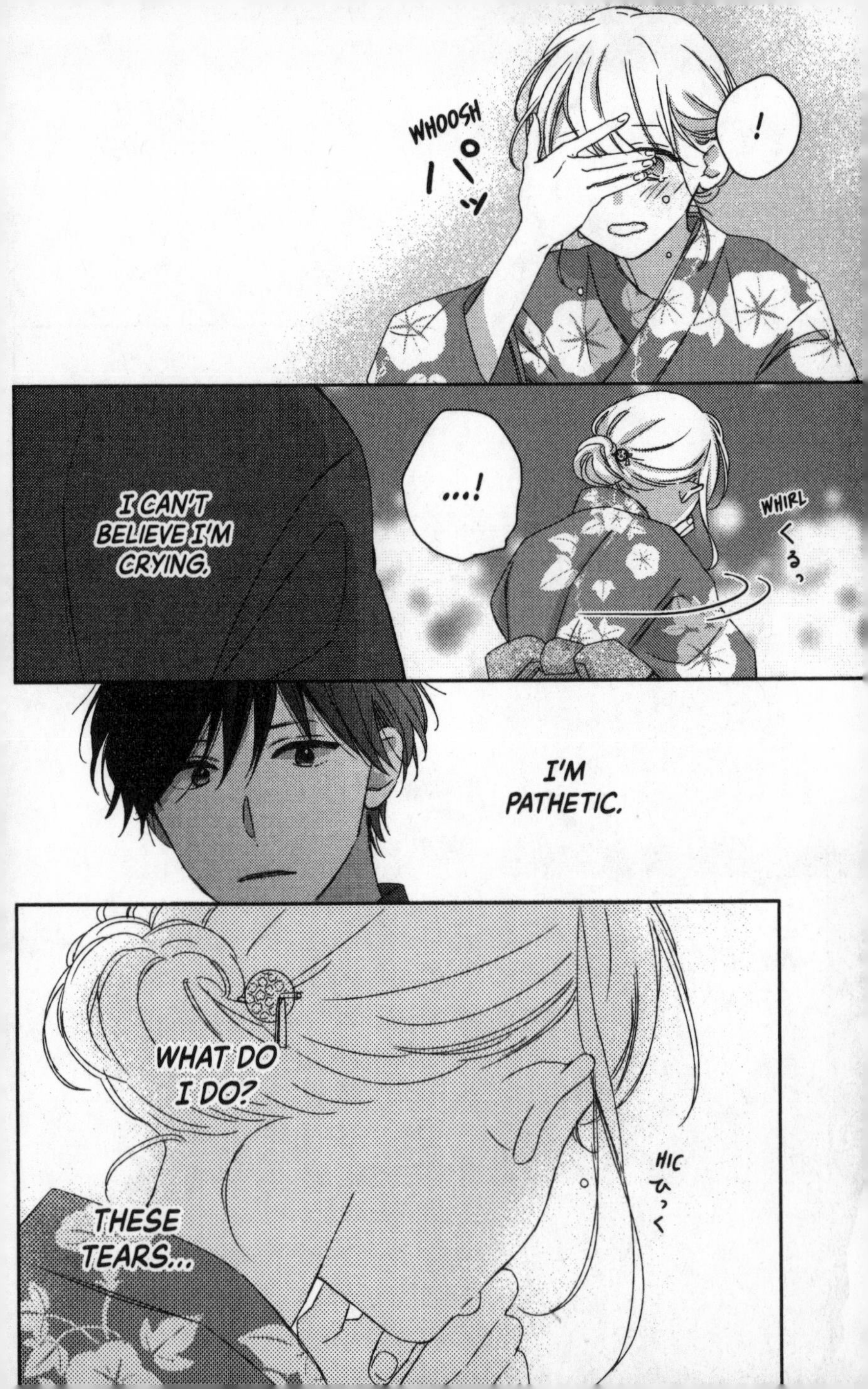
!
WHOOSH
パッ
WHIRL
くるっ
...!
I CAN'T BELIEVE I'M CRYING.
I'M PATHETIC.
HIC
ひっく
WHAT DO I DO?
THESE TEARS...

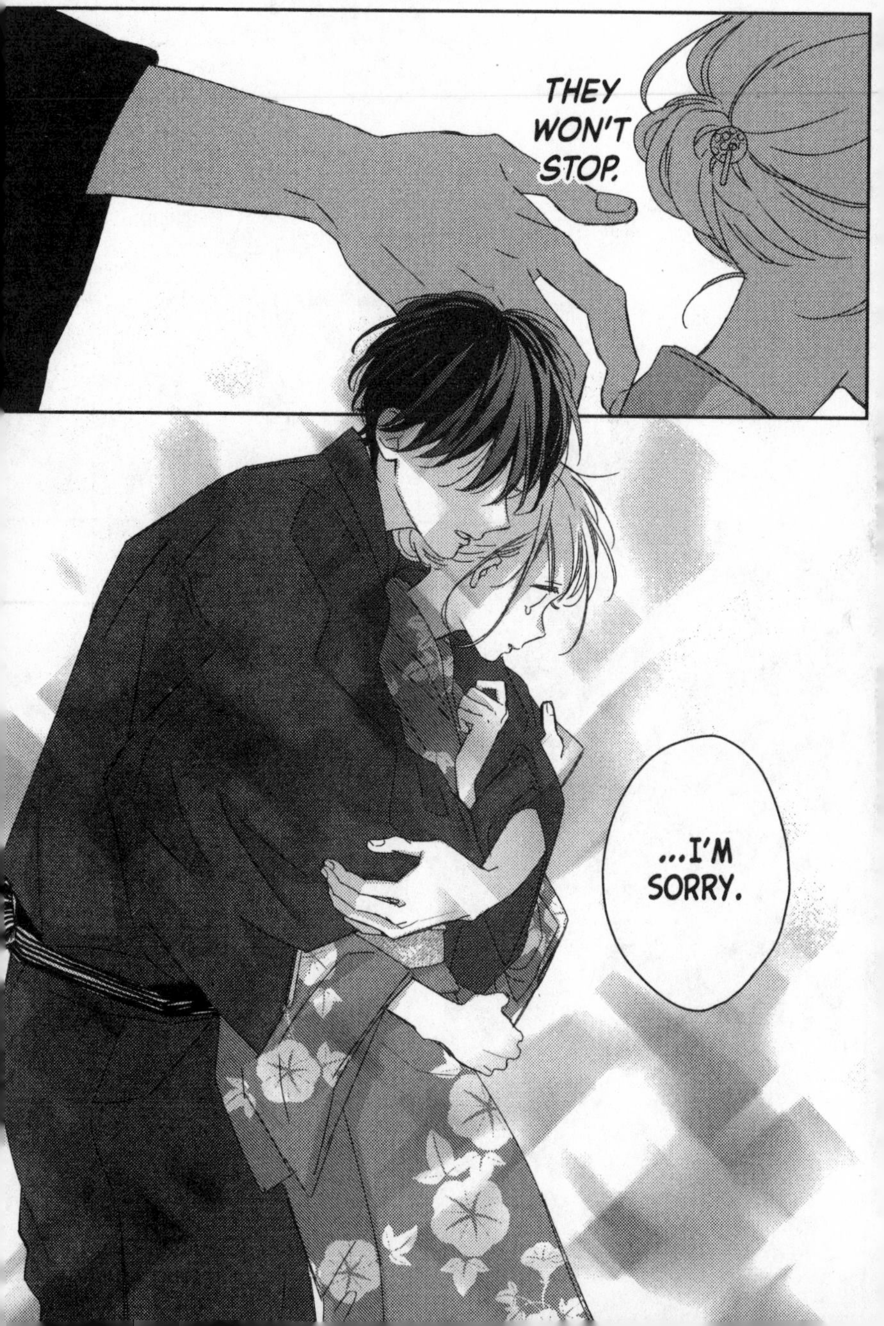
THEY WON'T STOP.
...I'M SORRY.

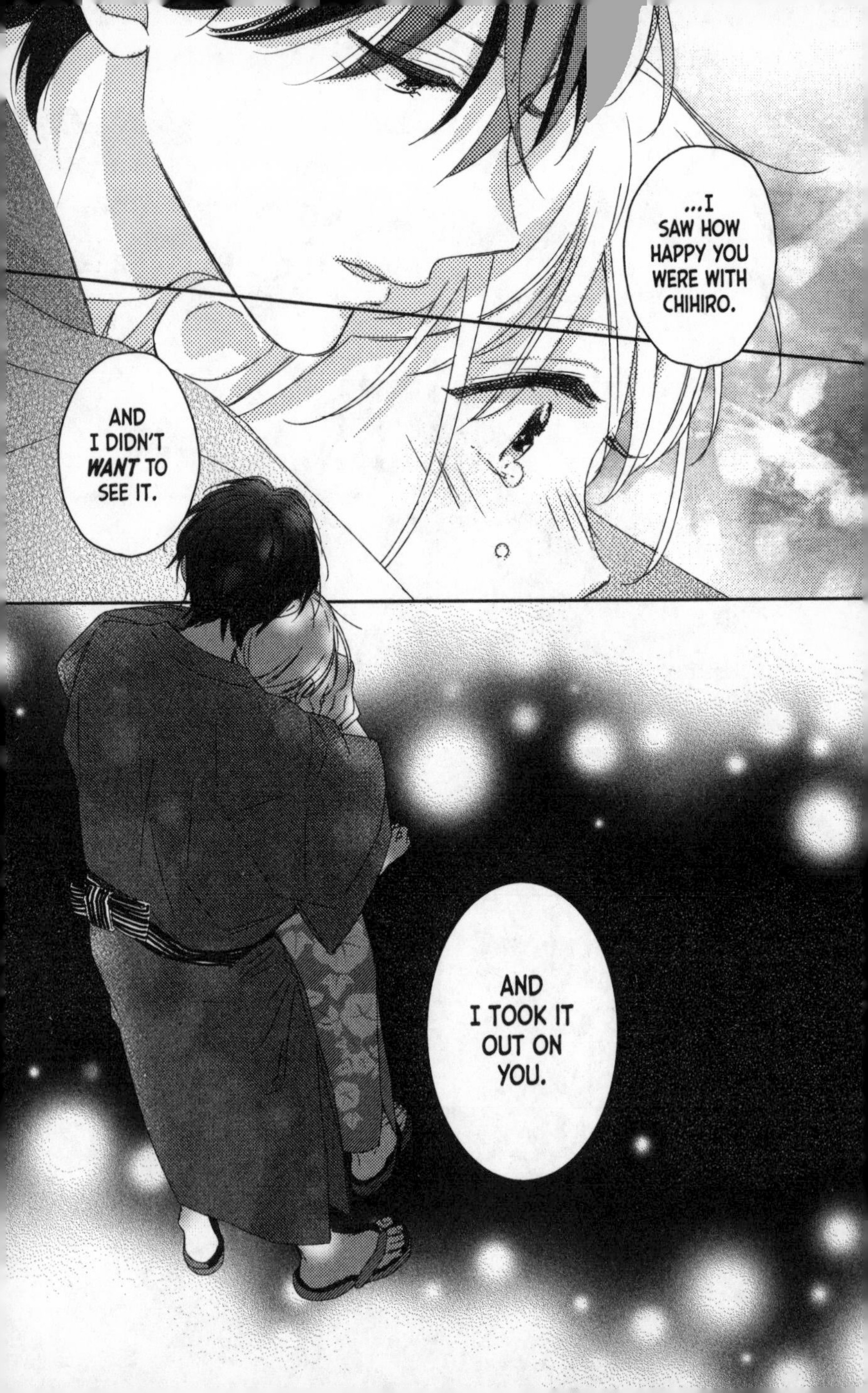
...I SAW HOW HAPPY YOU WERE WITH CHIHIRO.
AND I DIDN'T *WANT* TO SEE IT.
AND I TOOK IT OUT ON YOU.

Those Not-So-Sweet Boys

THE DOG SITTERS

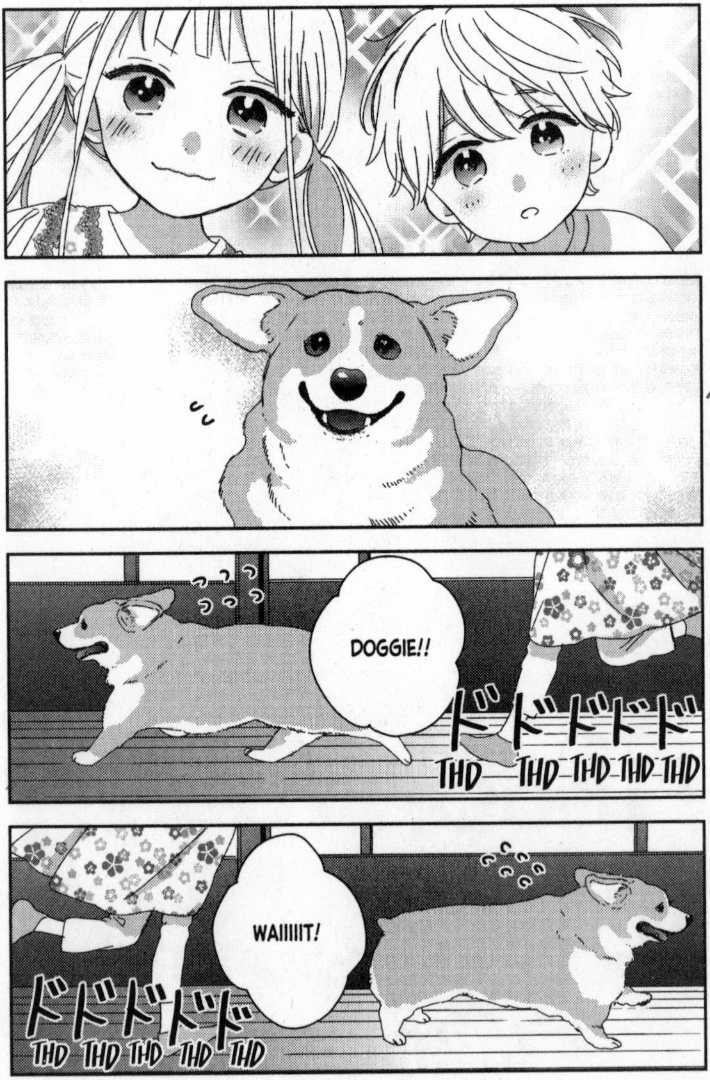
DOGGIE!!
ドドドドド
THD THD THD THD THD
WAIIIIIT!
ドドドドド
THD THD THD THD THD